HUMPHREY GIBBS: BELEAGUERED GOVERNOR

Humphrey Gibbs
Beleaguered Governor

Southern Rhodesia, 1929–69

Alan Megahey

Introduction by R. G. Mugabe

Foreword by Robert Blake

First published in Great Britain 1998 by
MACMILLAN PRESS LTD
Houndmills, Basingstoke, Hampshire RG21 6XS and London
Companies and representatives throughout the world

A catalogue record for this book is available from the British Library.

ISBN 0–333–72158–6

First published in the United States of America 1998 by
ST. MARTIN'S PRESS, INC.,
Scholarly and Reference Division,
175 Fifth Avenue, New York, N.Y. 10010

ISBN 0–312–21209–7

Library of Congress Cataloging-in-Publication Data
Megahey, Alan J.
Humphrey Gibbs, Beleaguered Governor : Southern Rhodesia, 1929–69 /
Alan Megahey.
p.   cm.
Includes bibliographical references.
ISBN 0–312–21209–7
1. Gibbs, Humphrey, Sir, 1902–1990.   2. Zimbabwe–
–History—1890–1965.   3. Zimbabwe—History—1965–1980.
4. Governors—Zimbabwe—Biography.   I. Title.
DT2975.G53M44   1997
968.91'02'092—dc21
[B]   97–38255
                                                                 CIP

This book is printed on paper suitable for recycling and made from fully managed and
sustained forest sources.

10   9   8   7   6   5   4   3   2   1
07   06   05   04   03   02   01   00   99   98

Printed in Great Britain by
TJ International,
Padstow

For Elizabeth and Ann
and in memory of Mark

Contents

List of Plates

1. In Scotland for the grouse shooting: Humphrey's parents, Lord and Lady Hunsdon.
2. Edwardian boyhood: Humphrey Gibbs and his brother, Geoffrey.
3. Colonial architecture: Government House in Salisbury, with the Governor's standard flying.
4. Full regalia: The Governor with tribal chiefs and Stan Morris, Secretary for Native Affairs.
5. The Art of the Possible: Greeting R. A. Butler during his visit to Rhodesia in 1963 when he promised (or didn't promise) dominion status for the colony.
6. The Commonwealth's longest-serving premier: at Government House with Huggie (Viscount Malvern) after his retirement.
7. Grasping the nettle: Harold Wilson, watched by the Governor, greets Ian Smith at Government House, October 1965, during a last face-to-face attempt to avert UDI.
8. Formal dinner while under siege: The Governor and Lady Gibbs with the Archbishop of Central Africa and the Bishops of Mashonaland and Matabeleland, March 1966.
9. Plain sailing? The Governor and the Chief Justice (Sir Hugh Beadle) aboard HMS *Tiger*, still hoping for a peaceful settlement.
10. The end of the road: Sir Humphrey Gibbs walking his dog in the aftermath of his resignation as Governor, June 1969.

Plates 1 and 2 are reproduced from photographs in the Gibbs Archives (Peterhouse, Zimbabwe).
Plates 3, 4, 5, 6, 7 and 9 are reproduced from *The Herald* with permission from Zimbabwe Newspapers (1980) Ltd.
Plate 10 is reproduced from *The Star* with permission from Independent Newspapers Gauteng.

Introduction

This biography of Sir Humphrey Gibbs, as indeed any other attempt to assess his life and work, would be deficient if it failed to pay attention to the major political and social upheavals taking place in Southern Rhodesia in the epochal decade of the 1960s.

This was the decade of a resurgent African nationalism not only in Zimbabwe but all across the continent and even beyond. This was the decade which at its dawn saw the beginning of the end of the Central African Federation and the subsequent emergence of the independent states of Malawi and Zambia. This was the decade of a triumphant Pan-Africanism. Indeed, it was with good reason and a large measure of realism that the then British Prime Minister, Harold Macmillan, spoke in the South African Parliament in Cape Town in early 1960 of the "wind of change" then blowing irresistibly throughout the length and breadth of the entire continent.

Yet, to change the metaphor, the handwriting on the wall was neither recognised nor read by some. This was particularly in evidence among the then rulers in the very South Africa where Macmillan had spoken so eloquently and in Southern Rhodesia which had also been on his itinerary. Buoyed by an electoral victory in a virtually whites-only political contest for power in late 1962, the Rhodesian Front party set itself on a collision course, not only with the African majority but also from 1964 under Ian Smith, with Britain, the colonial power. Regarding Africans as inferior humans and as, in any case, quite undeserving of anything approximating full rights of participation in their own governance, much less national independence, the Rhodesia Front erected or reinforced the machinery of an apartheid-style regime in the country and proceeded to declare independence unilaterally and illegally on 11 November 1965.

Sir Humphrey Gibbs, as Governor of the colony, had essentially two choices; to succumb or to resist. He, to his credit and to the admiration of many, chose the latter. He would not endorse the unilateral declaration of independence (UDI). He would not recognise the authority of the government born of the illegal act. He would stand for constitutionality and the rule of law. He would only obey the directives of those with the lawful constitutional authority over him and the colony, namely Her Majesty's Government of the United Kingdom.

It took a man of courage and principle to assume the stance that Sir Humphrey did. He, as this book shows, not only opposed UDI on constitutional grounds, but he also saw it as politically fatally flawed. It would, he reasoned, lead to greater conflict and strife in the country. The African majority could not meekly submit to the dictatorship and oppression of the Rhodesian Front regime. Even before the UDI, scores of young men had already begun military training in preparation for the protracted armed liberation struggle which was to culminate with the recovery of sovereign national independence on 18 April 1980.

Sir Humphrey, as a Christian, a farmer, a political leader and statesman, stood for compassion, humanity, fairness and justice. He fought those whose philosophy and actions ran counter to these humane values. We honour him because he was a man of principle and commitment. This book appropriately describes the virtues of the man and his outstanding accomplishments. It certainly deserves a place on every shelf, especially in Zimbabwe.

R. G. Mugabe
PRESIDENT OF THE REPUBLIC OF ZIMBABWE

Foreword

Sir Humphrey Gibbs was the last Governor of Rhodesia. He was appointed in 1959 and had to deal with ten years of turbulent politics when that landlocked white-dominated colony was in the eye of an international storm. Dr Megahey, who was Rector of Peterhouse, one of the best Rhodesian schools, knew him well as Chairman of the school's governors. He is a scholarly historian and a lucid writer. He disclaims his biography as being 'official' but he has had access to a mass of papers private and public, he has had the support of the Gibbs family, and he has talked to many of those in and outside Rhodesia who were involved. The result is a highly readable and impartial book, unlikely to be superseded; and incidentally a welcome corrective to the tendentious version of events in Ian Smith's recently published autobiography.

I met Sir Humphrey for the first time in 1968. I was in Salisbury doing preliminary work on my History of Rhodesia. I knew many members of his wealthy family who had been at Christ Church, Oxford, where I was a don from 1946 to 1968. But Humphrey bypassed Oxford, emigrated to Rhodesia and became a highly successful and respected 'farmer' in the Rhodesian sense, i.e. a landowner in Matabeleland.

He went into politics rather reluctantly and was a member of the Legislative Assembly – 'Parliament' – from 1948 to 1953 for the Wankie constituency. He was a supporter of Godfrey Huggins (later Lord Malvern), the leader of the United Party. Gibbs retired in 1953 just when the Federation came into being. Six years later he accepted appointment as Governor on the basis that it would be temporary. It was an honour he could hardly refuse. He was the first 'Rhodesian' to hold it. He little guessed that he would be there for ten years and that he would be embroiled in a prolonged political and constitutional crisis culminating in UDI in 1965 followed by the vain attempts on *Tiger* and *Fearless* to reach a settlement.

This was all in the past by the time I dined with him for the first time in Government House. He was still in office, strongly pressed by Harold Wilson as he had been all along to stay there as a possible link with London for some sort of settlement. The Smith regime had cut off all his financial and logistical support, but he still kept up the style of Governor financed by himself and loyal friends. Loyalty was the key to his career. It was a strange experience to dine in this last isolated legitimate bastion of the Crown in the first colony that had rebelled since the American War of Independence. There was a uniformed ADC, there were, as always, neatly dressed servants. The port – or its equivalent – circulated. We drank the toast of the Queen. This can be in Britain something of a perfunctory formality, but there and in these circumstances it really meant something. I shall never forget it.

A year later Smith declared a republic and Humphrey Gibbs was released from a bondage which had grown increasingly irksome and humiliating. The legal position of the Governor of Rhodesia had never been clear-cut. He was not an executive Governor as in Zambia and Malawi before independence. Neither was he quite like a Governor-General as in Australia or Canada. There were many obscurities and grey areas. But, although Humphrey Gibbs was by no means a constitutional expert and although his previous career had not prepared him in any way for these complicated issues, there is general agreement that he never put a foot wrong. Of course he took advice, but he had instinctive appreciation of who were good and who were bad advisers. This is a fascinating account of the career of a man whose guiding star was loyalty to the Crown and who followed it to the end.

Robert Blake

Preface

Saturday 10 November 1990 was a warm, sunny day in Harare, the capital of Zimbabwe. At mid-morning in the Cathedral Church of St Mary and All Angels, in the centre of the city, the funeral was taking place of a man whom President Mugabe had hailed as "a hero in his own right". The Rt Hon Sir Humphrey Gibbs, sometime Governor of the Colony of Southern Rhodesia, had died five days previously, a few weeks before his eighty-eighth birthday.

The Cathedral was crowded, as it had been on occasions in the past when Humphrey had occupied the Governor's pew at the front for the memorial service for Sir Winston Churchill, or at the wedding of one of his sons. He and his wife had sat there regularly each Sunday from 1959 until 1969. During those years he had been the Queen's representative in the colony; during the last four of them he had been a governor unrecognised by the rebel regime which controlled the country.

Few who attended the service could look back to 1928, when Humphrey Gibbs had arrived as an immigrant in southern Africa. Virtually the whole of the continent was then under the control of the European powers, and there was a steady flow of immigrants into South Africa, Southern Rhodesia and Kenya – those parts of British Africa which, far from being the white man's grave, were widely regarded as idyllic places to settle. Humphrey had made his life as a farmer in Rhodesia during the period of world depression. He had continued to farm during the Second World War. His experiences and convictions had led him to assume a position of leadership not only within the farming community, but within the wider life of the colony. He had been an MP after the war, and had become Governor of his adopted country in 1959. There followed ten years in that role, during times of grave political difficulties. He had become the 'beleaguered governor' during the Unilateral Declaration of Independence (UDI) years, and only left Government House when Rhodesia voted in 1969 to become a republic. Ten years after a retirement spent on his farm while his country endured a long and bitter war, he welcomed the peace and independence which finally came in 1980. It was a short-lived respite. After a few years, the troubles in Matabeleland led him and his wife to move to Harare. Now, from his home in the northern suburbs, his funeral was taking place.

Many of those who attended were well-known figures in the Republic of Zimbabwe: Victoria Chitepo and Nathan Shamuyarira were Cabinet Ministers, as was Denis Norman, a former president of the Farmers' Union which Humphrey had co-founded. Others had played a prominent role in public life while Humphrey was Governor: Bob Williams and Evan Campbell had been frequent visitors at Government House. Colonel Grainger, and other elderly men in their robes as Knights of the Order of St John, mourned the passing of the man who had been their Knight Commander for many years. Many of the numerous organisations and schools with which he had been associated sent their representatives. Captain Christopher Owen had come from London to be present; he had been aide-de-camp to the Governor before and after UDI.

Her Majesty the Queen was represented by the British High Commissioner in Zimbabwe, Mr (now Sir) Kieran Prendergast. A moment of alarm was experienced before the service began when Dame Molly, Humphrey's widow, said that she intended to curtsey to him, since he represented Her Majesty. She was dissuaded by a rather embarrassed High Commissioner.

The service was short. Humphrey had requested that no sermon or eulogy be delivered. The priest got around this by speaking some words as a bidding to prayer:

> We are here today to give thanks for the life and work of Humphrey Gibbs:
> We give thanks and remember him as a father, a friend and a farmer, and as a founder and a patron of so much that is good in the new Zimbabwe; as a devoted servant of the Crown and as a loyal citizen of Zimbabwe; as a committed churchman, who gave an example of Christian living.
>
> He wanted no tributes, no eulogy; but we offer this service as a tribute to a great man, and as an act of loving support for Dame Molly and the whole family.
>
> We offer it too as an inspiration to all those, who, like Sir Humphrey, strive to put others before self, and to serve God in their daily lives. We offer it in sure and certain hope that as God our father accepts the soul of his servant, so he will accept this offering of praise and thanksgiving.

The Russian Contakion of the Dead was sung by the choir. The congregation sang 'Now thank we all our God'. The country's first black diocesan bishop gave the blessing. The coffin was borne out, down the steps at the great west door and past the plaque commemorating Humphrey's laying of a foundation stone for an extension to the cathedral. The coffin was attended by six young blue-blazered pallbearers, black and white prefects from Peterhouse, the school Humphrey had helped to found nearly forty years before. On a cushion on the coffin was just one decoration: the Order of the Epiphany, awarded by the Church of the Province of Central Africa, and of which Humphrey had been the first recipient while he was the beleaguered Governor in Government House.

Two months later, a memorial service was held in the Chapel of the Order of the British Empire in St Paul's Cathedral. The former Bishop of Mashonaland, Paul Burrough, said of him:

> He went to Africa in 1928 when he would have been called a colonialist in an outpost of Empire, but he lived and stayed as a white African enormously enhancing the true wealth of Africa and so adding richness of life and new opportunities in agriculture, art, economics, and, above all, in Christian living for black and white alike.

The British Empire had long gone. Its departure had been marked by many imperial 'last' things – last posts, last lowerings of the flag, last British troops. By 1991 there were few outposts left. Perhaps the funeral of Sir Humphrey Gibbs, and his subsequent memorial service, could be added to that list of final events in the long drawn-out obsequies of empire. It marked the end too of a long life, which had begun when the empire was in its heyday.

A. J. Megahey

Acknowledgements

While this book is not an official biography, I owe an enormous debt of gratitude to the Gibbs family, and in particular to Dame Molly Gibbs, Sir Humphrey's widow. Her decision to donate her late husband's papers to Peterhouse, the school of which I was then head, enabled me to begin work on this biography without even having to leave my own home. Sadly, she died just as this book was going to the publishers.

I am also grateful for help, advice and material to the following: Sir Nicholas Bacon, Mr Tim Everard, Mr Justice Fieldsend, Mr and Mrs Bruce Fieldsend, Mr George Gibbons, Professor Keith Jeffery, the Revd Richard Holderness, Mr Jeremy Lewis, Mr Peter MacSporran, Mrs Bridget Perry, Sir John Pestell, Lord Plunket, General Sam Putterill, Mr James Ramsden, Mr Ian Smith, Mr Anthony Swire-Thompson, Lady Tredgold, Mrs M. van Hoffen, Mrs Pamela Welch, Dr and Mrs Bob Williams, Bishop Bill Westwood, Sir Oliver Wright.

In Zimbabwe, the staff of the National Archives were most helpful, as was the curator of the Anglo-American Archives. The President and staff of the Commercial Farmers Union (formerly the Rhodesia National Farmers Union, co-founded by Sir Humphrey) allowed me unrestricted access to their minute books, and were ever helpful in providing photocopying – especially of the magazine *Vuka*, which is unobtainable elsewhere. Mrs Pamela Douglas (now Welch) introduced me to the Harare Diocesan Archives, and I hope we gained mutual inspiration from our all too few days working in them.

In England I was greatly helped by the staff of Rhodes House in Oxford, the Borthwick Institute in York, the British Library's Newspaper Repository at Colindale, and the Public Record Office. The Cambridge University Library was as ever a joy to work in, and its newly acquired Royal Commonwealth Society collection provides the scholar with yet another invaluable facility there. The Macmillan staff, especially Mr T. M. Farmiloe and Ms Aruna Vasudevan, have been most helpful, as has Mr Christopher Paterson, whose encouragement from the beginning did much to ensure that the book was written.

My wife has been living uncomplainingly with the life of Humphrey Gibbs for the past six years. Without her enthusiasm and support this book would not have been completed.

A Note on Place-names

The country in which Humphrey Gibbs spent most of his life underwent a number of name changes:

1890–1898	Mashonaland and Matabeleland (British South Africa Company)
1898–1923	Southern Rhodesia (British South Africa Company)
1923–1953	The Colony of Southern Rhodesia
1953–1963	The Federation of Rhodesia and Nyasaland
1964–1970	Rhodesia
1970–1979	The Republic of Rhodesia
1979	The Republic of Zimbabwe-Rhodesia
1979–1980	The Colony of Southern Rhodesia
1980–	The Republic of Zimbabwe

Names of some places within the country have changed; in the text I have used whichever name was appropriate at the time.

Rhodesian	Zimbabwean	Rhodesian	Zimbabwean
Fort Victoria	Masvingo	Marandellas	Marondera
Gatooma	Kadoma	Que Que	Kwe Kwe
Gwelo	Gweru	Salisbury	Harare
Hartley	Chegutu	Sinoia	Chinoyi
Inyanga	Nyanga	Umtali	Mutare
Melsetter	Chimanimani	Wankie	Hwange

Southern Rhodesia in 1959: Map of Places Mentioned in the Text

Chronology

(Key dates in Humphrey Gibbs' (HVG's) life given in italics)

1923 Southern Rhodesia became a Crown Colony
1928 *HVG arrived in Southern Africa*
1929 *HVG settled at Bonisa, a farm in Matabeleland*
1930 Land Apportionment Act
1931 Godfrey Huggins founded the Reform Party
1934 Huggins – now leading a new United Party – became Prime Minister
       HVG married Molly Peel Nelson in Bulawayo
1939 Bledisloe Report on amalgamation of the Rhodesias
       Huggins won general election
1940 *HVG founded* Vuka, *a magazine for farmers*
1941 *HVG became a member of the newly formed Natural Resources Board*
1942 *HVG co-founder of the Rhodesia National Farmers Union*
1946 United Party under Huggins again returned to power, with reduced majority
1947 Visit of the Royal Family to Southern Rhodesia
1948 Huggins won general election with increased majority
       HVG became MP for Wankie
1949 Victoria Falls Conference called for Federation of the central African colonies
1953 Federation of Rhodesia and Nyasaland with Huggins as Prime Minister
       HVG retired from Parliament, but became Chairman of the United Party
       Garfield Todd became Prime Minister of Southern Rhodesia
1956 Roy Welensky succeeded Huggins (Lord Malvern) as Federal Prime Minister
1957 University College of Rhodesia and Nyasaland opened in Salisbury
1958 Todd ousted; succeeded as Prime Minister by Edgar Whitehead
1959 *HVG became Governor of Southern Rhodesia*
1960 Kariba Dam opened by HM The Queen Mother
       Macmillan's visit to Salisbury and his 'wind of change' speech in Cape Town
1961 Zimbabwe African People's Union (ZAPU) founded
       Whitehead's 'Build a Nation' campaign began

1962   Rhodesian Front won general election, with Winston Field as Prime Minister
1963   Federation of Rhodesia and Nyasaland dissolved
1964   Ian Smith replaced Winston Field as Prime Minister
       Northern Rhodesia became independent as Zambia
1965   Britain's declaration of the 'Five Principles'
       Unilateral Declaration of Independence by Rhodesian Front government
       HVG 'dismissed' RF government and became isolated at Government House
1966   First major battle (Sinoia) between government forces and nationalist forces
       Tiger talks between UK and Rhodesian governments
1967   'Constitutional Case' opened in the High Court in Salisbury
1968   *HVG and Chief Justice Beadle parted company*
       Fearless talks between UK and Rhodesian governments
1969   Referendum found in favour of a republic
       HVG resigned as Governor and returned to his farm
1970   Rhodesia declared a republic, with Clifford Dupont as first President
1971   Anglo-Rhodesian settlement proposals agreed upon by Smith and Home
1972   Pearce Commission found proposals unacceptable to majority of Africans
1974   Smith announced agreement for cease-fire and talks with African nationalists
1975   Independence of Mozambique, led by Samora Machel
1976   Robert Mugabe and Joshua Nkomo formed the Patriotic Front (PF)
1977   Anglo-American plan for a settlement
1978   Internal settlement (Smith, Sithole, Muzorewa, Chirau) denounced by PF
1979   Zimbabwe-Rhodesia established with Muzorewa as Prime Minister. Lusaka Accord agreed at Commonwealth Conference
1980   Southern Rhodesia again a colony under the Crown; Soames as Governor
       Zimbabwe independent: Banana as President; Mugabe as Prime Minister
1981   Beginnings of 'dissident' troubles in Matabeleland
1983   Nkomo fled to Botswana, after increasing dissident unrest in Matabeleland
       HVG decided to leave Matabeleland and move to Harare
1987   Mugabe and Nkomo signed a unity pact
       Mugabe became President of Zimbabwe, and Nkomo Vice-President
1990   *Death of HVG*

1   The Early Years

FAMILY BACKGROUND   .

Humphrey Vicary Gibbs was born at the beginning of the twentieth century. Viewed from the end of the century, that period seems utterly remote. It is a different world – a world that has been variously described as a 'golden age' or an 'age of innocence' or as a time of 'crisis'.[1] For those who were young then, and who lived on into the later twentieth century, it was a world past recall, a world separated – as it were – from later years by the trauma of the First World War. Humphrey's boyhood was firmly set within that pre-war period, and also within what Violet Bonham Carter called a 'world which belonged to the few'.[2] She looked back on those early years of the twentieth century and described how it seemed to those who belonged to that small, upper-class English world:

> It was a stable and a civilised world in which the greatness and authority of Britain and her Empire seemed unassailable and invulnerably secure. In spite of our reverses in the Boer War it was assumed unquestioningly that we should always emerge 'victorious, happy and glorious' from any conflict. There were no doubts about the permanence of our 'dominion over palm and pine', or of our title to it. Powerful, prosperous, peace-loving, with the seas all around us and the Royal navy on the seas, the social, economic international order seemed to our unseeing eyes as firmly fixed on earth as the signs of the Zodiac in the sky.[3]

In 1902 Humphrey was born into that secure, upper-class world of people who lived at the heart of the British Empire. Queen Victoria had died just two years previously. Humphrey's grandfather, Henry Huck Gibbs, had gone to Rugby under Arnold in 1832, the year of the Great Reform Bill, five years before Victoria ascended the throne. He had become a force in the City of London. Like so many other London bankers, he had his country – or suburban – seat in Hertfordshire, close enough to London to commute. This residence, Aldenham House, was part of Henry's inheritance, and much improved by him with the addition of a billiard room and campanile. Finally in 1882 it was almost doubled in size with 'among other improvements, the addition of a chapel for Victorian family prayers, and a "court room" for the dispensing of justice by the resident JP'.[4] Henry Huck Gibbs was Conservative MP for the City of London in the early 1890s, and was created first Baron Aldenham in 1896. Humphrey's uncle Alban was also elected in the

Conservative interest for the City of London. He was persuaded to stand down when he had only just won, to make a safe seat for his party leader, Arthur Balfour, who had lost the general election disastrously, and his own seat humiliatingly, in the Liberal landslide victory of February 1906, while Humphrey was still a toddler.

The Gibbs family was comfortable and secure. It was a well-known in the City, where the firm of Antony Gibbs was a finance house of repute. Humphrey's grandfather had been the first merchant banker to become Governor of the Bank of England.[5] It was from their secure positions on the commanding heights in the City that both grandfather and father had written extensively on what must now seem to be the utterly arcane subject of bi-metallism. This was the belief that a gold-silver standard, rather than merely a gold standard, would be beneficial to the country, since the price of gold – and hence the price of British products – had increased sharply in the decades after the Franco-Prussian War.[6] For A. J. Balfour, 'the arguments for a gold-silver standard were conclusive',[7] but by the time he became Prime Minister in 1902, four months before Humphrey was born, the world supply of gold had increased and he had lost interest in the question. Nevertheless, the men at the top of Antony Gibbs and Sons were significant members of the City elite, and formers of opinion in Tory circles and among the banking fraternity at a time when the City was experiencing its 'Golden Years'.[8]

Humphrey's uncle Vicary – after whom he was named – had different interests. He was the noted editor of the second edition of *The Complete Peerage*. For Vicary it was a 'labour of love and the chief delight of his life'.[9] His other passion was his garden, at Aldenham House which he occupied as a tenant for forty years. His garden, which had 'long been one of the best kept in the country',[10] included an arboretum, 'the largest privately owned collection in the world'.[11] Another uncle, Kenneth, was a clergyman, a member of the Athenaeum, and later a chaplain to the King. Neither of these could remember their brother, Walter, who had died in 1858 at the age of eight, from typhoid fever: the wealthy in Victorian England were not immune from the awful fact of death in childhood. But they were of course protected from much of the squalor and disease which afflicted a large part of the population. They were surrounded by servants. They lived in big houses. There was a sense of continuity: two of the family houses – Aldenham House and Aldenham Hall – changed in shape and use but 'only one of them ever changed hands by sale in the more than three centuries since 1540'.[12] The Gibbs family was part of Edwardian England's 'very small and very exclusive caste'.[13]

One historian of that caste's 'decline and fall' has noted the historic connection between the Church and the landed classes.[14] But he has nothing to say about the Christian *values* which were upheld by many such families.

The Gibbses were a faithful Anglican family; they were also a strongly Christian one. That is, their relationship with the Church did not end with the fact that there were clergymen, Church Estate Commissioners and patrons of livings within their ranks. They certainly maintained such relationships, and in that sense they typify the connection between the upper classes and the Established Church. This was particularly true of Humphrey's grandfather, the first Lord Aldenham. He was a patron of Keble College, Oxford, and on its Council from 1873 to 1907. He restored and reseated Aldenham Church in 1882, and gave a new choir screen in 1902. He restored the high altar screen in St Alban's Abbey in 1884–9, and donated a reredos and a reconstructed organ.[15] He contributed to the building and endowing of Christ Church, Elstree. He was a member of the English Church Union from 1862, and a council member 1886–1907. He was a member of the house of laity of Convocation from 1887 until 1907 and a life member of the Corporation of Church House, Westminster. The connection with the Established Church was notable also in his eldest son, the second Lord Aldenham. He had a connection through his wife to the very substantial Beresford endowment of the Church of Ireland. As a result of the Napoleonic Wars, the King of Portugal had given a very generous pension to Viscount Beresford, which was to be paid during his lifetime and that of his two successors. The pension had been assigned, by the recipient, for the benefit of 'the Irish branch of the United Church of England and Ireland'. The second and last of his successors died in 1916, thus leaving his son-in-law, Aldenham, as the sole surviving trustee. A legal judgment – which was required as the Church of Ireland was now disestablished and no longer a 'branch of the United Church of England and Ireland' – made over the control of the fund to other trustees, and although the Portuguese income had now ceased, the Church of Ireland benefited to the tune of some £110,000.[16]

Lord Aldenham's fourth son, Herbert Cockayne Gibbs, was Humphrey's father. He too carried on the tradition of close involvement in the life of the Church. But he also exemplifies strongly what is perhaps a much more profound and important relationship – not so much between the landed classes and the Established Church, as between individuals and the Christian faith. While the former relationship is often taken to imply nepotism, self-interest and power politics, the more profound relationship is that between people and the faith they professed. This was evident in the lives of many provincial Methodists who formed virtually the backbone of the nineteenth-century Liberal Party. It was evident in the dynamism that sent a Robert Moffat or a David Livingstone to Africa. But it was not confined to those whose 'Nonconformist conscience' formed their terms of reference in their dealings with political or social issues. It was not confined to those whose evangelical zeal led them to become missionaries whether in Africa or in 'darkest England'. It was evident also among many in the upper classes, whose Christian beliefs can too often be mistaken for a mere formality or a mark of upbringing and caste. For the family in which Humphrey was to grow up, Christian values – and not merely 'Victorian' values – were a central principle, a guide to behaviour, and the well-spring from which sprang the integrity and honesty which informed the lives of members of the family, and for which many, not least Humphrey himself, were highly regarded. When Lord Hunsdon (as his father became in 1923) died in 1935, the Bishop of St Albans described him as 'the finest type of English Christian gentleman'.[17] He went on to talk of a man who 'loved his country', who was 'straight as a die in his private as in his public life', and who 'won the loyalty and affection of all who worked for him'. These sentiments, nearly sixty years later, were to be repeated at the funeral of his son Humphrey.

BOYHOOD

Into that family Humphrey was born on 22 November 1902, at 9 Portman Square, the family's town house in London. The house has gone, replaced by a branch of Barclays Bank.[18] But the gardens are still there where he played as a child, as is the drinking fountain – alas no longer issuing water – which stood just across the street from the front door. On the other side of the square lived Mrs Keppel, the King's mistress, and the royal brougham often drew up outside Number 38. Humphrey left no record of ever having seen it. Undoubtedly the liaison was not talked about in the Gibbs household, certainly not in front of the children. Mrs Keppel's daughter remembered Portman Square as 'elegantly constituted, mainly of eighteenth century houses to which had been added few concessions to modern comfort inside'.[19] The upper classes in Edwardian England lived in great style, but with an absence of the home comforts which ordinary folk eighty years later would take for granted. Humphrey went to school first in a small establishment in Somerset Street, behind Selfridges, and once a week went off by horse-drawn carriage to play football at Wormwood Scrubs. The family kept two pairs of horses in Portman Square Mews, and Humphrey with his elder brother Geoffrey got to know the fashionable neighbourhoods as they accompanied the coachman and footmen taking Mrs Gibbs around delivering her visiting cards. The eldest brother, Walter, was at Eton when Humphrey was born, and went up to Cambridge in 1907, so it was Geoffrey – just sixteen months his senior – with whom Humphrey grew up.

The boys were delighted when in 1908 their father acquired Briggens, in the parish of Hunsdon in Hertfordshire. It was a grand establishment, centred on a large drawing room which housed Romney's portrait of Lady Hamilton. It was well staffed, with a butler, two footmen, a trainee footman, three housemaids, a cook and other kitchen staff. There were numerous gardeners for the extensive parkland, and, from the boys' point of view, best of all there were two tennis courts and a river where they could keep a canoe. That almost spelt disaster for the young Humphrey one day when he was joining his mother and sisters for a picnic, they in the canoe and he arriving by donkey and cart. The donkey backed suddenly tossing the cart and Humphrey into the river. Barbara, who was six years older than her brother, leapt into the river to extricate him from the cart, a feat for which she was awarded a gold medal by the Royal Life Saving Society.

The familiar upper-class rhythm of life was maintained: in London for the winter months, and at the country estate for the spring and summer. And while their parents went to Scotland for the shooting in August/September, the young boys were farmed out to nanny at a boarding house in Littlehampton. It was run by Mr Greenfield when he retired from his post as the Gibbses coachman at Portman Square. They were in London however for the funeral of Edward VII in May 1910. It was to remain one of Humphrey's first memories of a national event. He remembered seeing the King's 'disconsolate fox-terrier Caesar',[20] following the coffin in charge of a Highland servant. That was probably more interesting to a young boy than the fact that the dog was followed by George V, the German Emperor and seven other kings, as well as by the ill-fated Francis Ferdinand of Austria-Hungary. He also remembered watching from his privileged position in a stand on the Edgeware Road while a thief went along collecting umbrellas from watchers who were too taken with the spectacle to notice what was happening.

That other aspect of upper-class life soon obtruded, and Humphrey followed his brother as a boarder at Ludgrove, the preparatory school where he would be prepared for entry into Eton. There, during that year when the First World War broke out, he played football for the 2nd XI, jumped 3'9" in the high jump and won Mr Wilkinson's prize for Music. He was placed higher than his friend Alec Douglas-Home in Classics, French and Mathematics, but lower in History and Geography. Alec was to follow him to Eton and to remain a lifelong friend. Charles Ponsonby was another friend, much older than Humphrey, who came into his life while he was at Ludgrove. Ponsonby was an Old Etonian who worked in the city for Antony Gibbs and Sons. He was a well-connected young man: his paternal grandfather was Lord de Mauley, and his maternal great-grandfather was the Earl of Bessborough. In 1912 he married Winifred, Humphrey's much older sister.

It was while Humphrey was relaxing on a hot day after the end of the summer term, watching Ponsonby score eighty runs in a cricket match at Hunsdon, that the First World War broke out.[21]

A year later, the war that was to have been over by Christmas was still raging. Humphrey's eldest brother, and his brother-in-law, were at the front. Ludgrove could already name twenty-six of its old boys who had fallen in the service of their country, among them Fergus Bowes-Lyon, brother of the future Queen Mother. 'The slaughter of so many young men, mere boys often, was heart-rending',[22] and that was as true of Ludgrove as it was of the school about which it was written, and to which Humphrey was now heading. He was to follow his brother to P. V. Broke's house at Eton. However, in the early summer of 1915, when he should have been sitting the entrance examination, he was ill with scarlet fever. He was admitted anyway, and went to Eton in September 1915, but sat the examination after he had got there. He always believed that he had only succeeded because his father was a friend of the headmaster, Edward Lyttelton. The headmaster was soon to leave Eton. He had just preached his 'unfortunate' sermon at St Margaret's, Westminster, which was thought to be too sympathetic to the Germans and which led to his being replaced as Headmaster by Cyril Alington.[23] Not only did Humphrey experience two headmasters (plus an interregnum); he also had two housemasters: P. V. Broke, 'kind and helpful to a new arrival', was replaced after two years by A. W. Whitworth, who was later described as 'scrupulously fair to all the different types in his House'.[24] When one of his old boys – Alec Douglas-Home – became Prime Minister in 1963 Whitworth was among the first to congratulate him.[25] Maybe there was also a letter of congratulation when Humphrey Gibbs became Governor of Southern Rhodesia in 1959; if so, it has not survived.

Humphrey enjoyed Eton, and while he did not shine particularly either at work or games, he did manage to receive his 'Oppidan Wall', that is his colours for that most arcane of pursuits, the Eton Wall Game. More importantly, he was popular and personable. He became a member of the Eton Society, or 'Pop', in September 1920. This, in the inter-war years especially, was the apex of an Eton career, and a privilege enjoyed by only two dozen boys at any one time. Bernard Fergusson remembered affectionately that 'the Society is an awe-inspiring sight; a line of Pops marching down the street arm-in-arm, talking and laughing, umbrellas swinging, has as much pomp in the eyes of the small Etonian as the opening of Parliament'.[26] Little wonder that decades later one such small Etonian, by then the British High Commissioner in South Africa, should write to Humphrey Gibbs remembering the time when 'you kindly paused to watch my efforts to play fives when strolling with your pop friends'.[27] It is a nice comment on the English 'Establishment' to note the destiny of some of those friends: Alec Douglas-Home was Prime Minister 1963–4; Sir Richard Jackson was President of Interpol, 1960–3; Ronald Aird was Secretary of the Marylebone Cricket Club, 1952–62; the Revd J. S. Bewis was Rector of St James's, Piccadilly, 1954–68; and the Hon David Bowes-Lyon was another of the future Queen Mother's brothers.

But just as the beginning of his Eton career had been overshadowed by illness, so too was the end. Humphrey based himself at Portman Square for the 1921 Eton and Harrow match, with his schoolfriend Edmund Bacon and with Charles Ponsonby. They all went out to a dance after the close of play on the first day. Returning home at about 1.00 a.m. they all fell into bed, but Humphrey woke about an hour later with acute stomach pains. He called out to Charles to go and fetch a doctor. His brother-in-law, thinking he had simply over-indulged, told him to go to sleep. By about 6.00 a.m. however he became convinced that Humphrey really was ill, the doctor was called, and a burst appendix was diagnosed, whereupon he was carted off to hospital. The problem did not quite end there, for it had to be resewn a year later.

Memories of other more pleasant events in his Eton career would remain. He remembered saying goodbye to his Officers' Training Corps Commanding Officer after his last camp, and taking off his cap instead of saluting. He remembered the visit of the Prince of Wales in 1920 and of Prince Hirohito of Japan in 1921. The latter proved the more memorable, as Humphrey watched H. Babington Smith – Acting Captain of the School and a fellow member of Pop – pronouncing 'clearly and effectively a form of welcome in Japanese, to which the school responded with a shout of "Banzai!", followed, as was right, by complete silence'.[28] So his school career closed with two brief and distant contacts with royalty. He was to have closer ones in the years ahead.

THE STUDENT

On 1 October 1921 Humphrey was admitted as a 'Pensioner' at Trinity College, Cambridge. It was the grandest college in the university, and intellectually its strongest. Walter had read History there, graduating in 1910. Five years before Humphrey went up, the anti-war Bertrand Russell had been deprived of his fellowship, having been convicted under the Defence of the Realm Act, but the twenty-one fellows who remonstrated against that decision are 'a remarkable index of Trinity's academic distinction at the time'[29] – men like A. N. Whitehead, F. M. Cornforth, F. A. Simpson, D. A. Winstanley, J. R. M. Butler and E. D. Adrian.[30] The Master of the

College was the outstanding physicist, Sir Joseph John Thomson, who 'was responsible for the fundamental change of outlook which distinguishes the physics of this century from that of the last'.[31] Other senior members in residence included the poet A. E. Housman, and Sir James Frazer (of *The Golden Bough*). But these men impinged little upon the life of Humphrey Gibbs. He had gone up to read agriculture. He shared lodgings in a little house at 9 Portugal Street with his schoolfriend Edmund ('Mindy') Bacon, who was to become one of his closest friends, and eventually a relation by marriage. Bacon's biographer comments: 'Apart from work it was a good life. Newmarket races were close at hand and Mindy was able to arrange shooting for them both. The carefree undergraduate existence which characterised the immediate post-war world both at Oxford and Cambridge was a pleasant contrast to the restrictions of school's rules ....'[32]

But the two friends got bored with the academic approach to farming, and decided to leave in June 1922. Mindy Bacon always regretted this decision – though some forty years on, as premier baronet of England, he was to become Pro-Chancellor of the University of East Anglia. Humphrey never expressed any doubts about the decision. Indeed he was amused thirty-seven years later to be described by the College of Arms, in the award of his knighthood, as an 'MA of the University of Cambridge'. And he was pleased to learn forty-seven years after his departure that the Fellows of Trinity 'were very desirous of doing you honour', as Lord Butler told him.[33] But in 1922 more active pursuits beckoned, and the two young Etonians went off to become pupils on the Duke of Newcastle's estate at Clumber in Nottinghamshire, in the Dukeries. There they spent a 'very enjoyable two years', as Humphrey recalled it. They lived in a cottage and were looked after by a housekeeper. There was plenty of tennis, cricket and shooting. They were near the estate of the Duke of Portland, whose son – Morven Cavendish-Bentinck – had been at Eton with them. They managed at least once to dine in great style with him while his parents were away, but only after having negotiated a rather tricky interview with the butler who was dubious about admitting two young men who arrived at the front door on their bicycles.

The foreign trips which Humphrey managed to undertake in the three years after leaving Eton illustrate well the lifestyle of, and the opportunities open to, a young man of the wealthy classes in those years after the First World War. Soon after leaving Eton, he went on a trip with Sam Bicknell (a fellow member of 'Pop') and his father to the West Indies by banana boat. They spent two weeks in Jamaica visiting the sugar farms and factories, and Humphrey had his first lesson in colonial governorship. They were invited to lunch with the Governor, Sir Leslie Probyn, a distant relative by marriage. Being a young man with more interesting things to do, Humphrey told the aide-de-camp (ADC) that they were otherwise engaged on the suggested day. Sir Leslie (who had been a colonial governor for almost twenty years[34]) was having none of it, and personally rang his young kinsman with a lesson in etiquette. Sixty years later Humphrey was able to recall the lesson: 'When one gets an invitation from The Governor one accepts and cancels any previous engagement!' They moved on from Jamaica, toured the Panama Canal, and caught a Dutch boat home, which called in on Trinidad and Tobago.

The next adventure, with Mindy Bacon, was to take time off from their Clumber apprenticeship and take 'a long Easter weekend' in Portugal. They landed at Lisbon on Easter Monday, and visited a bullfight which they were delighted to learn did not involve killing the bull; they were even more delighted when the matador got his come-uppance at the end of the fight, for while taking a bow he was tossed high in the air to the delight of the crowds, and to the satisfaction of the young Englishmen. They toured up to Oporto where they stayed with friends, and savoured the delights of being wakened in the morning not by a cup of tea, but with a glass of port. On a rather different note, Humphrey took himself off to Zebrugge, because he believed that the blocking of the canal on St George's Day 1918 was, as Churchill put it, 'the finest feat of arms in the Great War, and certainly an episode unsurpassed in the history of the Royal Navy'.[35] Later scholarship has cast some doubts on the importance of this episode,[36] but for a young man hearing about the drama, and the award of eleven Victoria Crosses as a result of the action, it was a great thrill to see with his own eyes the ship that had been sunk to block the passage of German U-boats.

People at the end of the twentieth century tend to think that the world is now a smaller place than ever before – and would probably identify television and jet aircraft as the main causes of this. We are told that we live in a 'global village'. But to the moneyed classes after the First World War, especially given the power and security of the British Empire, the world was very much open to inspection. While Humphrey was planning the West Indies trip, the Beit Professor of Colonial History at Oxford, Reginald Coupland, was giving his inaugural lecture, in which he told his audience:

> The War, in fact, has taught us, as nothing else could have done, how the sundering spaces of the world have shrunk before the swift advance of science. The lives of all its peoples have been brought intimately close together ....[37]

For most people in Britain that closeness was only evident via newspapers and newsreels. For the wealthy classes, it was a matter of first-hand experience. Perhaps Humphrey's visits overseas had given him a wanderlust, but there was more to learn before he could test his skills and indulge in more travel overseas.

In 1924 Mindy and Humphrey parted – though remained the closest friends thereafter. Mindy had the prospect of taking over the family estates in Norfolk, so his future was clear. Humphrey had no such option, so he set about acquiring a wider range of farming skills. He learnt about pig farming during six months at Manningtree, and went to Devizes to learn chicken farming. This particular assignment was useful in a number of ways. He was able to learn more about Africa. His brother-in-law, Charles Ponsonby, had been singing the praises of east Africa where he had business interests, and he had been awarded a medal in 1914 by the Royal Society of Arts for a paper he had written on Nyasaland. The owner of the chicken farm had returned recently from Kenya, with stories of European settlement there. The farm also had a small dairy unit, and while working there Humphrey met Robert Boutflour, who was making a name for himself as Wiltshire Chief Agricultural Officer, with very decided views on the management of dairy herds – ideas which Humphrey found very useful in years to come.[38] It was at Devizes too that Humphrey got into the habit which he was to find essential when he started farming in Africa – early rising. He lodged with an old baker and his wife in the village, and the baker rose at 3.00 a.m. to start his bread-making. This made Humphrey feel guilty that he was only rising when it became light.

The next move was to Gloucestershire, to the Bledisloe Estate. It was something of an experimental farm, with dairy, pig and chicken units. There were six other 'pupils'. One was Arthur Peel, the heir to the Peel earldom, who had been Humphrey's senior at Eton, and with whom now he formed a close friendship. Humphrey was often joined by Mindy Bacon in discovering the joys of shooting on Peel's Gunnerside estate in Yorkshire. Another fellow pupil was John Done, from South Africa. He farmed – mainly sheep – at Sandflats near Grahamstown in the Eastern Cape, in an area mainly inhabited by descendants of the 1820 settlers. It was Done, and his stories of life and farming in Southern Africa, who turned Humphrey's overseas interests away from east Africa and further south. Another aspect of his time at the Bledisloe Estate was significant. In 1925 Charles Wood was Minister of Agriculture in the new Baldwin administration – and was soon to become Viceroy of India, as Lord Irwin (and later still, Foreign Secretary as the Earl of Halifax). 'There was nothing auspicious about Wood's time at Agriculture', his biographer tells us.[39] However, Wood's Parliamentary Secretary at the Ministry of Agriculture was Lord Bledisloe, who suggested that they take young Peel and Gibbs along with them on a proposed inspection of Danish farming methods. This confirmed Humphrey's interest in dairy farming, in co-operative ventures and in agricultural efficiency – interests which were to become a major part of his life in the 1930s and 1940s. In addition to learning something, Bledisloe's young pupils also managed a holiday, travelling from Denmark to Stockholm, then through the Baltic states to Berlin.

Humphrey returned to England, and then soon to Briggens, where he ran the home farm from 1925 to 1927. There was a small Jersey herd, some South Down sheep, and chickens and pigs. But farming in Britain held out little by way of prospects for Humphrey. Briggens was not primarily a farm but a country home which his eldest brother Walter would inherit when he succeeded to the title. In November 1927, on his birthday, Humphrey's father made over to him a capital sum provided he only used the income. This focused his mind on what he had been considering for several years now – that he should go to Africa and see what farming opportunities there might be there. The contrast between farming in England and in Africa was not so stark then as it was later to become. Briggens was almost completely unmechanised; agricultural wages were 25/- (£1.25) per week. These features of farming – low labour costs and low levels of mechanisation – were true of Africa as well. Wage levels there, as Done would obviously have told Humphrey, were even lower. In 1928 farm labourers in Rhodesia were receiving between 7/6 and 32/- per month, though with food and lodging in addition.[40] For a young man with some capital but few prospects in England, the idea of farming in Africa was obviously attractive. As a prelude to emigrating, Humphrey spent a few weeks touring North Africa with his parents, and noticing in particular how a great civilisation had declined and lay buried under the sands – as a result, he noted, of the bad farming and erosion of once fertile land. He became an early convert to the now fashionable concept of 'conservation', and it was to be a major concern throughout his life. And that life, he had now determined, would be spent in southern Africa. He visited the 1820 Settlers Association in London and obtained some introductions. He told John Done, who had already gone home, that he was coming. And in January 1928 he boarded the Llanstephen Castle, on which for the cost of £35 he was to spend three weeks travelling via Ascension and St Helena to Cape Town.

2   Into Africa

EMPIRE SETTLEMENT

Victorian England, or more correctly Victorian Britain, had been, in George Kitson Clark's phrase, an 'expanding society'.[41] It expanded in terms of economic muscle and of creativity; and in terms of overseas settlement. Missionaries, colonists and merchants carried British culture, values, trade, influence – and the English language – over the globe. A whole variety of motives lay behind that overseas expansion. There were colonisers who wanted to begin a new life in new and exciting surroundings. There were those who saw personal and national economic advantages in trading across the world, protected as they were by the Royal Navy. There were those who saw in that Navy and that colonising the surest guarantee of Britain's influence and greatness. There were those who wanted to spread the Gospel.[42] For a whole variety of reasons, and with varying degrees of enthusiasm, men – and women and children – found themselves living far from home, on a temporary or permanent basis, but with the English language and the Union flag to remind them that they were still members of what was often called 'our great imperial family'.[43] While the internal dynamism of Britain had begun to wind down in the latter part of the nineteenth century, and while Germany and the US overtook her in terms of economic growth, the expansion in terms of people continued. 'Mass emigration, which showed no signs of diminishing, meant that by the beginning of the twentieth century, 20 per cent of the Empire's white population was living in the dominions.'[44]

The First World War now appears, in a long perspective, to have contributed to the 'winding down' of Britain as a great power, and to have placed intolerable strains on her economy. But while other empires had fallen – the German, the Russian, the Habsburg, the Ottoman – Britain's was intact, and indeed enlarged as a result of the post-war treaties. France's empire too was thus enhanced. It 'still seemed a Eurocentred world'.[45] The pattern of emigration from the mother country to the various parts of the British Empire still seemed a desirable, or some said essential, policy. The Royal Commission on the Dominions, which had first been appointed in 1912, spent much time on the question of migration, and when it finally reported towards the end of the war (during which migration had largely ceased) it was enthusiastic in its support of Empire Settlement schemes.[46] As a result, the Tennyson Committee was appointed in 1917 to suggest ways and means of encouraging empire settlement, though the bill which it recommended to the House of

Commons (Emigration Bill 1918) never made it to the statute book. However in 1918 the Secretary of State for the Colonies, Milner, set up the Government Emigration Committee, later called the Oversea Settlement Committee, with its own secretariat. In charge of the women's side of its work was Miss Gladys Pott, grand-daughter of the Revd Joseph Gibbs, who was the youngest son of Antony Gibbs, Humphrey's great-grandfather. Whether this tenuous family connection with 'oversea settlement' influenced Humphrey Gibbs in any way, we do not know.

When in February 1922 Milner's successor as Colonial Secretary – Winston Churchill – received a delegation from the Royal Colonial Institute on the subject of state-aided empire settlement, he said:[47]

> I would point out that there is nothing more true about Empire Settlement than that continued persistency and perseverance are required. A year will show practically nothing. Ten years will begin to show results. In fifty years, great and lasting changes may be set on foot, and in a century a revolution may be effected in the balance of population.

It was to effect those changes that the Oversea Settlement Committee was working. The Free Passage Scheme for ex-servicemen ran from 1919 to 1922 and assisted the emigration of over 82,000 people, some 6000 of whom went to South Africa and Rhodesia. Private enterprise was also at work. The Royal Empire Society's 'Empire Emigration Committee' included representatives from thirty different organisations with an interest in placing people overseas, such as the YMCA, Dr Barnardo's, the British Empire Service League, the Devon and Cornwall Migration Committee and the Church Emigration Society.[48] The 1820 Association was established a century after the first English emigrants had settled in the Grahamstown area of the Eastern Cape in South Africa. It had a galaxy of imperial luminaries – Milner, Selborne, Beit, Kipling – on its London committee. Its aims were quite straightforward: 'the strengthening of the white races in South Africa by the introduction of primary producers and the strengthening of the ideology of Empire by the introduction of British settlers'.[49] And there were also schemes for 'Junior Imperial Migration'. One of these was inspired by Kingsley Fairbridge, who had grown up in Rhodesia and had a 'vision' there of 'little children shedding the bondage of bitter circumstances and stretching their legs' on farms and the wide open spaces of Canada, Australia and Rhodesia.[50] The last parties of child emigrants under the Fairbridge arrived in Rhodesia in 1958. To go abroad and settle in the empire was a way of strengthening the position of Imperial Britain. But it was also a way of dealing with Britain's 'surplus population'. The impetus behind it – so strong still in the 1920s – seems to suggest that the dynamic which had helped forge Victorian England and which had sent Britons all over the world as conquerors and colonisers still had some life left in it. Indeed as late as 1965 the *Handbook of Commonwealth Organisations* still listed four organisations dedicated to encouraging and facilitating emigration: the Big Brother Movement (founded in 1925 to promote the emigration of boys to Australia), the Commonwealth Migration Council (founded in 1950 'with the principal object of increasing the flow of British migrants to the Dominions'), the Fairbridge Society, and the Overseas Migration Board (run jointly by the Commonwealth Relations Office and the Ministry of Labour).[51]

While the 'climax of Empire' may have been the Diamond Jubilee of Queen Victoria in 1897,[52] the imperial theme was much to the fore in the 1920s – and not only in terms of settlement. The Empire Marketing Board, with albeit a short life from 1926 to 1932,[53] and the advent of air travel, seemed to be strengthening the sinews of empire in those inter-war years. The housewife in Britain could create an 'Empire plum pudding' for Christmas, and was encouraged to feel a glow of pride that the ingredients all grew in British territories. The newsreels, first silent and flickering, and then with upbeat commentaries, could bring the images of empire alive in the Gaumonts and Regals of the home country. Letters to and from the colonies travelled faster now, by air. The sea plane added a touch of romance and glamour to imperial travel. Little wonder that there were still people who wanted to be an active part of empire, and not merely spectators. The Colonial Service – and the more up-market Indian Civil Service – had long been a career offering a chance to live and serve overseas before retirement back at home. But the men, women and children for whom 'imperial settlement' seemed to offer opportunity and hope, sunshine and a new life, were to contribute hugely to the changing face of Africa in the 1920s and indeed right up until the 1960s. And 'without doubt the greatest imprint upon the colonial landscape was wrought by settlers who came to Africa to establish a permanent home'.[54]

But what sort of settlers were required? The problem this question raised was very much in evidence at a luncheon held in Liverpool in December 1927, just as Humphrey Gibbs was purchasing his ticket to sail for South Africa. The lunch was sponsored by the Liverpool Branch of the Royal Colonial Institute, soon to become the Royal Empire Society, and later still the Royal Commonwealth Society with Charles Ponsonby as its President. The Liverpool Chairman – a local worthy, Mr Robert Rankin – 'said Empire migration transcended in importance almost any other question now before the public, since 1,000,000 unemployed remained idle, and £60,000,000 was being paid annually in relief, while virgin lands of the Empire were calling for settlers'. The Guest of Honour, Sir Archibald Weigall – a leading light in the Institute and a former Governor of South Australia – hastened to point out that there 'must be no suggestion that you are going to dump the humanity that you don't want'.[55] It was people with skills, and particularly young people, who were in demand in the empire. That was a crucial theme, taken up by Sir John Allen, a Liverpool MP, who pointed out that 'it has been increasingly realised that the greater number of those who are out of employment are not the kind of migrants best fitted for settlement in the Dominions'.[56] 'The ideal emigrant', he went on to say, 'is, of course, the one who is prepared to pay his way out ... and fend for himself.' That, indeed, was the sort of emigrant envisaged by the 1820 Settlers Association: Englishmen with talents and skills, and some money, who could contribute to the Englishness of South Africa, and form a counterweight to Afrikaans influence. Humphrey Gibbs could pay his way out; his varied farming experience had done something to teach him how to 'fend for himself'. And he had some capital. But before settling down, he was to spend over a year travelling, learning, planning and prospecting, first in South Africa, and then in Southern Rhodesia.

SOUTH AFRICAN DIARY

Humphrey Gibbs kept a diary for only one short period in his life: for the thirteen months after he set foot in Cape Town in March 1928. It is not a description of his impressions and experiences; it is more a record of what he had learned – details that he could use when he himself settled down to farming. For the first six months – which account for three-quarters of the entries in the diary – he was travelling round South Africa, learning about farming and keeping an eye open for a possible purchase. Then from August 1928 the diary deals with his experiences in Rhodesia, where he settled and bought a farm.

Fortunately, he had the time, money and contacts to make his stay in South Africa interesting and informative. This was not the South Africa of apartheid and bantustans. This was an earlier South Africa where often when men spoke of 'racial antagonism', they meant the conflict between English and Boer.[57] And the Union-Castle's *Year Book*, which Humphrey may have glanced at during his long voyage to South Africa, was more interested in the relationship between white people of British and Dutch descent – at political, farming and social levels – than it was in the relationship between whites, blacks and Coloureds. The guidance and statistics given in the *Year Book* were for the use of white people. The underlying assumption in it was that the facts and figures would be of use not only to visitors, but to those coming to settle in the Union.

While in Cape Town, which was and is the least black part of South Africa, Humphrey dined with the MP for Albany, the area around Grahamstown where he might possibly settle. He spent an afternoon at Somerset West with Sir Lionel Phillips, colleague of Rhodes, Beit and Jameson. He had been one of the four Uitlanders who had been condemned to death – but subsequently fined and released – after the Jameson Raid.[58] Phillips' appearance in the dock had not set him back too much. He had extensive mining interests and directorships, though for him farming was more a hobby than a business. He suggested that Humphrey might try Southern Rhodesia in preference to anywhere in South Africa, if he wanted to farm successfully. But Humphrey wanted to have a good look round before committing himself.

He based himself at John Done's farm, Bickley, at Sand Flats, about fifty miles north of Port Elizabeth and thirty miles west of Grahamstown. Just ten or twelve miles away at Selborne, near Addo, was Rietfontein Farm. This was a citrus estate run by the brothers Henry and Joseph Gibbs, second cousins of Humphrey's father, a family relationship which played a significant part in his life. From March until May 1928 these two farms were home to him. During these months he filled his diary with hints and lore which he picked up from local farmers – almost all of them Englishmen. He learned about tobacco growing, and about the problem of overproduction in Southern Rhodesia, and also the difficulty empire tobacco was facing trying to make inroads into a market dominated by American producers. He learned about cattle, though both at Cape Town and Grahamstown he was disappointed with the quality of the stock on show. He looked at wattle plantations and drew detailed diagrams of planting to maximum effect, and discovered one of the advantages of farming in Southern Africa – that wattle produced there could be exported to Australia and sold more cheaply than their own product, because African labour costs were so much lower. Used though he was to the low wages paid on English farms, he was nevertheless surprised at just how low they were in Africa. He looked at cotton and cattle, and especially at maize, which provided the staple diet for most people in southern Africa, as well as being a basis of flour production and cattlefeed. But most of all, he looked at sheep. This in the end proved to be one aspect of farming which he was not to take up in Matabeleland when he established his own farm, for Rhodesia in general was not a great sheep-rearing area. The fact that he did a short course in sheep management at a college in Grootfontein shows that even just before he went up to prospect Rhodesia, he was not certain in his own mind that he would settle there. But meanwhile he learned about, and dealt with, some of the diseases and parasites which afflicted sheep – blue tongue, nodular worm, wire worm. He discovered that the working capital needed to start a 1000-acre farm, mainly concentrating on sheep, would be in the region of £6500, giving an annual return of some 8 per cent. This scale of return seemed to be generally agreed, though many of the people he met – including Joseph Gibbs – were gloomy about farming prospects generally, perhaps a state of mind not uncommon in farmers. But Joseph's experiences were a warning to Humphrey, who had arrived at Selborne to find the Gibbs' farm suffering from years of drought, yet within a month or two, the problem was flooding, a bursting dam, and an orchard covered in four or five feet of silt.

There was, he found, far too much talk for his liking of 'politics' among the farmers, Dutch and English, but particularly among the latter. He gives tantalisingly few details of what exactly it was that put him off, and in retrospect made him decide not to return to South Africa. But it was obviously the 'native question' which was at the heart of these political debates. One problem he was told of by farmers in the Natal area was the practice of employing the native labourers during the six months they were required to work the land, allowing them to go off and find work elsewhere – perhaps in Johannesburg – for the rest of the year. But meanwhile the families and cattle remained on the farm, the kraals were overstocked with cattle, and the labourers were prone to returning if they did not find work, to cause trouble and steal stock or mealies. The Ladysmith Farmer's Association was trying to find a solution: it might involve employing the labourers all the year round, and finding some regulations which would limit the number of cattle they could hold in their kraals. Another problem, which he found in the Grahamstown area, reminds us that these were the days long before apartheid had redrawn the residential map of South Africa. Some white farmers were suffering from rampant theft on account, he recorded, of 'the neighbouring farms belonging to Hottentots'.

In Port Elizabeth he paid £60 for a car – which as he later ruefully admitted, cost him more in broken springs than in petrol – and set off via Natal and the Transvaal for Rhodesia. He stopped off in Johannesburg – this was in August 1928 – and purchased a pistol, not for the security reasons which we might now think of, but to defend himself against lions. He also had a talk there with the local 1820 Settlers representative, which helped to convince him he was heading in the right direction, as this man 'is a terrible pessimist and is rather depressing about anything to do with the Union, saying that the Dutch are getting far too strong'. That was a sentiment which had only recently been shared by the whites in Southern Rhodesia when they voted for self-government rather than for incorporation in South Africa. It was a sentiment too which was alive twenty years later when the whites there voted for Federation with the territories to the north.[59]

RHODESIAN DIARY

On Sunday 26 August 1928, Humphrey Gibbs drove from Louis Trichardt in the Northern Transvaal, over the Limpopo River to West Nicholson in Southern Rhodesia, 'through scrub forest all the way nearly, [and] very few farms on account of the poor soil and partly the wildness of the country – lions, leopards etc still being a great curse'. He had visited this part of the world briefly with his sister Barbara who had stopped over with him in April. They had taken a sleeper up to Victoria Falls, getting out at Bulawayo on the return journey, and going out to see the Matopos – the wild, stony country near the city where Cecil Rhodes was buried. Now he was returning with his car, with money in his pocket, and with the growing feeling that this was the place to settle.

   He stayed in Bulawayo for the remainder of August, and then during September set out by car to prospect other parts of the country. He travelled via Shabani and Gwelo to Salisbury, where he found people insistent that Mashonaland was the place to farm. The rivalry between Salisbury the capital of Mashonaland, and Bulawayo the capital of Matabeleland, was as strong then as now. Then, Bulawayo's European population was 11,000 to Salisbury's 9000. By 1990 the position was reversed, and Bulawayo's total population was some 400,000 to Salisbury's 600,000. Doris Lessing, looking back over half a century to her childhood in the 1920s remembered that: 'Salisbury said Bulawayo was commercial, crude, lacking in graces. Bulawayo said Salisbury was boring, and "civil service", respectable, snobby. Now Bulawayo is saying Harare [Salisbury] is full of Chefs getting rich and the smell of bad money. Harare says Bulawayo is a backwater. To the outsider both cities seem to fizz with energy and interest.'[60] But in 1928 Bulawayo was the larger city, and Salisbury had only had a parliament building for six years since the grant of responsible government to the colony. So the contrast was less stark then than now. However, it wasn't the cities that Humphrey Gibbs was interested in, but rather the farming prospects. So he drove from Salisbury eastwards towards Umtali, looking at Marandellas, Wedza, Rusape, Headlands and Odzi – all good farming areas – and indeed some of the families he stayed with on that excursion still farm there in the 1990s. He ventured out to Gatooma, and to Trelawney, Barwick and Banket to the north of Salisbury. But although he saw some good farming areas, he concluded generally that this part of the world did not appeal to him, and he returned to Matabeleland. Perhaps a young man brought up in the English home counties found the big open spaces of Matabeleland, with their thorn trees and blazing summer days, more attractive than the green rolling landscapes of Mashonaland, which could sometimes be mistaken for home.

He picked up an important piece of information in Salisbury. Mundy, the Secretary for Agriculture, recommended the farm of Major Sharp, near Bulawayo. He suggested that Sharp might be prepared to take Humphrey on as a pupil. So in October 1928 he found himself learning the tricks of the trade with this somewhat eccentric farmer. Sharp had spent twenty years in the Congo, and was 'one of the old pioneers who had discovered radium and uranium' there.[61] He had been in Rhodesia only for six years, and was a progressive farmer. His ideas on production and also on conservation appealed to Humphrey, who was delighted, after so many gloomy conversations with farmers throughout southern Africa, to find someone 'frightfully keen about the farm'. It was a mixed farm – tobacco, cattle and maize. And it was hard work: Humphrey had to hang an alarm clock inside a petrol tin over his bed to ensure that he woke to fulfil the exacting demands of his master. But it was a good apprenticeship, during which the possibility came up of purchasing a neighbouring farm. He took up an option on it, and that settled in August 1929 he returned to England to join his father in Scotland for the grouse shooting, and to stock up on equipment for his new acquisition.

RHODESIA IN 1929

So in 1929, Humphrey Gibbs was committing himself, and his capital, to Southern Rhodesia, the 'Empire's Youngest Colony'.[62] The country had first succumbed to European settlement as a result of the 'Pioneer Column' sponsored by Cecil Rhodes which had raised the Union Jack in what became Salisbury in September 1890. It did not, however, become a colony until 1923 when the British South Africa Company's overall responsibility for the territory passed to the legislature in Salisbury, with a Governor appointed by the Crown, and a constitution which placed it in 'the anomalous and contradictory status of a "self-governing colony"'.[63] The Governor of Southern Rhodesia was thus different from the usual. While he had the prestige and the pay – and the cocked hat with ostrich feathers – of the normal colonial governor, he did not have the political power. He did not head the legislature – a situation which led to a crisis in 1927 over the attempt by the first Governor, Sir John Chancellor, to have a say in the choice of a successor to the first Rhodesian Premier, Sir Charles Coughlan.[64] Questions about the relationship between the Governor of the colony and the elected government did not arise again until some thirty-five years later when Humphrey Gibbs himself was governor. Questions about the status of the colony itself, however, were high on the Rhodesian political agenda, and the answer which politicians came up with in the 1960s were to dominate Humphrey's governorship.

During its comparatively short history, and more especially in the late 1920s as a result of Rhodesian government publicity, the colony exercised a strong appeal. Back in the 1890s one traveller had written in a genre which was to become widespread thirty years later. He described his journeyings in the territory: 'One who travels across the Matabele or Mashona Highlands in the winter months has cold nights and heavy dews for his bivouacs; but by day he rides or walks like the old Athenians "through most pellucid air", with generally a keen health-giving breeze blowing and a cloudless sky overhead.'[65] Often the motive for going to Rhodesia was purely materialistic – the hope of finding mining possibilities to rival those which had made men rich on the Witwatersrand. But such a motive could be given a romantic gloss: 'if Rhodesia be in truth the Ophir of old, if Solomon found his gold where we, too, seek for treasure, there is an echo of poetry in our most modern industry to which the pioneer cannot be deaf'.[66] Those words were written at the beginning of the twentieth century; towards its end the interested visitor would still be shown the primitive gold workings on the Wedza Hills, which inspired Rider Haggard to identify the spot as the location for King Solomon's mines.

It was as much as anything the romance of this new country. 'The sun sets in a glory of cloud effects, and our Rhodesian night begins, warm, scented, peaceful, melodious with a thousand sounds', as one settler of twenty years' standing gushed in her book published in 1928.[67] And she went on, in words which whites would echo throughout the century:

> I know if I went for a trip now, I would be longing for my Rhodesian hill-top in no time, for there is no doubt about it, the place gets a grip on one, and it seems, no matter how definitely anyone shakes the dust of Rhodesia from their feet, and retires on a pension to live happily in England ever after, they invariably reappear.[68]

Another writer, who lived in Rhodesia in the mid-1920s but had left by the mid-1930s, confirmed that: 'Economic reasons caused my departure from this loving and loveable land and even now, after my short but happy sojourn there, I sometimes feel the pangs of separation. Strange tuggings at my heart come and go. The call of the veldt is always there in the hearts of those who have tasted its elusive charms.'[69] It was to be a recurring theme for the whites. Sixty years later, when Rhodesia had become Zimbabwe, a hard-bitten reporter who had grown up there was admitting that 'in sleep I wandered again ... through the blazing tropical gardens and the cool verandahs of my childhood ... I dreamed of the beauties of the veldt and mountain streams

....'[70] He had left while the country was still Southern Rhodesia. One who left soon after it became Zimbabwe wrote: 'What is it about this land, I ask other African people who, like me, no longer live there. What is this thing which, like the tug of an invisible chain, keeps pulling us back?'[71] 'It is the good magic', she concludes, as does another woman brought up in the 1940s near Bulawayo who recollects: 'Those were magical days, and little wonder for we lived in a land of magic.'[72]

Was it the sheer beauty of the place that attracted, and indeed almost drugged, the Europeans who came to settle? Or was it something simpler? Was it, as one observer suggested, 'sheer scenic sentiment, for parts of Rhodesia do resemble closely some of the more beautiful aspects of Britain – Rhodesia remained in many ways the most British of all the colonies'?[73] You could recreate, on a huge scale, the pleasing aspect of English parkland, with an added piquancy in the un-Englishness of the msasa trees. You could imagine, up in the Eastern Highlands, that you were in Scotland, or perhaps the Lake District, with even a scent on the air akin to heather. Or perhaps the sunshine, and the resonances of English landscape within this tropical setting, became a seed bed for a particular kind of Englishness. Noel Brettell, the Rhodesian poet who was an Englishman from a humble background, asked himself the question: 'Were we transplanting and trying to keep alive in Africa as an exotic, a mode of life that was no longer viable in England itself? ... not necessarily shall we put the clock back, but, coming to a country where the clock was already slow, should we be content to keep it fixed at "ten to three"?'[74]

Unlike England, it was an underpopulated country. It was the size of France – bigger than the whole of the United Kingdom – but with a population of under two million, of whom not 50,000 were Europeans. 'We have more or less vast areas that are empty', warned Godfrey Huggins in the mid-1930s, arguing for increased immigration lest 'hostile overcrowded countries ... cast their eyes on our resources'.[75] Even in the mid-1950s, John Gunther found the same thing. '"The greatest wealth of Southern Rhodesia", an Indian friend in Salisbury told us, "is its emptiness". The country is, virtually speaking, still a vacuum.'[76] This emptiness appealed to the British, who had long lived on an overcrowded island where, although more people lived in the towns than in the country, the rural myth persisted. Writing of 'ideas of nationhood in English poetry', John Lucas comments that: 'The world which is shook with the grandeur of God has nothing in common with London or Liverpool or Sheffield or Dublin. The "health" of England is therefore "rooted" in country living.'[77] For many, the Rhodesian countryside offered what England could scarcely offer any longer – wide open spaces and a closeness to 'nature'. And it offered what other African countries could not match: 'pleasant it is, and spacious and humane, and there is nothing there of that stark hostility that mars African landscape in the desiccated regions'.[78] Nor the stark hostility that was to be found in the grimy industrial landscapes of much of Britain, one might be tempted to add.

This 'romance of past and present'[79] was to exercise a strong influence on whites in Rhodesia, and to contribute to a growing sense of identity and patriotism. Other influences were at work as well. Of the total European population of some 50,000 in 1931, almost 19,000 were under twenty-one.[80] And Rhodesian children were – in this period – acquiring an accent of their own, 'which itself formed one of the elements which went into an emergent "proto-nationalism", linked to British patriotism, but based on an open-air ethos and an enduring faith in the white man's mission in Africa'.[81] Englishmen found themselves in a land surrounded by great empty spaces, by Afrikaner settlers, and by a large and as yet quiescent mass of black humanity. And yet, as one commentator noted in 1930, 'The best thing about the country – an asset more valuable than its potential wealth and great undeveloped resources – is the steady, cheerful, warm-hearted Englishness of Rhodesia.'[82] And that Englishness was reinforced by Godfrey Huggins, as yet a back-bencher but soon to be the long-serving Prime Minister of the colony (and indeed the longest serving in the history of the empire and Commonwealth). Huggins was an Englishman to the core. When he was raised to the peerage in 1956 he took as his title Viscount Malvern of Rhodesia and of Bexley in the county of Kent. Thus he commemorated not only his birthplace and his adopted country, but also his old school, Malvern College. Like so many men of his class and generation, his public school days exercised a powerful influence on him, as when he declared in the Legislative Assembly that what the country needed 'were young men who had "fagged at school and have been flogged at school", people who had learned how to command and obey'.[83] If those were the criteria, it would seem that the young Humphrey Gibbs might have the qualifications to become a successful settler in this new colony.

3 Farming in Peace and War

BEGINNING TO FARM

The farm which came on the market while Humphrey Gibbs was working for Major Sharp was called Bonisa. He took out an option on half of it, 3000 acres lying between the Bulawayo–Wankie railway line and the Kame river, some twenty-five miles north-west of Bulawayo, at Redbank, in the Nyamandhlovu district. The district's name is Ndebele for 'flesh of the elephant', said to have been so named by King Mzilikazi, the great nineteenth-century Matabele ruler. Having spent the shooting season of late 1929 in Scotland, Humphrey returned to his new farm in a Ford model truck which he purchased in Johannesburg and loaded with provisions. His sister Barbara accompanied him, and they spent their first night at Bonisa on their newly purchased camp-beds on the verandah, and being kept awake by an infestation of black ants.

Edgar Whitehead was another young Englishman who had arrived in Cape Town just the month before Humphrey. Later, as Prime Minister of Rhodesia in the late 1950s, it was he who invited Humphrey to become Governor. He recorded his experience of what it was like to be transplanted from England to Southern Africa: 'it was a great change for anybody coming from English country house life in the 1920s, spending approximately half the year at home and about half the year at an Oxford College, to come to a life where luxuries simply did not exist'.[84] At least Humphrey had had nearly two years of acclimatisation before he settled to fend for himself on his own property. Nevertheless, life at Bonisa in the late 1920s and early 1930s was not at all like country living in England. The farm had to be created from practically nothing. Much had to be imported. He soon took delivery of a Fordson tractor and cultivator which he had bought in England. A steel wagon, plough discs and furrow ploughs were purchased locally, as was a span of trained oxen. Twelve Friesland heifers were put on order from South Africa. And at the end of the first year, Humphrey had to decide whether to take up the option on the farm, so he approached the creditors and asked them to throw in the 2500 acres on the other side of the railway track. They agreed, so the whole farm, of 5500 acres, was purchased finally for £3500. Edward Green, whom he had met aboard ship on his journey out, had been pupiling on a neighbouring farm, and he now joined Humphrey and started a chicken farm at Bonisa. Farming was a risky business. They were pleased to reap 150 bags of maize in the first year and 300 in the second. In the third they went for 3000 but again managed only 300. However, they were also selling milk in Bulawayo, taken there by train from the siding which was on the farm, and where in those more relaxed days the train would wait if the churns were not ready. They were soon growing beans, sunhemp and monkey nuts as well. Late in 1932 Humphrey was invited to enter seed maize cobs for the world grain exhibition in Regina, Canada.[85] In early 1933 he discovered that he had won twenty-second place in the world, best of the Rhodesian entrants, beating all Australian entries, and making a big contribution to the success of the Rhodesian entries which overall had the best percentage rate of success in the whole exhibition.[86] Characteristically he did not boast of his success, not even to his family, who only found out months later. 'You really are too absurdly modest', his mother chided him good-naturedly in a letter.[87]

In 1930 an article on farming in Rhodesia appeared in the Royal Empire Society's journal, *United Empire*. The writer claimed that 'it is almost impossible for the newcomer not to make a success of farming if he starts on the right lines, and is prepared to *work*'.[88] Underneath these words was a photograph of 'What a Settler's Home Looks Like', showing a couple of white men with their black staff outside two rondavels (round, thatched mud huts). Perhaps this was to warn the unwary that they should not expect a life of luxury. But there was also the warning that the settler must be prepared to *work*. It was the period of the great depression. Bishop Paget reported gloomily, having toured his vast diocese, that 'capital – in vast sums – has gone into the ground, and it has not been returned. The European settlers are really hard hit: retrenchment is in the air.'[89] Humphrey was fortunate: he was working hard, and producing staples – maize and milk – which were always in demand. In addition, unlike the farmers of Mashonaland who were far more vulnerable to world recession because of their dependence upon tobacco, the Matabeleland farmers were less hard hit, and were able to maintain a native workforce earning higher wages than that in Mashonaland.[90]

One lesson the farmers learned, though, was the need for better organisation,[91] and indeed it has been claimed that 'European agriculture in the period 1926–36 was remarkable more for its political than its economic successes'.[92] Humphrey Gibbs was a successful farmer, but he was also soon convinced of the need for better organisation of farming interests. The government's interest in the good regulation of the agricultural industry was reflected in the legislation of the period. In 1931 there was a burst of government intervention: the Maize Control Act, the Cattle Levy Act, the establishment of a Dairy Control Board, and the Land Apportionment Act were all passed or implemented in that one year.[93] But the farmers, by contrast, had weakened their own power base. At the annual congress of the

Matabeleland Branch of the Rhodesian Agricultural Union (RAU) there were serious proposals to break away from the parent body, and they did indeed become financially autonomous, thus weakening the farmers' cause nationally, but on what to them seemed the good grounds that the RAU was too biased in favour of Mashonaland.[94] Humphrey Gibbs watched and learned lessons. They were to be acted upon nationally in the years ahead, but for the moment resulted only in a small-scale revolt organised by him and his sister Barbara. The local farmers were persuaded to bring pressure to bear upon the new Dairy Control Board to induce it to add some local farmer representation, or face the threat that the milk and cream supplies would be sold through other channels. They were successful, and a useful lesson was learnt.

But meanwhile Humphrey's personal life was undergoing change. At Easter 1933 he met a young local girl, Molly Nelson. She was twenty-one, and had been born and educated in Johannesburg. Her father was an English-born engineer, who, despite having travelled the world and finally settled in Southern Africa, was still English enough to send his one son back home for education at Haileybury. Molly and Humphrey met at a tennis party. Tennis was now Humphrey's sole sporting activity, and one of the few ways he met other people socially. Molly was training, by drawing in her father's office, with a view to becoming an architect. She and Humphrey met every so often at the Sly's farm which was halfway between Bonisa and Bulawayo, and when Humphrey set off back to England with Barbara later that year, Molly suggested he could write to her. His rather unromantic response was that Barbara would keep her updated with all the news. However, when he reached Mombasa he wrote, and the courtship proper began. On his return – via Nairobi where he bought a car and drove down – they decided to get engaged, and in November telegrammed the family with the good news. They were married on 17 January 1934 by Bishop Paget, in St John's Church (later Cathedral) in Bulawayo. The bride 'looked extremely pretty all in white georgette with a big picture hat, long mittens and a victorian posy'.[95] And after a hurried reception held at the train, they journeyed down to South Africa for their honeymoon in Sea Point, at the Cape. The Gibbs family had hoped the honeymoon might be spent in England, but the couple decided to wait for some months before making the trip. Humphrey knew that for Molly their first visit to England would involve the somewhat daunting prospect of meeting the very extensive Gibbs clan. They went in the (English) autumn of 1934, and Molly 'endeared herself to all'.[96] The couple were able to bring back from England the wedding presents and silver which would help to establish their home.

They had returned from the Cape to what was a fairly primitive home at Bonisa. It was a long building of three rooms in a row, each about 12 feet square, with a verandah along the front, and at the back some lean-to rooms providing store room, bathroom and kitchen. After their first son, Jeremy, was born in May 1935, plans were drawn up for a rather more substantial farmhouse, which was a thatched building with concrete foundations, built from bricks baked on the farm. They could then enjoy the luxury of piped hot water produced by their new 'Rhodesian Boiler'. This was simply a 44-gallon drum with a wood fire underneath, and appropriate piping to carry the hot water to kitchen and bathroom. It was a simple method of producing hot water, in a land where there was a plentiful supply of wood, and of labour to cut it and stoke the fire.[97] At the start the new house was supplied by water drawn by windmill, and lighted by oil lamps. Soon however, with the help of Molly's engineer father, a bore hole was sunk with the water drawn up by a pump, and a second-hand electric lighting system was installed. And of course they had staff. The wonderfully named 'Breakfast' was there when Molly arrived, and as soon as Jeremy was born, a nanny had to be employed. Later in the twentieth century, white families were quite happy to employ a black nanny, a luxury many of them could not have afforded in England. But in the inter-war years the better-off families could turn to the Society for the Overseas Settlement of British Women, and employ an English (or British) one. So they acquired Nanny Turner, who had worked for the Mountbattens, and also a nursery maid called Maisie. Unfortunately Nanny got malaria after three months, gave up and went home. Maisie took over instead.

Other children were born: Nigel in April 1937, Timothy in December 1938, Kenneth in May 1941, and finally Simon in October 1947. By the time Simon was born, Humphrey had been back to his old school, and had seen his old housemaster; but he had decided that although the boys might be put down for Eton ('in case anything unforeseen takes place') they would not go there.[98] They were a Rhodesian family – indeed they had been for many years.

THE SECOND WORLD WAR

'We were the first people in the whole Empire to be on active service ... Led by our Prime Minister, we are in this war, by our own free will, up to our necks.' That was the proud declaration of Rhodesia's High Commissioner in London, speaking during the dark days of 1940.[99] There were a number of messages in this simple statement. He was making the point that Southern Rhodesia was not merely a colony; it was more like a dominion. And unlike the dominion to its south, it had no hesitation about joining in the war. In South Africa there had been a strong move for 'benevolent neutrality' and only after the Prime Minister had resigned and been replaced by General Smuts, his deputy, had war actually been declared.

The war – remote as it was from Rhodesia – brought dramatic changes. Bulawayo itself was different now. One young woman recorded the impact of war there. 'Suddenly the whole face of the town changed with the arrival of the Royal Air Force in their blue uniforms ... We were all swept up in a hurricane of frenetic enjoyment, brought to earth only by the announcements in the papers of fatalities and losses.'[100] During 1940 and 1941, five different centres were established in and around Bulawayo to sustain the influx of men and machines for the Empire Air Training Scheme, which at its peak employed 12,200 white personnel and 5000 blacks. In all some 7600 pilots received training in the skies over Rhodesia, and about 2300 navigators, bomb aimers and air gunners.[101] Many of these men found their way out to Bonisa for recreation and refreshment – as the Bonisa visitors book attests. As they flew in the dangerous and hostile territory of occupied Europe, many of them must have thought back to their training in the peaceful skies of Rhodesia. Little wonder that many found their way back to the colony after the war under a Land Settlement Scheme which was one of the last of its kind.[102]

It was a cause of some distress to Humphrey Gibbs that he was medically unfit for active service, as a result of varicose veins, and of the botched appendix operation when he was at Eton. When he tried to circumvent the regulations, he was told firmly that he was in an exempted category anyway on several counts. He was exempt because of the size of his family: only men with one child (or exceptionally, with ministerial permission, two) were taken into full-time training. And, even more importantly, he was exempted because he was a farmer – with a productive farm.[103] So as second best, he served as a Local Defence Force commander, using his influence locally to ensure that men – especially farmers – attended the district camps for short-term training. But he also fashioned for himself an even more important role, throwing himself into the job of organising the farmers for war production. Huggins had spoken of people 'who had learned to command'. Humphrey had already demonstrated his leadership skills during the dairy protest. Now he had a chance to undertake a campaign with national repercussions. At the local level, this meant forming local food committees in support of the government's Central Food Production Committee, and Humphrey's drive effected this in Matabeleland in double-quick time. Fodder banks were established to ease feeding problems during the winter months – the Nyamandhlovu district built up a huge bank of hay. Humphrey took on the task of persuading some of the local farmers to diversify. The Binghams, for instance, who were neighbours, had been growing nothing but maize year after year since the First World War; Humphrey managed to press old Mrs Bingham to grow beans, which she did somewhat reluctantly. There is little doubt that his charm did the trick, and the Gibbses were welcome guests at her birthdays which she continued to celebrate well into her nineties, with cocktails on the verandah and a dining table groaning with silver.

Other dining companions, who lightened these war years, were the Barings. Evelyn Baring had been born some months before Humphrey in Manchester Square, just a few hundred yards from Portman Square, and the families were on the same social circuit. The Barings were part of a great imperial clan. Evelyn Baring was the son of Lord Cromer who had been virtual ruler of Egypt from 1879 to 1907. His wife was a grand-daughter of Lord Salisbury, and her grandfathers were Lord Selborne and Lord Grey who had been a friend of Cecil Rhodes. Evelyn had just turned forty when he arrived in Southern Rhodesia as Governor at the end of 1942. They found that the Gibbses were about the only people they could mix with easily and socially, and there was an attractive Government House in Bulawayo which they could make use of when they wanted to escape from Salisbury. Molly Baring accompanied Humphrey and Molly when they went fishing and camping on the Zambezi. They left, after only two years, when Sir Evelyn was appointed British High Commissioner in South Africa – a rather wider stage on which he could employ his talents. After the formal leave-takings in Salisbury, the Barings stopped off in Bulawayo in October 1944, where 'the farewells were rather more jolly and less maudlin'.[104] Subsequently Humphrey wrote to them: 'We are losing real friends. What a difference the last two years has made to the colony to have a couple who took such a real interest in everything that we are trying to do – not just figureheads.'[105] One of the lessons Humphrey learned from this short but significant period was how 'Evelyn's liberal views',[106] and his courage in putting them forward, had won him respect among the younger generation, and he admired the attempt by the Barings to influence white Rhodesian attitudes.

FARMING POLITICS

But social life and the local campaign to grow more food were less time-consuming and less important than Humphrey's activities on the national scene. His foray into farming politics – organising the creamery revolt to ensure proper prices for farmers from the Dairy Control Board – had shown him that he had something of a talent for organising and rallying people. He was chairman of the Matabeleland Farmers Union when the war broke out, and he launched what he described as the 'President's Monthly Letter',

which was a cyclostyled circular that in June 1940 became a printed magazine.
A month later it had been renamed *Vuka* (Awake!). In retrospect, he could
smile at the way the farmers would dub this 'The Rector's Monthly
Newsletter' or 'Uncle Hum's Letter to the Tiny Tots', but it had a serious
purpose. It was produced in a little room lent to him by the Farmers Co-op
in Bulawayo, and printed with the co-operation of C. F. Mitchell, the editor
of the *Sunday News* in Bulawayo.[107] The copies were carted out to Bonisa
where they were folded and labelled by himself and Molly – and nanny –
and dumped on the passing train for immediate distribution. In the first
issue, Humphrey spelled out what he himself had already come to terms with:
'The Government's views are that the majority of farmers, young and old,
are being of greater service sticking to their jobs than they would be by joining
the armed forces at the present time.'[108] Two issues were vital: 'organisation
and education'. These words could well be taken as the theme running
through *Vuka*, and indeed through Humphrey's activities over the next
decade.

Organisation meant ensuring that the farmers – by profession and by
inclination an independent breed – should join their local District Associations.
It meant that the Matabeleland Farmers Union should be stronger, and that
it should co-operate more comprehensively with the parallel organisation in
Mashonaland. To this end Humphrey organised tours of Mashonaland by
Matabeleland farmers. He established good personal relations with John
Dennis, President of the Rhodesia Agricultural Union, which represented the
Mashonaland and Manicaland farmers, and from which the Matabeleland
farmers had declared virtual UDI in 1928. Throughout 1941 Dennis and Gibbs
were pressing for a new national union of farmers. By October a constitution
had been prepared for discussion at the district farmers meetings throughout
the county.[109] New cattle regulations proposed by the government in early
1942 gave rise to discontent among farmers, and gave Humphrey the
opportunity yet again to drive home his point: 'Perhaps this very matter will
make us realise what fools we are and make us put our backs right into the
organisation of our own affairs.'[110] In July 1942, he was able to report with
great satisfaction that the National Farmers Union was about to be given a
formal and legal existence, with the passing of a Bill which would 'legalise
the constitution and make our finances secure'.[111] In November the Farmers
Licensing Act was in place, and a Congress was held in Salisbury to adopt
a constitution and elect officers to a new Rhodesia National Farmers Union
(RNFU). John Dennis became its first President, and Humphrey Gibbs its
first Vice-President, thus acknowledging the work done by these men in
creating the national body, and maintaining a nice balance between
Mashonaland and Matabeleland. After the Congress held in September 1944,

Humphrey became its second President, while retaining the editorship of *Vuka*. The theme of his presidential address – as had been the theme of his interventions as Vice-President at the previous Congress – was his belief that 'it is absolutely essential for us all to work whole-heartedly together in order to bring in an agricultural policy which will prevent further destruction of our soils'.[112] The idea of a national agricultural policy, adopted by government on the advice of the RNFU, had been the subject of much discussion within the Council since its formation, and the success of the war-time food production committees was pointed to as an example of what might be achieved by co-operative effort.[113] Such a strategy was still being debated in 1950, but 'while still prepared to come to the rescue of white farmers, the Government knew very well how far the balance of economic and political power had shifted within the colony over the past few years'.[114] Secondary industry was becoming more significant; the national importance of the farmers in producing food not only for the colony but for the mother country was less crucial. The mining, commercial and industrial sectors were becoming more significant within the Rhodesian economy. Humphrey now moved his focus of attention away from the RNFU. He gave up the presidency at the end of 1946, and in 1947 handed over the editorship of *Vuka*, which became *The Rhodesian Farmer* – and has continued as *The Farmer* up to the present time. But his interest in educating was to continue within a different organisation.

From its beginnings as a cyclostyled news-sheet, *Vuka* contained articles to help farmers improve their efficiency. Ralph Palmer contributed articles on forestry; Charles Murray at the government's research establishment in the Matopos contributed monthly articles instructing farmers on best techniques and the latest advances. All this was not quite enough for Humphrey. Ever since his visit to Denmark and his training with Bledisloe he had been interested in 'scientific' farming. And in Rhodesia, that meant for him a greater awareness of conservation. Long before this became a fashionable concept, he was carrying out practical experiments on his own farm. He had discovered during his first two years at Bonisa that land which was very productive could easily become eroded by wind, especially given the light sandy soils with which he was working. He experimented with various techniques, including contour ridging and better ways of irrigation. He would have agreed with Lewes Hastings, a leading tobacco farmer, who raised the whole question of conservation in the Legislative Assembly in 1938, and concluded that the 'typical Rhodesian attitude' was 'After me, the desert'.[115] The conservation drive was to take two different, but complementary routes.

The conservation of game had become an issue in the nineteenth century, when the depredations of the big game hunters had obliterated game herds in many parts of Africa. Towards the end of the century game reserves had been established in South Africa, while the Convention of London in 1900 'provided for the protection of wild animals in that part of the continent lying between 20°N and the Zambezi River'.[116] The Wankie Game Reserve was created by statute in 1928. It was run from then until 1958 by the legendary Ted Davidson – or 'Dumbanyika' ('the one who goes through the wilderness').[117] There have been criticisms of game reserves (and national parks which were legislated for in 1949) on the grounds that they have 'excluded African communities from resources which they believed to be their own', and have reinforced the Europeans' view that Africans were naturally anti-conservationist – 'that Africans were cruel to animals and cut down trees while Europeans were kind to animals and planted trees'.[118] Humphrey himself was a keen hunter – though he preferred fish to big game – but he was also very aware that Wankie was only a partial answer to the whole question of conservation, and that even more important than conserving game was the question of conserving the land. Twenty years later a commentator was highlighting this: 'The urgent problem in Africa is not to find land for everyone, but to protect the basic resources of soil, water and vegetation which are drastically threatened by present practices.'[119] It was this problem that Humphrey Gibbs had tackled through the columns of *Vuka*. Now, much to his satisfaction, he was able to address it on a national platform through the Natural Resources Board. He had campaigned for this, and was appointed to serve on it when it was set up in October 1941. Chaired by Sir Robert MacIlwaine, a water court judge, its other members were William Benzies, a retired Native Commissioner (who had been one of the firing squad at Cecil Rhodes' funeral), and Walter Sole, a leading farmer from the Mazoe Valley. Its appointment, as the Permanent Secretary in the Department of Agriculture wrote, was 'a momentous step in the history of the Colony'.[120]

It was not an easy task – to start a conservation drive in the midst of the war. Nevertheless by the time Humphrey took over as Chairman of the Natural Resources Board, in January 1947, it had already achieved much. It had a Public Relations Department, and in 1946 appointed an officer to make films 'for propaganda purposes'. The war had taught much about using film in this way, and Africans as well as Europeans had become used to absorbing information and watching action through this medium.[121] The government also accepted the recommendation that there should be a Price Advisory Board, and prices for all agricultural products would include 'a figure to cover conservation work'.[122] An Agriculture Department Extension

Service was to be set up to help disseminate 'the vast amount of knowledge
and information that has accumulated ... and should have the effect of rapidly
improving the standard of farming'.[123] Intensive Conservation Areas were
being established, with fifteen declared by the end of 1947, and seventy-two
established by 1950. When a group of farmers (usually eighty or ninety)
petitioned to have their areas so declared, a committee was elected locally,
with certain statutory powers to oversee the work of conservation in that area.
They were in a sense district committees of the Natural Resources Board.
Their effectiveness is demonstrated by the fact that they were still active forty
years later. The Board summed up its mission and purpose in its Annual Report
in 1947:

> If the natural resources of the country are lost through thoughtless use they
> can never be recovered and part of the country's means of prosperity in
> the future will be lost for all time. Some of the older established countries
> have found to their cost that they have lost for all time some of their most
> valuable assets and have taken very strong measures to preserve what they
> have left. It is fortunate that Southern Rhodesia has woken up before the
> position has become desperate, but the situation in many parts of the
> country is very serious and natural resources are being lost. Any expenditure
> of time and money now will save the country many times as much in the
> future and will help to conserve irreplaceable valuable resources.[124]

That is as good a summary as any of Humphrey Gibbs' own philosophy,
and it was thanks very largely to his efforts that action was taken swiftly and
in time – and long before such action had become fashionable elsewhere. It
was in large part due to his efforts that over thirty years later President Nyerere
of Tanzania, impressed by what he saw in the country that had just become
Zimbabwe, should say to Robert Mugabe, 'You have inherited a jewel in
Africa; don't tarnish it.'[125] Humphrey's activities, however, were not confined
to these areas of farming and conservation.

HELPING THE CHURCH

The Anglican Church, to which Humphrey Gibbs belonged, was the largest
Christian denomination among Rhodesian Europeans during the war years,
with some 30,000 members, or nearly half the white population. Probably
twice that number of Africans belonged, making it second to the Roman
Catholic Church among the black population. The diocese of Southern
Rhodesia was still a part of the Province of South Africa. William Gaul, the
diminutive Irishman who had been Bishop at the turn of the century, used

to claim that he 'was the smallest bishop with the largest diocese in Christendom'.[126] The Bishop from 1925 had been Edward Paget, son of the formidable Francis Paget, Dean of Christ Church and then Bishop of Oxford.[127] There was no doubt that Francis was formidable. In 1906 he refused to ordain the Archbishop of Canterbury's son, on the grounds 'that he could not unquestioningly assert the truth of the two great gospel miracles'.[128] Thus was William Temple, the great war-time Archbishop of Canterbury, almost lost to the priesthood of the Church of England. Francis did however, five years later in 1911, and just before his death, ordain his son Edward. In 1914, after working as a slum priest in the East End of London, Edward became Vicar of the parish of Benoni, near Johannesburg. After eleven years there he was elected Bishop of Southern Rhodesia.[129]

Paget had been at Christ Church with Major Sharp, and Humphrey first met him on the tennis court at Sharp's farm in 1928. They got on well. For Humphrey, service to the Church was almost in the family genes, and throughout his time in England after he left school, he continued to go to church, as he did in South Africa. It was more difficult from Bonisa, especially before the road was made up, and the journey into Bulawayo was a major undertaking. But his connection with the Church was reinforced by the fact that his cousin, Michael Gibbs, was already well-known in the diocese. Michael had been head boy at Lancing (as had his younger brother, Thomas, who had pipped Tom Driberg for the position).[130] Michael had arrived in Bulawayo in 1928, had been attached to the Cathedral there until 1934, and was Dean from then until 1941. So the name Gibbs was well-known in the diocese. Humphrey claimed that wherever he travelled in Matabeleland, he was met by people who had been either baptised or married by cousin Michael.

While Humphrey was settling in at Bonisa, the diocese was facing financial difficulties. A diocesan report in 1931 lamented that 'for some years past there have been frequent warnings that the diocesan income was insufficient'. It went on to warn that 'except for the money the Bishop raised in England, there would not have been a sufficient balance in the diocesan account to meet even cheques for stipends'.[131] As the Bishop's secretary once put it, Paget's 'vision always outran the money to hand'.[132] Nevertheless, Paget was a realist, and he took note of an analysis which suggested that 'the decline of the Anglican community' was a cause of concern.[133] 'The Christian Church', he wrote, 'needs a change of heart and of outlook.'[134] He was making both a theological and a practical point. A greater commitment to the life of the Church would have practical implications. The Church must begin to pay its way, or its work would suffer. There had been a deficit of 10 per cent in 1930, during the depression, and then after some years of virtually balancing the books, the 1939 figures looked grim – expenditure of £15,948 and an income of £14,692 – a deficit of 8 per cent. Paget called on Humphrey Gibbs to chair a Finance Commission. During early 1940, Humphrey and another member of the commission – Leonard Tracey, a farming friend – toured the whole of the vast diocese. They visited every parish and mission, and produced, by mid-1940, a long and detailed report. It was a hard-hitting one. It criticised the 'haphazard systems and unbusinesslike methods' employed throughout the diocese. This applied to the financial administration, but had wider implications. The report pointed out that the work of the Church was being hampered by understaffing, which in turn was a result of a lack of financial resources. This had the effect not only of hampering the missionary work of the Church, but had pastoral implications as well. Clergy did not do enough visiting because they were too busy and overstretched. The end result was a lack of 'family spirit' within the diocese, and a lack of contact between church leaders and church people. The twenty-four-page report then went on to spell out possible solutions, based on better fund-raising, better organisation, and other initiatives, including the appointment of a full-time diocesan secretary-treasurer.[135] Perhaps Humphrey Gibbs' hand can be particularly seen in the section on the Diocesan Magazine. This had a circulation of only 450 copies in a church population of 10,000. More articles, a circulation drive, better illustrations and more advertisements were called for. As Humphrey had fathered *Vuka,* so now he was the godfather of what soon became *The Link* – the new diocesan magazine.

Paget had been impressed by the 'spirit of goodwill and co-operation' engendered by the Gibbs-Tracey visitation of the parishes.[136] In order to sell their report and encourage the parishes to feel involved, the two men were persuaded to do a further visitation in December 1940, before the Diocesan Synod met in January 1941 to finalise implementation of their recommen-dations. While the financial problems of the diocese were by no means solved, at least in 1941 the accounts showed a small surplus. In 1942 this 'heartening state of affairs' delighted the Bishop, and Humphrey was able to write to all priests and all parish and mission councils to thank them for 'the steady improvement brought about during the past two years'.[137] But he also warned them that unless they kept the Finance Board informed of their ability to raise additional funds, there would have to be a scaling down of the work of the diocese in the current year. The Diocesan Secretary-Treasurer, the Revd G. E. P. Broderick, wrote an article in October 1942 for *The Link* trying to explain the details of the diocesan finances and needs. To his frustration, he found that parishes were still claiming not to know what was going on. He wrote to Humphrey saying that all this was 'too ridiculous and depressing beyond words'.[138] As a result, the lay members of the Board of Finance – including Gibbs and Tracey – felt moved to produce an article for *The Link* reminding church people of their obligations, and setting out once again the rationale for fund-raising.[139] As he had been doing with farmers, so now Humphrey found himself doing with parishes: cajoling them, encouraging them to greater efforts, and trying to instil among them more of a sense of corporate identity and common purpose.

At the beginning of the Second World War, Synod had raised an issue which was not entirely unrelated to the question of finance. Humphrey and his team reported on the 'lack of family spirit' within the diocese, and given the vastness of the area it covered, this would probably continue to be the case – unless the diocese were sub-divided. This issue had been raised during Bishop Gaul's episcopate, but no progress had been made. Paget himself knew the toll it must take on a bishop to confirm some 10,000 people each year, and to travel the vast distances from the Zambezi to the Limpopo, trying to keep in touch with a diocese larger than France. He appointed a committee in 1943 'to consider and report on the proposed division of the Diocese of Southern Rhodesia'. Humphrey was a member. It reported in 1946 recommending the establishment of a Diocese of Matabeleland.[140] Synod agreed in principle, but felt that this Committee had been too exclusively concerned with the impact on Matabeleland. So a sub-committee of Standing Committee was set up to 'consider the effects of the division upon the present Diocese as a whole'.[141] It was not until 1952 that this committee had finally finished its work, and the decision was taken to implement the division forthwith. Humphrey had meanwhile become an MP and had dropped out of active involvement in the planning of the sub-division. Family involvement continued however, as Humphrey's cousin Michael, now Dean of Cape Town, was one of two people delegated to assist the Archbishop of Cape Town in the choice of a first bishop for the new diocese.

Other activities on behalf of the Church had meanwhile occupied Humphrey's time. In 1939 he was invited to head up a committee to support a new Mission in the diocese, run by Ned Paterson. Missions were vitally important to the colony. They were run by all the denominations as centres of evangelism, as hospitals, and as places of education, particularly for the black population. In 1936 it was reckoned that the financial input in education of the nine largest missions in the colony almost matched that of the government.[142] The new venture which Humphrey now headed was Cyrene Mission, near Bulawayo, which became a 'great new venture ... the centre of African Arts and Crafts'.[143] It had become sufficiently well-known to have a visit from her Majesty the Queen during the Royal Tour of Southern Africa in 1947.[144] Humphrey's connection with it was to become even stronger when in 1967 his second son, Nigel, married Paterson's daughter. He also became involved in another initiative. It was an imaginative one launched by Bishop

Paget, and which appealed greatly to Humphrey the farmer – a meeting of black and white farmers under the Bishop's chairmanship. Humphrey spoke at this 'Inter-Racial Farmers Meeting' held at the Bishop's house in 1945. He was able to dwell upon a topic very dear to his heart, and to do so at a time when he was Chairman of the RNFU. He 'began by emphasising that the soil is God's gift to man, our biggest asset both for the present and for posterity'. He went on to plead for better soil conservation, and diversification of crops beyond the traditional staple of mealies. At a further such meeting, held in 1947, Humphrey 'spoke with authority as Chairman of the Natural Resources Board', and again he 'emphasised the close connection between religion and the land, and the dangers of laziness and ignorance in a land where much of the soil was good'.[145]

In December 1952 representatives of the old and huge undivided diocese met for the last time in Synod. It was held at Whitestone School in Bulawayo, to which Humphrey and Molly later sent their son Simon, the other sons having gone to the older but far distant Ruzawi in Mashonaland. Ruzawi and Whitestone were, along with Bishopslea for girls in Salisbury, Anglican preparatory schools managed by a common Board of Governors on which Humphrey sat. At the Whitestone Synod, the diocese was sub-divided, and the names Mashonaland and Matabeleland were chosen for the two new ones. Having been involved in the Division of the Diocese Committee in 1946, it must have been pleasing for Humphrey to see their work finally come to fruition. He was to have particularly strong associations in the future with the cathedral in Salisbury and with the Diocese of Mashonaland. There is a plaque in the cloisters of what is now Harare Cathedral to celebrate his life, and his work for the Church in Rhodesia and Zimbabwe. It was dedicated in 1992 by the black Archbishop of Central Africa, in the presence of the black Bishop of Harare (as the diocese of Mashonaland had recently been renamed). Dame Molly Gibbs (as she had then become) was present, though she had recently moved to England. As the guests at that occasion took tea in the Cathedral cloisters, the sirens of the presidential motorcade could be heard from the direction of Africa Unity Square – formerly Cecil Square. Thus, in so many ways, had things changed in the sixty years since Humphrey had first become involved in the Church in Rhodesia. But that is to anticipate.

4 Politics and Federation

Humphrey Gibbs was now something of a national figure, given his work in founding the Rhodesia National Farmers Union (RNFU) and his membership of the Natural Resources Board (NRB). He was also something of an 'establishment' figure, given his background and social contacts. He was therefore sought after in the years following the end of the Second World War. Politically, they were years of some confusion in Southern Rhodesia. In 1946 Godfrey Huggins had been Prime Minister and leader of the United Party for thirteen years. It was a remarkable period of stability given that during these years Britain had five different Prime Ministers – MacDonald, Baldwin, Chamberlain, Churchill and Attlee. Huggins had been knighted in 1941. His government had, during the war, engaged in the kind of state intervention which had marked the experience of all countries fighting a 'total war'. But in fact, such interventionism had begun – as it had in many Western countries – in the early 1930s. Under Huggins' predecessor the impact of the depression, and the influence of developments in South Africa 'drew the Southern Rhodesian state still further down the path of intervention and control'.[146]

After the war there was a 'marked swing away from the interventionist programme associated with the United Party'.[147] This was evident in the election of 1946, and while Huggins did not share the fate of Britain's wartime leader, he now led a minority government. The United Party had thirteen seats, the 'Liberals' had won twelve, the Rhodesia Labour Party three and the Southern Rhodesia Labour Party two; subsequently on a recount and court action, the United Party (UP) gained one seat from the Liberals. So Huggins was faced with opposition parties which, because they represented different poles in the political spectrum, were unlikely to unseat him. But nevertheless he was under attack. The Labour Party was weak and split. The Liberals were the newest and obviously the most dangerous of the opposition parties, both because of their numbers, and also because of their policies. The party had emerged during the war. While 'Liberal' in name, its policies were illiberal, and it was in fact the ideological forerunner of Ian Smith's Rhodesian Front. The Liberals were keen on racial exclusiveness, and they opposed state intervention. These were policies which might well appeal to a section of the white population, and a section that was being enhanced by immigrants from socialist Britain.[148] But there was a widespread feeling within the

37

Liberal Party that it was unelectable while Jacob Smit was its leader. Smit
was an Afrikaner, with a distinctly Afrikaans accent when he spoke English.
He had the advantage of ministerial experience: he had served in Cabinet
under Huggins before joining the Liberals. But moves were soon afoot to
unseat him. A Liberal delegation which included Ray Stockil, one of the
party's founders, and Rubidge Stumbles, later Mr Speaker, met with Hugh
Beadle and Sir Ernest Guest of the UP to discuss the possibility of a coalition
under a leader other than Huggins. The discussions came to nothing. So
internal party moves were made to replace Smit. Humphrey Gibbs was
approached. He was visited by Ray Stockil, and thus the 'Bulawayo Plot'
unfolded. Humphrey was not one for intrigue, and indeed he felt loyalty to
the Prime Minister who had been so co-operative in the creation of the
Rhodesia National Farmers Union and the NRB. Besides, as George Rudland
recalled he was 'too much to the left'. Rudland, soon to face Humphrey in
an election contest, described him as a 'great friend', but many years later
his feeling was that the approach had been a futile one.[149] When Stumbles,
the deputy leader of the Liberals who was on holiday at Inyanga, heard about
the approach, he hurried back to Salisbury and learned more about the plot.
He determined that it must be foiled, so two Liberal Party members flew to
Johannesburg and leaked the story to the *Rand Daily Mail*. They reckoned
the source of the leak would be less easily traceable if it happened in South
Africa. It duly appeared in the press in Rhodesia. Not unnaturally, as Stumbles
later recorded, 'the close ties that had held the leading people in the Liberal
Party together were never thereafter quite the same'.[150] The approach had
been an ill-conceived one. Subsequently, Humphrey ostentatiously had a drink
with Huggins in the bar of the Salisbury Club to demonstrate where his
loyalties lay, and then agreed to stand as a United Party candidate at the next
election.[151] Although the parliament was only two years old, the next election
came in 1948.

The election of 1948 was precipitated by the defeat of the government by
an unlikely and temporary alliance of Liberals and Labour.[152] Humphrey stood
in the rural Wankie constituency, which stretched north-west from Bonisa
some 150 miles up to the Zambezi. His opponent was George Rudland, and
there was a Rhodesia Labour Party candidate as well. Rudland's career
demonstrated a remarkable capacity to change, chameleon-like, as his or the
national mood took him. He was later a Minister under Todd and Field,[153]
and subsequently Vice-President of Smith's Rhodesian Front Party. He later
claimed that the contest when he stood against Humphrey was an amicable
one, but that he had to try to attract trade union votes, since 'I couldn't get
a single vote from the Establishment because they were wedded socially to
the United Party.'[154] Not surprisingly, Humphrey won with 51 per cent of

the vote, an improvement (that was reflected nationally) on the 1946 result when his predecessor had won with 38 per cent of the vote, only narrowly defeating the Labour candidate. Huggins could be well pleased: he now led a party of twenty-four MPs, facing an opposition of five Liberals and one Labour.[155] And as his biographers comment, 'no one from now on seriously challenged Huggins's ascendancy'.[156]

Humphrey was now a member of the Legislative Assembly. It was a very small body – more like the Northern Ireland parliament at Stormont than Westminster. While it had all the Mother of Parliaments' trappings like a bewigged speaker, mace, leather-covered benches and dispatch box, its mood was more that of a city council. The members mostly knew each other, and most met regularly at the Salisbury Club just across the road. Even so, Humphrey always claimed afterwards that he had not enjoyed his time as an MP, and that his only intervention had been to say 'Hear, hear', a story repeated by others.[157] This was almost but not quite true. He was encouraged by another new boy, Garfield Todd, who as a missionary was well used to public speaking. Todd recollected that Humphrey 'used to get up and hesitate sometimes and I used to suggest a word to him'.[158] The new member for Wankie took the opportunity to speak up for causes dear to his heart. In November 1948 he was supporting the Native Development Fund Bill (later Act) which proposed a levy on maize produced by the European farmers which would be used to fund the development of native areas. 'I have been to most of the reserves when associated with the Natural Resources Board', he said, and 'I do not suppose the House realises their deplorable state and the enormous amount of work to be done.'[159] In the following month he was again speaking – at seven and a half columns' length, on subjects with which he was very familiar: the encouragement of food production, and further efforts in the field of conservation.[160] In 1949 he was vocal in support of the National Parks Bill. While Chairman of the Natural Resources Board he had overseen the creation of a National Parks sub-committee, tasked with collecting evidence and making recommendations as to which areas should be designated. The Act which was now passed created a National Parks Advisory Board, placed the parks under the control of the Minister of Internal Affairs, and gave the Governor power to create a national park in any area of Crown land or land donated or bequeathed to him. The immediate result was the creation of four parks – Wankie Game Reserve, the Robins Game sanctuary, the Kazuma Pan Game Reserve, and a portion of the Chimanimani mountains. A few months later portions of the Rhodes Inyanga estate were added to the list. These were not to be mere game sanctuaries; they were to be places for the study and preservation of objects of geological, ethnological, historical or scientific interest, as well as for the propagation and protection of wildlife – and all 'for the benefit, advantage and enjoyment of the inhabitants of the Colony'.[161] Humphrey Gibbs also spoke on the debate on the better regulation of the milk industry,[162] on the establishment of the Grain Marketing Board,[163] and on measures to increase food production via a subsidy scheme.[164] On all these topics, he was able to speak as one who had been intimately involved as a practical farmer and as an organiser of farmers.

The Liberal Party, which opposed the 'socialistic leanings' of the United Party,[165] had won only five seats in parliament, so the government was able to continue its programme of 'improving' the systems of control which the state operated. It continued its creation – and recreation in the changed post-war circumstances – of a 'formidable'[166] apparatus of statutory bodies for the better administration of the agriculture industry. Men who, in Britain, would have been Conservatives, were prepared in the African context to vote for an amazing, and growing, body of legislation covering both industry and society. One of the new boys on the Liberal side opposing this extension of state intervention after the 1948 election was Ian Smith, who as Prime Minister in the 1960s and 1970s was to enhance the powers of the state. The highly regulated society and state which Smith administered for fourteen years and further developed to cope with the problems of sanctions and internal unrest was then inherited by Zimbabwe's Marxist government of Robert Mugabe. And ironically again it was Mugabe who began its dismantling in the late 1980s in a World Bank supervised strategy called ESAP, or the Economic Structural Adjustment Programme.

FEDERATION

The question of government regulation was not the paramount issue after 1948, and indeed pales into insignificance beside the major concern that was to come before the Colony's seventh Assembly.[167] That was the problem of 'federation' or amalgamation with the territories to the north. Cecil Rhodes had dreamt of a solid block of British territory, and a railway, stretching from Cairo to the Cape. He himself had been responsible for pushing British influence north from the Limpopo into what became Northern and Southern Rhodesia. The peace settlement after the Great War had given Britain control, yet further north, of the former German colony of Tanganyika. There were now those who felt that an amalgamation of the British territories in central Africa would strengthen the imperial position in the continent. Cecil Rhodes' dream, viewed from the perspective of Salisbury rather than Cape Town, began to take on a specific political dimension. To the south lay the Union of South Africa with its large Afrikaans population. To the north on the other side of the Zambezi lay Northern Rhodesia, even larger than the southern colony; further north were the East African territories of Kenya, Uganda and Tanganyika. To the east and west lay Portuguese colonies. Why not amalgamate the Rhodesias? Nyasaland – small and heavily populated – was sometimes added in as another component in a British central African bloc. There were strategic and economic arguments to be mobilised to support the idea of a federation or amalgamation of these territories. These arguments had emerged in various different forms from time to time since the days of Rhodes. In the year that Humphrey Gibbs landed in Africa, a commission headed by Sir Edward Hilton Young had rejected the idea of amalgamation, though there was a suggestion that the railway belt of Northern Rhodesia be detached and added to the southern colony.[168] Rather more significant for the future was the conclusion that it would be wrong 'to place any further tracts with a large native population under the Government of Southern Rhodesia until that Government has demonstrated its ability to cope with the extensive native problems that already confront it'. Then in 1936 an informal Victoria Falls Conference had resolved, and the Legislative Assembly in Salisbury had agreed, that 'the early amalgamation of Northern and Southern Rhodesia under a Constitution conferring the right of complete self-government is in the interests of all the inhabitants of both colonies'.[169] Pressure from Huggins led to the appointment of a Royal Commission chaired by Viscount Bledisloe, which visited the territories and took evidence in 1938 and reported in 1939.[170] The commissioners favoured greater inter-dependence not only for Northern and Southern Rhodesia but for Nyasaland as well.[171] But it stopped short of recommending amalgamation, largely because 'the native policies of the three territories were at present too divergent'.[172] While he was in Rhodesia, Bledisloe met up with his old farming pupil, and later wrote to Humphrey's mother saying that he hoped her son would become an MP. She reported to Humphrey that 'it was obviously not for him to push you as a personal friend just when he had been sent out on this Commission – but he would do all he could to see you get a good job'.[173] Bledisloe was evidently much taken with Southern Rhodesia, and he established a trust fund to provide awards for chiefs who ' were judged to have encouraged their people into pursuing good farming habits'. Nine sterling silver medals were awarded between 1942 and 1957, which was just prior to his death.[174] One is left wondering whether Bledisloe's conversations with Humphrey Gibbs had inspired him to make this gesture, for it was a cause close to Humphrey's heart.

The Second World War put paid to any likelihood that the British government would take any further action for the moment, though Huggins himself tried to keep the issue alive, aided by the emerging leader of the whites in Northern Rhodesia, Roy Welensky, In 1949 these two men, each fresh from election victories in their respective territories, met with other representatives from the three territories, again at the Victoria Falls Hotel, and without the prior blessing of the British government. Welensky had been in London the previous year and had been told firmly by Arthur Creech-Jones, Labour's Colonial Secretary: 'Do you believe ... that any Government, either Tory or Socialist, would ever consider either granting Northern Rhodesia a constitution like Southern Rhodesia's, or, if there were amalgamation of the two, the kind of constitution which would place the control of several million black people in the hands of a few hundred thousand whites?'[175] Oliver Stanley, the opposition's spokesman on colonial affairs, had confirmed this that same day. So the challenge that faced Huggins and Welensky when they met at Victoria Falls was to find a formula which would be acceptable. Federation rather than amalgamation was adopted as the way forward, though when it came to arguing the case in London in 1951, the Southern Rhodesian delegates continued to press for amalgamation. There were others however, within the ranks of the United Party, notably Sir Ernest Guest, who favoured a different kind of amalgamation – joining up with South Africa.[176] But that was certainly not a policy which would appeal to any British government. Federation was the scheme that emerged, first while the Labour government was in power, and then after the general election of October 1951 with the Conservatives. The details were worked out at Lancaster House, under the chairmanship of Oliver Lyttelton, now Colonial Secretary, and Lord Salisbury, the new Commonwealth Secretary who had strong personal and emotional links with the 'white settlers' of Southern Rhodesia. Huggins attended for Southern Rhodesia, bringing along with him Jasper Savanhu, and Joshua Nkomo, who was destined to tread these same boards again nearly thirty years later when Zimbabwe, not Federation, was the object of the exercise. A White Paper[177] set out the interim proposals in June 1952, and these were debated in the Southern Rhodesian Assembly.

It has been claimed that the Churchill government 'presented it as an act of creative statesmanship within an imperial framework', but that the 'more cynical compared it with the increasingly desperate and drastic reorganisations that had characterised the Roman Empire in its terminal decline'.[178] Oliver Lyttelton, adamant that Federation was the right idea, at the right time, in the right place, maintained firmly that 'Our policy was and is one of partnership.'[179] Humphrey Gibbs agreed. On 26 June he told his fellow MPs:

'I am absolutely whole-heartedly in agreement with the principle of federation, and I want to see federation take place at the earliest opportunity.'[180] Before this could happen, however, Huggins put it to the electorate in a referendum in April. The almost entirely white electorate, with an 82 per cent turn-out, endorsed the Federation proposals by almost 64 per cent. Thereafter events moved swiftly, with the Rhodesia and Nyasaland Federation Act passing at Westminster and receiving the royal assent on 14 July. On 4 September, Lord Llewellin arrived in Salisbury to be sworn in as the first Governor-General of the Federation. Salisbury became a city housing two parliaments, two civil services, a Governor-General of the Federation and a Governor of Southern Rhodesia, and political parties geared for operation within the colony on the one hand, and within the Federation on the other. This complexity was mirrored in London. There were two High Commissioners, one representing Southern Rhodesia and the other the Federation. The Commonwealth Relations Office retained links with Southern Rhodesia, while the Colonial Office had responsibility for the two northern territories. Huggins' own biographers comment that the Federation was 'the world's most over-governed country'.[181]

John Gunther, exploring Africa in 1955, tried to explain why the Federation came about. He identified four reasons: that it would make for a better economy; that it would ensure British survival in this vital part of Africa; that it was bound to help African interests in the future, and that it would, if successful, provide a pattern for the evolution of racial partnership in other parts of Africa. Most of those who supported Federation would have agreed with these motives. Yet as Ronald Hyam has pointed out, there was another – and he claims overriding – motive. It was summed up by Oliver Lyttelton, not in his published memoirs (where the economic argument looms largest), but privately when he admitted that 'fear of South Africa was Number One for me'. This, Hyam claims, is the 'monocausal' explanation. The British government pushed Federation through 'to place the first line of defence against South African expansion on the Limpopo not the Zambezi'.[182]

For the ordinary, decent whites in Southern Rhodesia – people like Humphrey Gibbs who had made their homes and lives there – the feeling was that Federation offered the best hope of creating a fairer and more prosperous society. Just as in Britain where the austerity of the post-war years gave way in the early and mid-1950s to a more hopeful and more prosperous society, so in Southern Rhodesia the political and social and economic stresses and strains of the post-war years were becoming things of the past, and a new and more hopeful age was dawning.

'LEGITIMATE TO HOPE'

R. A. Butler, Macmillan's hatchet man for the winding up of the Federation just ten years after it began, wrote in his autobiography:

> It was legitimate in 1952 to hope that Africans' suspicion of the Federal idea might evaporate if, against a background of rising prosperity, room was given to them to play their parts in the territorial and federal governments. Indeed, the exalted concept of a partnership within a multi-racial community was sincerely held up not only as a moral idea and a Commonwealth necessity, but as a counter to the beguilements of Communism.[183]

There is no doubt that Humphrey Gibbs shared that hope. He hailed Federation when it was proposed in the Assembly. In August 1953, at the party congress held in Bulawayo, he was elected to the Chairmanship of the Southern Rhodesian section of the United Party.[184] Huggins was moving to become Prime Minister of the Federation, so the party had to come up with a candidate for the premiership in Southern Rhodesia. The two candidates put up for election were Julian Greenfield and Garfield Todd. Greenfield was a lawyer who had served as constitutional adviser to Huggins during the negotiations leading to Federation. He had been born in the Transvaal but had lived in Rhodesia since 1909. Todd was a New Zealander who had arrived as a missionary in the country in 1934. Greenfield later claimed that he let his name go forward merely to assess whether Todd had sufficient backing.[185] Garfield Todd remembers it slightly differently.[186] He claims that when the vote was taken before lunch, there was a tie, and the Chairman – Humphrey Gibbs – used his casting vote in favour of Greenfield, the man with more experience. Although he had entered the Assembly at the same time as Todd, Greenfield had been involved in party politics since 1933. But according to Todd, when Humphrey gave his casting vote there was 'pandemonium' and it was agreed that they should all go out to lunch and take the matter up again thereafter. After lunch what happened is clear. Greenfield stated that he wished to move into Federal politics, thus clearing the way for the election of Todd as party leader – and hence Southern Rhodesia's Prime Minister.

The Federation, and the concept of partnership, have had such a bad press since the 1950s, that it is important to recapture the atmosphere in Southern Rhodesia at this point. The decade had not begun auspiciously. Hugh Beadle, Minister of Internal Affairs, was reporting to the Assembly in 1950 that 'the social services are breaking down' as a result of the influx of immigrants, so the government was 'trying to reduce the immigration rate'.[187] In 1951 there was a severe drought which led to an almost £6 million government overspend, and there was talk of a 'period of austerity'.[188] The magazine *African Affairs* reported in 1952 that 'the tempo Southern Rhodesia life continues on a rather dubious note'.[189] But all was now to change, and change – it seemed – for the better. While just before Federation the whites of Southern Rhodesia seemed to be 'a small shoal of coelacanths sheltering in an amiable backwater from the storms ahead', now – as even a severe critic of Federation noted – it 'brought a generous infusion of rich food into the pool and re-established its connection with the affairs of a wider world. Commerce, industry, public enterprise and development of every kind forged ahead at a great pace.'[190]

There was, it seemed, a new mood of liberalism in the country. Hardwicke Holderness, a lawyer and a liberal, in July 1953 had launched an Inter-racial Association based on '(a) the aim that fullness of life, both spiritual and material, shall be available to all ... and (b) the means of utilising fully the capacity of each individual to contribute, irrespective of race, creed or colour'.[191] And when Todd was elected United Party leader in August, Holderness' reaction was that this 'surely, must signify a readiness for change in a liberal direction on the part of at least a substantial proportion of the white electorate'.[192] Todd went to the polls in January 1954 leading what was now called the United Rhodesia Party, and won twenty-six of the thirty seats. Years later, A. D. H. Lloyd, an Ulsterman who became a member of Todd's Cabinet, tried to explain what he called 'this extraordinary wave of liberal sentiment'. Was it, he was asked, 'indeed a wave of liberal sentiment'? His answer was: 'It was absolutely unpredictable. I have never been able to analyse it. I just don't know what it was.'[193]

There were those who would claim that such liberal views were 'vaguely interracial enough to affront many European prejudices without offering Africans solid grounds for hope'.[194] At the time, the hopes seemed real enough. But it was the time when Humphrey Gibbs gave up politics. He did not enjoy it. He was happy to get back to his farm, and to his other business and philanthropic activities. He was well aware that meanwhile friends of his were advancing the liberal cause. Colonel David Sterling, who had settled in Salisbury after the war and who had taken holidays with Molly and Humphrey, founded the Capricorn Africa Society in 1949. Its 'Contract' published in 1956 declared its aim to be 'uniting the black, the white and the brown man in one patriotism' and establishing 'a society free from racial discrimination'.[195] Support came from the press in the colony: 'Capricorn proposes cautious but steady integration of all', ran one headline.[196] The black nationalists Herbert and Victoria Chitepo lent their support.[197] So too did the South African guru, Laurens van der Post.[198] At the same time,

Humphrey's old friend Bishop Paget was declaring 'We believe that the only national policy which is morally defensible must be that which gives the fullest opportunity of development of the members of all racial groups. We believe that it is morally wrong to follow a policy which has as its object the keeping of a particular racial group in a permanent position of inferiority....'[199] The new mood must have been particularly pleasing to Paget. No radical, he was nevertheless a political realist with a progressive cast of mind. Writing to his flock before the 1946 election, he had urged them to vote 'for those whom we feel will think and act justly for the welfare of the whole body of citizens of all races, and will have in mind always the rightful ambitions of the great majority of voteless citizens'.[200] It now remained to be seen, with such candidates now in control, whether Lloyd's 'extraordinary wave of liberal sentiment' could bring about significant political and social change in Southern Rhodesia.

5 Southern Rhodesia in the Late 1950s

PERSONAL MATTERS

In 1953 as Federation began, Humphrey Gibbs retired from the Legislative Assembly. He had just turned fifty. He was a tall, good-looking man, with something of a twinkle in his eye, speaking with the upper-class English accent which was to become unfashionable in Britain itself in the 1960s, but which was to be preserved by people like him, and in the circles in which he moved. In those circles, whether in England or in Southern Rhodesia, one of the questions which loomed large was where to educate the children.

Jeremy, Nigel, Timothy and Kenneth all attended Ruzawi, the Anglican preparatory school, which had been founded in 1928. Its white 'Cape Dutch' buildings, with their red-tiled roofs, lay within a huge tree-filled estate near Marandellas, in a part of the colony which, as the school prospectus liked (and still likes) to boast, enjoyed the best climate in the world. When the boys congregated there on a Sunday after chapel, and in the evening just before sunset, there was the flag ceremony which parents often watched. The school lined up around the lawn – some hundred little white boys in shorts and sun hats. The hats were doffed; the Union Jack was raised or lowered. The poet Noel Brettell, remembered when he went to teach there in the 1930s, that 'the ritual ... I at first thought rather quaint and faintly absurd. I came to see that it was, with so many other innocent affectations, a gesture of maintaining an unknown perimeter, the only values of which we could be absolutely sure.'[201] Those values – 'of English Christian education' – were a profound reflection of the beliefs of people like Humphrey Gibbs. The sadness for them – people who in England would send their children to public schools – was that there was no senior school equivalent of Ruzawi. For thirty years men like Canon Grinham (who founded Ruzawi) and Bishop Paget had hoped for an Anglican boarding school which could educate boys after the age of thirteen, but for the moment, no such option existed. They could be sent back to England, which was what the settlers in Kenya tended to do. Or, more conveniently, they could be sent to 'little England on the veld', the schools of South Africa.[202] These were modelled on the English public schools, usually run by headmasters imported from England. There were sufficient numbers of such institutions to provide the healthy competition in sport which was part of the public school ethos. So the four eldest boys went off to Cape

Town, to the Diocesan College (or 'Bishops'). They were not too far in spirit
from their father's school. A chapter in the school's history begins with
these words:

> A century ago when the Guards marched past Eton College, William
> Cory, the schoolmaster-poet, would spring to his feet. 'Brats, the British
> Army!' And he would stand, looking, listening, the tears in his eyes.
> Schoolmasters like Cory fan the shy and hidden flame of patriotism in the
> hearts of their boys. They hold aloft the Grail. They transmute the tag *Pro
> fide et patria* into a dedication and a declaration of faith. Bishops has been
> blessed with a line of such masters.[203]

If the boys were not to be educated at Eton, and if there were no independent
church schools within the colony, then a place like Bishops was an obvious
choice. In 1953 Jeremy was about to leave school and go up to Oxford; Nigel
and Timothy were there, and Kenneth was about to leave Ruzawi and follow
them. Meanwhile their father was becoming involved in plans which would
mean that the youngest son, Simon, would go to a new Anglican Preparatory
School, and a new Anglican senior school. The new preparatory school,
Springvale, had already opened near Marandellas – another contribution by
Ruzawi's founder Robert Grinham to the educational life of the colony. A
senior school (soon to be named Peterhouse) was already in the planning
stage, and would provide a suitable alternative to Bishops, which was a long
way away. Humphrey and Molly, and others like them, had patronised
Ruzawi; now immigration was creating an even greater demand for schools
like Springvale and Peterhouse within the colony. Both schools were products
of the greater wealth that was around during the days of Federation, and both
were symptoms of the more mature – and perhaps more liberal – society that
was developing in Southern Rhodesia.

In 1954 family life was disrupted. Molly took a telephone call early in the
year from Bishops, to be told the devastating news that Nigel had contracted
polio. He was in an isolation ward, with an iron lung on stand-by. Fortunately
cousin Michael was in Cape Town as Dean. He had been there since 1947,
though he was about to move to England to become Dean of Chester. Molly
flew down that day, stopping off in Johannesburg for the night, because there
was no through plane. Humphrey got a chartered plane the next day. When
the parents met, Molly admitted she had been 'extravagant' and had taken
a taxi from the isolation hospital up to the Deanery. Humphrey trumped this
by saying that he had taken a taxi from Bulawayo. They decided to take Nigel
to England for treatment. Jeremy was to go up to Christ Church, Oxford in
October, so they travelled over with both boys by ship, lunching en route

with the Governor of Gibraltar. They then remained in the UK for six weeks while Nigel was checked up on, and Jeremy got started at Oxford.

Before leaving Bonisa for their sea voyage. they had been involved in a big effort for the new diocese of Matabeleland, which had come into being at the end of 1953. Paget – who had ruled over the huge diocese of Southern Rhodesia since 1925 – had now been joined by an episcopal colleague, James Hughes. Hughes had been Bishop of British Honduras, and then of Barbados, and since 1951 had been an assistant Bishop of Birmingham. From there he received the call to become the first Bishop of Matabeleland. He came from a relatively new English diocese that was short of money, into a brand new diocese that lacked funds altogether. Humphrey lent his support to the idea of raising money for an endowment fund. The Bishop asked him to target the farming community. Humphrey conceived the idea of a harvest thanksgiving service to be held in a church built out of hay bales on the farm at Bonisa. Farmers over a wide area were written to and asked to provide 'for purchase by other farmers, such things as dairy calves, seeds of all kinds ... sheep or pigs [and] for purchase by townspeople – beef, mutton, poultry, game (buck and birds), veal, vegetables, monkey nuts, eggs, citrus, biltong, fresh cream, jams and other home-made produce'.[204] About 5000 people turned up in the course of the day. The only crisis arose when the tinder-dry bush caught fire on a picnic site, and some 300 acres burned fiercely for about two hours, until brought under control by Sea Scouts and Scouts who were helping at the Festival. The only casualty was a helper who burnt his hand by picking up a smouldering log. The collection at the service, taken up in milk churns, was £222.11s. The total handed over was some £2500. This, as Humphrey ruefully remembered, did not in the end go towards an endowment fund, but was mopped up by the diocese in wiping out debts.

Humphrey's own financial affairs fared rather better. By 1954 he had accumulated a brace of directorships. In Salisbury he sat on the boards of Barclays Bank, the Rhodesian Assets Investment Company, Border Farms, Gibbs and Company, Divide Chrome Metals, and the Rhodesian Engineering and Steel Company. In Bulawayo he was a director of Premier Portland Cement, Rhodesian Strathmore Investments, Kenilworth Estates, Wankie Colliery, Glenara Estates and Mining, North Zambezi Coal, British Metal Corporation, and he chaired Founders Building Society. He was also a director of two companies from which he received no remuneration – Ruzawi Schools Limited, and the newly founded (but as yet unopened) Peterhouse. In the small society that was Southern Rhodesia, he played billiards at the Salisbury and Bulawayo Clubs, or stood at their bars, with men who also sat on these boards, whom he had met in the Assembly, and who formed what has been called the 'establishment'.

'ESTABLISHMENT' VALUES

This Southern Rhodesian 'establishment' had, as one writer claims, 'two
attributes. First, they were intensely British .... Secondly, they were, perhaps
unknowingly, disciples of Burke.' [205] That first attribute hardly needs
explaining: these were men who had brought their rather old-fashioned
'Britishness' to an outpost of the empire, or in some cases their parents had
done so. Their games and their accents, their manners and their aspirations,
and above all their patriotism expressed as intense loyalty to the Crown: these
were the attributes that made them 'intensely British'. By the second attribute,
'disciples of Burke', he means that 'they saw their roles, whether on the RAU
[Rhodesian Agricultural Union[206]] or in the Legislative Assembly, as twofold
– to fight for the interests of their local community and also, above all, to
contribute their own individual voice to any discussion of the national
interest'. These two attributes are not in fact unrelated. There was something
Burkean about their view of history as an organic growth; their own history
was the history of England, transplanted and growing still in the heart of
Africa. We might add another 'establishment' characteristic – they were, as
Rudland had found when he opposed Gibbs for the Wankie seat in 1948,
wedded to the United Party and to Huggins' leadership. In Britain the
Conservative Party could not have been elected had its support been derived
merely from the rich and the squires from the shires. So in Southern Rhodesia
the United Party depended for its existence upon more than the social and
economic elite. In the 1950s 'it was accepted, even expected, that the
schoolmaster or well-to-do farmer would vote for an Establishment man
supporting Sir Godfrey Huggins'.[207]

It was a growing establishment. The Actons had arrived from England to
settle in Umtali, endowing theatre and music there, and building up a fine
botanical garden, largely funded by money through their Courtauld
connection. Lord and Lady Plunket settled at Melsetter and set about creating
a grand garden in the foothills of the Chimanimanis, travelling regularly back
to the UK to see their family; Robin Plunket's brother was a courtier in the
Royal Household. There were locally born men too like Bob Williams, a
wealthy businessman and leading light in the sporting establishment, who
had taken part in the inauguration of the Inter-racial Association. There
were old families like the MacIlwaines – Sir Robert had been first chairman
of the Natural Resources Board, and was responsible for starting Troutbeck
Inn, and thus opening up Inyanga as a holiday destination, particularly for
those who found the surroundings there powerfully reminiscent of Scotland.
And there were the Worsely Worsicks, who farmed near the MacIlwaines
at Marandellas. Sir Robert Tredgold, who became Chief Justice of the

Federation and then of Rhodesia, was a grandson of Robert Moffatt, the missionary pioneer. It would not be possible to list the members of the establishment, nor perhaps precisely to define who was 'in' or 'out'. But there were enough such people now – and others who aspired socially to speak the same way and retain the same British values – to patronise something new in Southern Rhodesia: independent schools.

For whites in Southern Rhodesia, the school system provided by the state was extremely good.[208] The oldest 'government' schools, as they were called – places like Prince Edward in Salisbury and Plumtree south of Bulawayo – were in style and ethos very much like the public schools in England. Or rather they were a curious amalgam. They were like the public schools (of that era) in that there was an enormous emphasis on games, and a devotion to rituals (like caning) and to sartorial extravagance. One English boy who ended up at Churchill, the new secondary school in Salisbury in the 1950s, described his pride at 'our splendid purple blazers with silver threaded Marlborough crest badges which could only be ordered from an expensive public school tailoring establishment in England ... pale straw boaters for town and little purple caps for cricket ... grey poplin shorts for day wear ... worsted "longs" at night'.[209] Nearly a quarter of a century later, at the end of the guerrilla warfare which helped turn Rhodesia into Zimbabwe, David Caute found a similar ethos at Umtali High School: 'In the school hall, a photograph of Churchill. Boys clad in white shirts and khaki shorts respectfully remove their green caps', at a school described (by itself) as 'a paradise of games fields, athletics facilities, tennis and squash courts, set down in 120 landscaped acres'.[210]

But there were parents who were prepared to pay for something different. There was an element of snobbery involved, no doubt. When Evelyn Waugh visited Southern Rhodesia in the late 1950s, he had a conversation with Sir Edgar Whitehead (whom he does not identify by name). Waugh said to him: 'I think you are a bachelor. I should not care to bring up children here.' Why not?, asked Whitehead. 'The accent', said Waugh, who records, 'I think there was a glance of sympathy in his eye.'[211] And of course the accent to which Waugh and Whitehead were referring was the clipped colonial vowels of Southern Rhodesia – an accent similar to that of the English South Africans. So snobbery may have played a role. But the provision of independent schools was an important issue. In the rest of British Africa – outside South Africa – English families sent their children home to boarding school in England. In the only other colony which had 'settlers' – Kenya – there were preparatory schools, but thereafter children were sent to Britain for their schooling. If Southern Rhodesia was actually home for people like the Gibbses, then the provision of independent boarding schools within the colony could be seen as a further sign of its maturity and its Englishness. But there were also pressures for the creation of specifically Christian, or Church schools. Already there was an old established Roman Catholic boys' secondary school in Salisbury – St George's, run by the Jesuits. There was a similar Roman Catholic school for girls, the Dominican Convent. Doris Lessing was sent there; 'it was a snobbish choice', she remarks.[212] As we have seen, Canon Grinham – who had founded Ruzawi in 1928 and then moved some eight miles away and founded another Anglican preparatory school at Springvale, in 1951 – had long felt the need for an Anglican senior school to which boys from Ruzawi could proceed. But he, and the Governors of Ruzawi, of whom Humphrey Gibbs was one, decided that 'it would not be wise to launch out until an adequate number of Preparatory schools had been established to feed it'.[213] By the early 1950s, this condition had been fulfilled. Ruzawi had been joined by Whitestone, in Bulawayo, and by Springvale near Marandellas. Several others existed already or were projected: a Roman Catholic one (St Thomas Aquinas) had opened in 1950 to join the old established Hartmann House which was a feeder for St George's. There was a mainly Afrikaans-medium one, Bothashof, founded in 1948.[214] St John's in Salisbury opened in 1956. These were all boys' schools.

In 1951, the Rector (headmaster) of Michaelhouse in Natal had begun to look north. Along with Bishops (Hilton) and St Andrews (Grahamstown), Michaelhouse was one of the leading public schools of the Union. Its Rector was an energetic and fervent Anglican called Fred Snell, who had been there since 1939 and felt it was time for a change. A boyish looking (he was forty-nine) and intellectually able old Wykehamist, he had already been at Michaelhouse longer than any other Rector in the school's history. His energy and restless – if somewhat combative – enthusiasm needed further challenges. He had visited the colony and managed to get Bishop Paget, the Governor of Southern Rhodesia, Sir Robert Hudson (Chief Justice) and Colonel Ellis Robins (of the British South Africa Company) interested in the project.[215] It was agreed that Snell would move to Rhodesia, base himself (with a light timetable) at Ruzawi, and further the project on the spot. In April 1952 the Ruzawi Schools Board agreed to make a loan of £500 to fund a search for a suitable site for the new school – as yet unnamed. By the time of Snell's second visit, three months later, an informal 'Peterhouse Committee' was in being under the Chairmanship of Humphrey Gibbs, and it was he and Ellis Robins who did most to make the project financially viable. Robins, an American citizen by origin, and a Rhodes Scholar – who was to end his life as Baron Robins of Chelsea and Rhodesia – used his business contacts to secure support from the BSA Company, the Imperial Tobacco Company and the copper mining houses. Humphrey Gibbs used his government contacts to secure a loan from the Northern Rhodesian government, on the grounds that the new school would provide much-needed education for boys from that territory – an initiative on a Federal basis that preceded Federation.[216] The school opened in February 1955; Humphrey remained on its Board, for many years as Chairman, until his death. His youngest son, Simon, went there – and into Paget House. In a parallel venture, and just eight miles away, another school was established, with both Gibbs and Snell on the founding Board of Governors. This was Bernard Mizeki College, founded near the site of – and partly as a memorial to – the martyrdom of Bernard Mizeki in 1896. The idea of this school was that it was 'to be a boarding high school for boys, predominantly or entirely black, as a partner to Peterhouse ... for predominantly or entirely white boys'.[217] But the story of multiracial education belongs to a later chapter, when Humphrey Gibbs was not only Chairman of the Peterhouse Governors, but also Governor of Southern Rhodesia.

LOST CHANCE?

Humphrey Gibbs was Chairman of the United Party – or now, within the colony, the United Rhodesia Party – when Garfield Todd became Prime Minister, and then won the election of January 1954 with twenty-six seats, opposed by four independents. Humphrey was to play no part in the political manoeuvrings of the next five years before he became Governor; indeed he was happy to be out of politics. But these were critical years in the history of Southern Rhodesia, and we need to understand what happened as a background to the momentous events of the 1960s.

The Southern Rhodesian High Commissioner in London in 1949 had talked confidently of 'the growth of a more liberal attitude on the part of the European towards the African population'.[218] The advent of Garfield Todd seemed to confirm the changes in the air. At Governor's Lodge Sir John Kennedy – 'the best Governor we ever had'[219] – and his wife were for the first time inviting Africans to public and private functions. At Government House there was Lord Llewellin, ex-Conservative minister 'of dynamic ability',[220] who had made his communion at the Cathedral at an interracial ordination service. And at the Cathedral too there was Paget, now about to become an Archbishop, with a Province ('Central Africa') that was virtually the same territory as the Central African Federation. The inauguration of this new Province of the Anglican Communion seemed to give some moral and spiritual underpinning to the concept of Federation. Clayton, Archbishop of Cape Town, spoke at the inauguration ceremony in May 1955 and declared:

'You are a multiracial province. Christ came to break down barriers. It is for you to create a union of hearts. This cannot be done by force or regulation.'[221] Geoffrey Fisher, the Archbishop of Canterbury, came out for the inauguration. He too spoke with optimism: 'You have begun your federal life with a declaration of faith in partnership as a distant goal. You begin, African and European, on the basis of mutual respect, friendship and trust, and I have rejoiced to see many grand evidences of its fruitful application in the fields of administration, education and industrial organisation.' Note Fisher's 'distant goal'. The Archbishop was conservative; he declared during his African tour: 'all men are not equal in the sight of God though they are equal in the love of God'.[222] He thought of himself as something of an Africa expert, as he had a number of personal contacts. His brother Leonard, who lived in Grahamstown, had been a bishop in South Africa since 1921.[223] His niece Ann was a headmistress in South Africa, and later Rhodesia.[224] He himself had been a public school headmaster and while in Salisbury, took the opportunity to drive the 50 miles with Paget to visit Peterhouse which had just opened and where his son, Charles, was second master.[225] The school's ecclesiastical links must have pleased the two prelates: Charles, as well as being second master, was soon to move into the second boarding house to be built at Peterhouse, named after Paget.[226] The school, in the early 1960s, was to make that 'distant goal' rather more immediate, when it become the first school in Rhodesia to be multiracial.

An even more significant educational advance was the opening of the University College of Rhodesia and Nyasaland, which owed its origin to a meeting of the 'Friends of the University Association of Rhodesia' which met first in 1945. Fund were raised and land purchased. Oxford was approached to become foster mother. But despite its 'many-sided relationship with the Empire'[227] Oxford's rather parochial response was that it was too far away.[228] Instead, the University of London agreed to patronise the new institution, final plans for which were published in April 1954. It was to be a 'non-racial-island of learning', receiving its Royal Charter in February 1955, and its final seal of approval with the installation of Queen Elizabeth the Queen Mother as its President in July 1957.

So in and around 1955 it was possible to hope, and to see a chance that multiracial partnership might ensure peace and prosperity in central Africa. But then came the ousting – in early 1958 – of Garfield Todd, the Prime Minister who seemed in many ways to epitomise this new mood. There are those who see his downfall after just four years in office as 'the first blow struck in the planned murder of Central Africa's white liberalism'.[229] That verdict was delivered just a year after Todd's demise. Humphrey Gibbs played no part in those events, but as we have already noted, they are essential background to what was to follow. The bare bones of the matter are straight-forward. Todd's premiership was marked by two significant disturbances – a strike at Wankie colliery when the Prime Minister reacted (or some said overreacted) with a show of force, but with a subsequent wage adjustment. A similar adjustment followed the Salisbury bus boycott in favour of lower fares in 1956. But his reaction to these issues, and his tendency to criticise the Federal government, did nothing to undermine Todd's popularity with the mainly white electorate. More controversial was the amending of the Land Apportionment Act in 1954 to allow for the possibility of hotels, restaurants and clubs becoming multiracial. Then in 1957 the Tredgold Commission recommended changes in the franchise and Todd pushed through, on this basis, a Franchise Bill which many in the party regarded as too liberal.[230] There were changes to the racist Industrial Conciliation Act of 1934 in the pipeline, and proposals to tackle the plight of urban Africans. At the annual United Rhodesia Party (URP) congress in late September 1957, discussions were dominated by the proposal that the territorial and Federal political parties should merge – a proposal supported by Todd (even though it would cut his dash somewhat, as the United Party would be dominated by the Federal Prime Minister). The proposal was passed. But even before and during the congress, there were private mutterings among Todd's ministers. At the end of November one of them, Sir Patrick Fletcher, reported to him that there was discontent, and that the other ministers might resign. At the Cabinet meeting following, Todd made some concessions – he would talk tough about the newly inaugurated African National Congress (ANC), and he would tolerate an amendment to the Immorality Act.[231] The ministers seemed happy. There was, thought Todd, a 'new unity' among his ministers – Fletcher, Hatty, Ellman-Brown and Stumbles.

It was at this point, at the end of 1957, that Todd went off to the Cape. There was some consternation that he had, on the eve of his departure, met with the radical white Guy Clutton-Brock, and with the leader of the newly inaugurated African National Congress, Joshua Nkomo, whom he knew from his days as headmaster of the school at his Dadaya Mission.[232] African leaders have learnt in subsequent decades that it is dangerous to be out of the country while discontent is simmering. Todd had reason to suppose that the discontent had died down. It had not.

While he travelled south there appeared in London's *Spectator* an article by Charles Vambe, who wrote enthusiastically: 'In Southern Rhodesia the present administration is under the guidance of a very liberal man, Prime Minister Todd, liberal by conviction as well as from political expediency, and I would go along with him the whole way.'[233] Over Christmas, his ministers finally decided that they could not. It was Sir Patrick Fletcher again

who, on Todd's return to the colony on 9 January, met him with the news
that he had already heard – from reporters at Johannesburg – that his Cabinet
intended to resign en bloc. When Todd did not take the hint and himself resign,
they did and so the Prime Minister constructed a new Cabinet, and on 8
February a party congress (still the territorial division of the United Party)
met to decide his fate. It was chaired by the man whom he had defeated for
the leadership of the party back in 1954 – Julian Greenfield, now Federal
Minister of Justice. The voting on the first round gave the Prime Minister a
majority, but not an overall one. He took 129 votes. There were two other
candidates, Sir Edgar Whitehead who got 122 votes, and Fletcher who took
73. With Fletcher eliminated, the Todd vote held at 122, but Whitehead came
out well ahead with 193. Todd had to accept defeat by a man who was not
even in the country at the time.

Sir Edgar Whitehead was not even an MP when this voting took place.
He was the Federal High Commissioner in Washington, an ex-Minister who
had earned high praise from R. A. Butler for his handling of the Rhodesian
economy in the years immediately prior to Federation.[234] He was an
establishment figure, who had arrived in Southern Africa a month after
Humphrey Gibbs, and was from the same kind of background. He farmed
in the Vumba (near Umtali); he was a bachelor, hard of hearing, with failing
eyesight, and a remarkable capacity for consuming beer and showing no ill-
effects. Alec Douglas-Home recorded with wry amusement that 'he once
arrived to talk with me at Dorneywood, and between 8pm and midnight
consumed thirteen bottles of beer'.[235] He was, as one observer put it, like
'a character out of *Wind in the Willows*'.[236] Whitehead answered the summons
and returned to the colony. He constructed a Cabinet in which Todd agreed
to serve, and then set about getting into parliament. He stood for a Bulawayo
seat and was defeated by the Dominion Party candidate, in a contest which
was as much about Todd and his policies as about Whitehead. As a result
the new Prime Minister decided to go to the country – but without Todd,
now regarded as an electoral liability and who now revived his own 'United
Rhodesia Party' to contest the election. The results represent a marked
change in the voting patterns: Whitehead's United Federal Party took
seventeen seats, the Dominion Party thirteen, and Todd's URP was wiped out.

Looking back on it, Todd himself not unnaturally felt that this was the
end as far as his liberal policies went. Over thirty years' later he was
lamenting: 'The blacks would have talked to me ... They still would have
listened ... They wouldn't listen to Whitehead ....' [237] Todd's lieutenant, the
founder of the Inter-racial Association, Hardwicke Holderness, agrees; his
book on this is called *Lost Chance*, but at the time, it did not look that way.

Indeed 'the years between 1958 and 1962 while Sir Edgar Whitehead was in office were the great reforming period in Rhodesian history. More social and economic legislation was passed than by any earlier Rhodesian Parliament and the bulk of it was designed specifically to benefit the African.'[238] But perhaps the difference now was that what has come to be called the 'feel-good factor' was no longer there – either among Africans or among whites. In retrospect the reforming moves look like those in Russia before the revolution, or in the Apartheid state before its final collapse. Maybe Todd had fallen because, as the consummate politician Welensky said 'there seemed to be something in his judgement that was lacking, a lack of political perspective'.[239] Maybe it was his 'modestly liberal paternalism' that estranged him from his Cabinet colleagues.[240] Perhaps, as Lord Home considered, 'in spite of his later protestations he was exactly the same as his predecessors and successors'.[241] Maybe, too, there had been a shift to the right, to those who, as the *Spectator* forecast, 'would talk of partnership and practice white supremacy'.[242] But for the moment, hopes were still high. Only time would show that the feel-good factor was ebbing away, and that greater militancy on the part of blacks and of whites would undermine the achievements of these years.

THE COLONY IN EARLY 1959

The year 1959 opened auspiciously for the Gibbs family. Humphrey and Molly became grandparents for the first time on 9 January when Jeremy's daughter, Elizabeth, was born in Johannesburg. It opened hopefully too for the colony: On 3 February the Prime Minister addressed the Assembly for the first time in the new year, and outlined a comprehensive legislative programme.[243] There was nothing in his brief speech to indicate the sweeping nature of some of the changes that would be introduced. Indeed the opposition welcomed his statement, not because they would agree with the changes, but because they welcomed 'the new attitude of the Government' in forewarning the house of the legislative programme.[244]

The changes were significant. The new Industrial Conciliation Act was introduced in February and became law on 25 August. It had been discussed at length in 1957 while Todd was Prime Minister. It was based on 'the principle that there can be no differentiation among workers on grounds of race, colour or religion', and therefore it was the government's duty 'to provide the machinery for equal opportunity through training and apprenticeship for all'.[245] A parallel move tampered with that other pillar of European privilege, the Land Apportionment Act, the 'magna carta of the European', as the right-wing William Cary called it. In February the Minister responsible, Jack Quinton, proposed its amendment which would allow hotels to become multiracial. The amendment was approved, as were amendments to the Public Service regulations to remove discrimination in terms of pensions and privileges, a move calculated to assist Africans, and also women. Other changes removed discriminations in terms of Post Offices, theatres, and in the purchase of 'European' beers and wines. These moves, as Colin Leys noted, 'are surely changes in the right direction'. They were hardly revolutionary, but 'do stand in marked contrast with the hardening apartheid of the Union [of South Africa]'.[246]

But there was a darker side. On 20 February, at their regular meeting in Salisbury, under the chairmanship of Lord Dalhousie, the Governors of Northern Rhodesia and Nyasaland, and the Federal and Southern Rhodesian Prime Ministers were given details of what 'could be interpreted as plans for a sort of St Bartholomew's Day massacre of Whites and "quisling" blacks'.[247] The result was the greatest crisis the Federation had faced thus far. Federal troops were flown to Blantyre, the capital of Nyasaland. Whitehead had a state of emergency declared in Rhodesia in the early hours of 26 February and some 500 members of the ANC were arrested. Subsequently he introduced a whole range of security measures in Southern Rhodesia contained in six bills, the most important of which became the Unlawful Organisations Act. It was a blow to Whitehead's hopes for 'partnership', but he anticipated that within the five years during which the new laws would initially operate, he would have gained significant support from Africans on the basis of his liberalising measures and the pace of economic advance. But Southern Rhodesia and the Federation were not isolated from the rest of the world, and world reaction – and more particularly reaction in Britain – was to have an influence on the course of events from now on.

The Nyasaland emergency was a blow to British rule in Africa. One summary highlights the 'complete harvest of failure' reaped there by the colonial authorities and the British government: 'perpetrating a mini-Amritsar on day one; being forced into an imperial (not even a local) enquiry within days; selecting as chief inquisitor the judge [Devlin] who was least likely to take a relaxed view of boisterous colonial methods; suffering the inquiry's public dismissal of the official reasons for declaring the emergency and finding that the political views of the "extremists" against whom the emergency had been declared vindicated by the inquiry as an accurate expression of local opinion'.[248] Although the focus of the emergency was Nyasaland, it had the wider effect of profoundly undermining any hopes for partnership in Central Africa. It also came at a bad time for the Conservative government in Britain. Macmillan was setting up the Monckton Commission to look into the future of the Federation, and a general election was in the offing. Little wonder that when the Devlin Report was finally produced in July, Macmillan should confide testily in his diaries; 'Why Devlin?' – who had in fact been chosen by the Lord Chancellor. 'I have since discovered', Macmillan wrote, 'that he is (a) *Irish* – no doubt with that Fenian blood that makes Irishmen anti-Government on principle, (b) a *lapsed* Roman Catholic. His brother is a Jesuit priest; his sister a nun.'[249] This was perhaps the last occasion when a British Prime Minister gave vent (albeit privately) to the Englishman's centuries-old 'anti-popery' sentiments; it was probably not the last time that anti-Irish sentiments were expressed.

Within Southern Rhodesia itself, the emergency passed. The liberal *Central African Examiner*, at the end of March, struck a confident note. 'He would be a fool who said that all is now well within the Federation of Rhodesia and Nyasaland, but no more foolish than those who refuse to recognise the accumulation of signs for the better which have appeared during the last fortnight.'[250] Its editorial – entitled 'Out of crisis – into where?' – pointed to the government's withdrawal of its proposed Preventive Detention Bill, its release of fifty detainees, and Roy Welensky's elevation 'though as always a little belatedly' of an African, Jasper Savanhu, to ministerial rank in the Federal government. Its conclusion was that Sir Edgar Whitehead 'intends to make partnership work'.

Alec Douglas-Home, who was Macmillan's Secretary of State for Commonwealth Relations, had visited the Federation in September/October 1957. He had been 'distressed to discover how bad the Federal politicians had been at selling their achievements in development to the citizens of the Federation and to the world outside'.[251] He had conceived the idea of an all-party commission from Britain which would visit the Federation and by its report 'the Africans could be convinced that the federal structure would serve the peoples of the three countries better than any other'. This was the origin of the Royal Commission which Macmillan's Cabinet finally decided upon in March 1959.[252] Evelyn Baring, the Gibbses old friend, was initially asked to chair it, though he felt he was 'inexperienced and far from impartial'.[253] The task was shouldered by Macmillan's Oxford contemporary, Walter Monckton. Meanwhile Humphrey's other old friend, Lord Home, spent four days in Salisbury at the end of March and beginning of April selling the approach to Welensky in particular. On Home's return to London, Welensky was surprised to hear from Macmillan that 'my cautious acceptance in principle of Alec Home's original proposal had been converted by some magic in Harold Macmillan's mind into willing – indeed enthusiastic – alliance with him in carrying out an exercise whose dangers and difficulties made him exult'.[254] Whatever 'Wondermac' hoped to achieve in Central Africa, Welensky's own position was clear. He had spelled it out in a speech at Kitwe on 10 March: it was a 'fallacious argument' to maintain that the day of the white man in Central Africa was drawing to a close. Those who thought so 'should prepare themselves for a rude shock'.[255]

6 First Year as Governor

One Monday morning in mid-1959, a telephone call came through to Bonisa asking Humphrey to call and see the Prime Minister when he was in Salisbury next day for the Barclays Bank board meeting. That night, Molly woke up with the realisation of why Humphrey had been summoned; she said nothing to him. He returned to the farm the following evening with the news that Whitehead wanted to put his name forward as Governor in succession to William-Powlett. He had been taken completely by surprise, and had only agreed on the understanding that it might be a short-term appointment. It was a private understanding between himself and the Prime Minister that 'his term should be eighteen months, and not the usual five years'.[256] This in fact fitted in well with the plans which Whitehead had for the Governorship.

The United Federal Party hoped that as part of the Federal review in 1960, the British government might agree to combine the posts of Governor-General of the Federation and Governor of Southern Rhodesia. This proposal had been in the offing for some time. When Alan Lennox-Boyd, the Colonial Secretary, had heard of it back in 1956, he was firm that 'we ought not to entertain it'.[257] When Lord Llewellin died in 1958, there was some relief in Whitehall that there was no local candidate who could possibly replace him as Governor-General.[258] But the issue had arisen again at the end of 1958. Whitehead suggested that on the departure of Peveril William-Powlett, who was taking terminal leave in June 1959, Governor's Lodge should be closed and the Governor-General invited to act as Governor of Southern Rhodesia. This would be a step towards amalgamating the two posts. If this was not possible, Whitehead was intending to recommend a local man for the Governorship. The only local candidate whose name was being mentioned at this stage was Sir Andrew Strachan, Chairman of Rhodesian Railways. But Whitehead was unwilling to make a formal recommendation, hoping still for the amalgamation of posts.[259] The Governor-General, Dalhousie, arranged a meeting early in 1959 with Whitehead, Welensky and the Governors of Northern Rhodesia and Nyasaland to discuss this proposed amalgamation. Predictably, all except Whitehead and Welensky were against it.[260] The temporary solution was that Whitehead would agree with a local man to take over as Officer Administering the Government during Powlett's terminal leave, continuing until after the constitutional review of the Federation which was due to take place in 1960. Home, the Commonwealth Secretary, agreed to this formula.[261] The idea of amalgamating the posts was still being talked about it Salisbury. But as the *Rhodesia Herald* pointed out, it was most unlikely that the British government would agree to a proposal which, while saving the tax payer £35,000 a year, would also lead to 'increased suspicion ... in the minds of the Africans of the Northern territories'.[262]

Humphrey decided to go to England, and while he was there, on 10 July, the Commonwealth Relations Office announced the appointment. It was greeted with delight in Southern Rhodesia. 'A happy choice', was the title of one leading article which declared that 'the choice of a Rhodesian as the Queen's representative ... is in keeping with the growing trend among Commonwealth countries for the Governorship to be entrusted to citizens of their own. It thus forms another token of the "coming into its own" by the Colony.' The article went on to note that things might change in 1960, and that Humphrey's appointment might 'open the door to the eventual appointment of a Rhodesian as Governor-General of the whole Federation'.[263] Congratulations flowed in. Evelyn Baring wrote from Government House, Kenya, advising him 'that it is absolutely essential for a Governor to be pompous' and offered lessons, since he suggested that Humphrey 'may be a little lacking in this fundamental quality'.[264] John Maud, his junior at Eton, wrote from South Africa with delight and amazement that they should find themselves 'neighbouring Excellencies'.[265] While in England Humphrey was not only receiving these congratulations. He was also engaged in the rather more worrying business of visiting doctors because of back trouble. Alec Home introduced a lighter note even in this context, delighting to point out that 'stiffening the backbone of Governors is all to the good'.[266] One correspondent, however, sounded a warning note: 'we are rapidly approaching the dreadful sixties when the Whites in Africa have got to work out a satisfactory accommodation with the Blacks or get out'. But, as he noted, 'the only hope for the Whites is to have persons like you at the helm while the change is going on'.[267]

Humphrey had an audience with the Queen on 30 October, and Molly was received immediately afterwards. They were to meet her again almost exactly ten years later, when Humphrey took formal leave on relinquishing his post. In that autumn of 1959, they still believed the appointment would be a short-term one. They did not dream that the governorship would last for a decade.[268] Several days later, a proclamation announced that while his predecessor was on leave, Humphrey would be the Officer Administering the Government. On 16 December he became Governor of Southern Rhodesia in succession to Vice-Admiral Sir Peveril Barton Reibey Wallop William-Powlett.

Humphrey had received the OBE (Order of the British Empire) in 1959, before he became Governor. Now he received the KCMG (Knight Commander of the Order of St Michael and St George) – 'automatic' for a colonial governor, as he deprecatingly put it. He also became a new Knight of the Order of St John, in the same list that contained the Chief Scout, Lord Rowallan, and the Governor of Bermuda, Sir Julian Gascoigne.[269] The Governor-General was head of the Order in the Federation, and when it ended Humphrey became the head, and remained so even after he ceased to be Governor.[270] Humphrey – now a knight twice over – and Lady Gibbs took up residence in Governor's Lodge. This 'horrid house', as Molly described it, became the Governor's residence during the time of Humphrey's predecessor. Built in bright red brick in 1929 at the corner of Enterprise Road and Glenara Avenue, it was one of the first houses in the new suburb of Highlands, originally designed for the general manager of the Imperial Tobacco Company and eventually acquired by the government in 1950. The extensions made for the William-Powletts 'changed the character of the house from a home to an institution', though it still retained the look of a grand neo-Georgian villa of the type found in the eastern states of the US.[271] With the ending of the Federation in 1963, the Gibbses were able to move into Government House, which for ten years had been the residence of the Governor-General. Situated in pleasant and reasonably secluded gardens between Chancellor Avenue and North Avenue, it was an attractive single-storey Cape Dutch building, of which Molly approved.[272] From there, and from the much superior Government House in Bulawayo, the Gibbses must now lead a very different life to that which they had enjoyed at Bonisa.

'It was nearly over now', says Jan Morris of the empire around 1960.[273] But there were still imperial echoes. There were still colonies where 'the Governor and his lady pottered through their generally uneventful terms of office'.[274] In the first few months of 1960, the pattern emerged for Humphrey and Molly. They had every expectation that for the next few years, it would vary little. There would be a fairly unhurried round of visits and stone layings, punctuated by occasional investitures at Governor's Lodge. In January there was the opening of the new Reps theatre (for the Salisbury Repertory Company) in the capital. The Governor and his wife attended, along with a whole glittering array, including the Governor-General, and the Federal and territorial Prime Ministers.[275] In that same month, there were the Australia Day celebrations to attend at the High Commission, and a summer flower show to open.[276] February saw Sir Humphrey meeting African police recruits at the British South Africa Police (BSAP) depot in Salisbury, attending a civic dinner in his honour, opening the new Queen Victoria Museum in the capital, and attending the dinner of the

Commonwealth Parliamentary Association as its guest of honour.[277] His programme for March included visits to three schools: Domboshawa and Goromonzi (African schools), and Arundel (a sort of sister-school to Peterhouse). There was lunch with the British South Africa Company, dinner with the Soroptimists and a dance at the Civil Service Club. There were factory visits: to Lion matches, Turner asbestos and Rodea fertilisers.[278] In April there were visits further afield. The first venture outside Salisbury was a very low-key visit to Gwelo – 'his escort was one police car'[279] – visiting local hospitals. A few days later their Excellencies were reported to 'have charmed Que Que'.[280] From there they went on to Bulawayo, where they stayed at Government House for three weeks, and toured the African townships.[281] In June it was reported that the Governor would entertain William Deedes and Lord Balniel to lunch. But already preparations were in train for the visit by a more important guest, the Queen Mother.

ROYALTY IN RHODESIA

The first royal visit to Southern Rhodesia had been by the Prince of Wales in 1925, though it was a minor interlude in what he described as his 'boring and monotonous' tour of South Africa – a tour adjudged to have been a great success, largely, as his biographer remarks, because 'there was little in the way of temptation'.[282] His youngest brother had a better time in March 1934. Prince George, later Duke of Kent, visited Bulawayo, and had opened the 'native' hospital in Gwelo which Humphrey visited in April 1960. He had toured the country seeing most of the sights, and had telegraphed afterwards to say that his one regret was that he was unable to stay longer.[283] We can believe this was more than the usual politeness of royalty. We read that he had met a man who had attended the opening of the Alfred Docks in Cape Town by his uncle Prince Albert in 1870. And in Umtali he met not only the Hon Lionel Cripps, Speaker of the House of Assembly who had arrived in the colony in 1890,[284] but also Major Wiegand, who crossed the border from Portuguese territory to meet the Prince, resplendent in iron cross which he had won for his work with Big Bertha in the siege of Paris during the Great War. Such delights were more likely to appeal to George than to his more hedonistic eldest brother.

When George VI visited Southern Rhodesia in 1947, accompanied by his wife and daughters, it was the first time a reigning monarch had set foot in Britain's African possessions, and the visit to South Africa had been regarded as particularly significant and politic. It was a long and exhausting tour, despite the comforts and air conditioning of the 'white train' in which they travelled. The King was very concerned that while he and his family enjoyed the sunshine and hospitality of the Southern Africans, his subjects back in Britain were shivering in a gloomy winter of austerity. He even telegraphed his Prime Minister asking if he should cut the tour short, but Attlee assured him that the presence in Africa of the King-Emperor was of national and international significance. The royal family's arrival on 14 April in Bulawayo was witnessed by Humphrey and Molly. Humphrey felt that the welcome being accorded the royal visitors was rather too subdued, and he climbed a tree shouting 'hooray', thus encouraging a more rousing reception. This perhaps accounts for the newspaper report that 'the citizens of Bulawayo disproved the belief that they could not cheer and show their feelings'.[285] The royal family's own feelings of pleasure at their reception in Southern Africa were significant too. For the first time, Africans (black and white) had seen their monarch and his heir. For Princess Elizabeth, about to be married, and all too soon to become monarch herself, the significance was not limited to a feeling of pleasure. The tour had, her biographer records, 'profoundly affected her outlook, helping to establish a Commonwealth interest and loyalty that became a consistent theme of her reign'.[286] It was a theme which was to re-emerge dramatically, as far as southern Africa was concerned, on many occasions – both happy and sad – in the course of the subsequent half-century.

King George's wife, Queen Elizabeth, was back in Southern Rhodesia six years later, in 1953, on a visit tinged no doubt with some melancholy. She was no longer Queen Empress, but Queen Mother. Her elder daughter's coronation had taken place just a month earlier, and she was accompanied by her younger daughter, Princess Margaret. The Princess's infatuation with Group Captain Peter Townsend – an equerry who had accompanied the tour in 1947 – had become obvious at the time of the coronation and was now at least temporarily suspended, both by her visit to Rhodesia, and by his being sent as air attaché to Brussels.[287] The arrangements for the royal visit, to which Humphrey was not privy but which he would experience at a future date, were awesome in their complexity. Rhodesian Railways produced a thirty-six-page booklet in which 'the precise instructions for the working of the trains was detailed to the minute when discussing time, and the quarter inch in relation to length'.[288] The Queen Mother opened the Rhodes Centenary Exhibition in Bulawayo on 3 July, and she and the Princess visited Gwelo, and Umtali, where a memorial was unveiled to Kingsley Fairbridge, the young Rhodesian whose empire settlement scheme for children was to attract much attention half a century later.[289] In Salisbury the Queen Mother laid the foundation stone at the site of the proposed University College. The Gibbses were summoned to a ball at Government House, to which a young set had been invited, no doubt to distract the Princess. This had left out of the reckoning the fact that the Queen Mother would also want to dance, and Humphrey was pressed into service, he nervous, and Molly more nervous still. No doubt Humphrey's friendship with her brother at Eton came up in the conversation. And they were to meet again when the Queen Mother returned to Salisbury in July 1957, to be installed as President of the University College of Rhodesia and Nyasaland.

Plans for a visit to the Federation by the Queen herself had been in train since 1955. Her Private Secretary, Sir Michael Adeane, had advised the Commonwealth Office that a visit might be possible in 1959 or 1960.[290] In 1958 Welensky was making moves to have the Queen come and open the Kariba Dam, due to be completed in 1960. Privately this was agreed in early 1959, but no announcement was to be made as yet.[291] This was just as well, for two reasons: first, the tensions within the Federation were hotting up, which might cause embarrassment; second, the Queen was in fact pregnant. The proposed visit was cancelled in June 1959, and the birth of Prince Andrew, later Duke of York, took place in February 1960. Fortunately no public announcement had been made, so the cancellation too was confidential – unlike the cancellation of her proposed visit to Ghana, which involved her Private Secretary being dispatched to Lagos to explain to President Nkrumah – 'a notoriously tricky personage' – why Her Majesty could not visit his country in late 1959.[292] Meanwhile, someone else must be found to open the Kariba Dam. So on 22 February 1960, just three days after Andrew's birth, the *Rhodesia Herald* was exulting in the fact that the Queen Mother was expected once more – on a visit to what it described as her 'favourite country in the Commonwealth'. Whether this is true, and whether as one chronicler of royalty claims, 'she has never made any secret of her sympathy for what the whites of Southern Africa stand for',[293] the fact was that she was to make a fourth visit, this time with the particular purpose of declaring open the Kariba Hydro-electric project. In preparation since 1954, this was to be the Federation's greatest – perhaps only lasting – achievement. Garfield Todd had managed to overturn Huggins' original Kafue scheme which would have been cheaper but which would have situated the new facility entirely within Northern Rhodesia. The Kariba Dam – then the largest man-made lake in the world, 180 miles long – was situated on the Zambezi between the Northern and Southern territories. Critics saw it as another example of *bambazonke* (take all!),[294] whereby Southern Rhodesia was getting the best of the Federation bargain, as had been the case when Salisbury was chosen as the site for the Federal capital. Critics also said that Kariba would 'have at completion a capacity far in excess of the anticipated requirements of a future Federal economy'[295] – a prediction which looked very dated thirty years on.

Before the grand opening at Kariba, the Queen Mother arrived at Bulawayo airport. She was accompanied by Humphrey and Molly from there to Government House, where she was to stay the night. In the afternoon she opened the Trade Fair, and attended a reception in the evening at the Civil Hall – she resplendent in crinoline and tiara. On the next day they accompanied her to an Interdenominational Church service, and for the rest of the day Humphrey and Molly had the – perhaps daunting – task of entertaining Her Majesty privately. She left the next day for Thornhill Royal Rhodesian Air Force base at Gwelo, and thence to two more weeks of touring the Federation and opening the Kariba power station.[296] For the Governor and his wife, it had been a charming and indeed triumphant episode at the start of the governorship. The Governor picked up two lessons which he put to good use soon after. On the Tuesday after she departed from Bulawayo, Humphrey spoke at a great Scout rally held at Milton School, Bulawayo – where he 'made history by becoming the first governor to attend a rally wearing scout uniform'; and he was able to base his speech on the lesson of devotion to duty exemplified in the Queen Mother.[297] Just as the Queen Mother, in tiara and crinoline, had made an impact – every inch the Queen Empress which she had been – so Humphrey made an impact with his Scout uniform. The least pompous of men, he was fortunate in having the looks and stature to appear magnificent in uniform. The cocked hat and tailcoat of a governor's full uniform, or the flowing robes of a Knight of St John, and equally the more humble khaki shirt and shorts and wide-brimmed hat of Chief Scout, all suited him and added style to an occasion. Black tie occasions were even more frequent. On Wednesday he was back in Salisbury speaking to the local branch of the Royal Commonwealth Society, where he spelled out the other lesson he had learnt. He described to them how he had felt obliged to admit to Her Majesty that he could speak no local language, and went on to advocate the learning and teaching of Shona and Ndebele.[298] The lesson about duty was hardly one that Humphrey Gibbs needed to be taught. Ingrained in him was a sense of duty. But his espousal of the other lesson – that local whites ought to learn native languages – was a significant one. It was one that no governor sent out from England would have taken on board so readily.

AFRICA YEAR 1960

In late July 1959, while Humphrey Gibbs was receiving letters of congratulation on his appointment, the British House of Commons was discussing Central Africa. 'A long session was drawing to an end. Members of Parliament and Ministers were in a restless mood.'[299] On 24 July the government published the results of the inquiry into the Hola incident, a *cause célèbre* which had blown up in Kenya in March, when eleven Mau Mau prisoners at Hola Detention Camp had died after a clash with warders. The White Paper exonerated the Governor, Humphrey's old friend Sir Evelyn Baring, and the Colonial Secretary, Alan Lennox-Boyd, and recorded the compulsory retirement of the ex-commandant of the camp, and the voluntary retirement of the Commissioner of Prisons. Macmillan records, somewhat dismissively, that 'it had been an anxious, if minor, incident, exaggerated by the hysterical attitude of some critics and the not unnatural desire of others to gain political advantage'.[300] By no accident, the Devlin Report on the Nyasaland disturbances was published on the same day. Macmillan breathed a sigh of relief when it was debated the following week and 'the Colonial secretary ended with a fine defence of his administration. We had a very good division – sixty-three majority.'[301] He turned his mind to a more important objective – that of winning the general election of October 1959. To the relief of the politicians in Salisbury, the Conservatives were returned with an increased majority. Perhaps it was a misplaced relief. In the new government, Lord Home was replaced at the Commonwealth Office by Duncan Sandys, and the Colonial Secretary, Alan Lennox-Boyd – who had retired from the Commons – was replaced by Iain Macleod. 'As a result of these changes', James Callaghan noted, 'we began to detect a rather different note in the speeches of the new Ministers' with regard to Africa.[302] One change of personnel, however, went unnoticed. A new Member of Parliament had taken her seat on the back-benches: Margaret Thatcher was to have a key role in the affairs of Rhodesia twenty years later.

While the results of the British general election were awaited, the Dominion Party held its annual territorial congress – at the Convent Hall in Gwelo – under a large glossy picture of Pope John XXIII in an attitude of benediction. The ruling United Party might have its internal disagreements, in terms of policy regarding partnership and in terms of style between the pugilistic Sir Roy Welensky and the taciturn Sir Edgar Whitehead. But the Dominion Party was even more in need of papal blessing. Its leader in the Legislative Assembly, Ray Stockil, had resigned in February. He disagreed with what the party's Federal leader, Winston Field, called the Central African Alliance, his vision for the future of the Federation. The plan was adopted by the divisional executive meeting in Salisbury, but its secretary resigned and at the end of March had formed the Southern Rhodesia Association, to fight for white rule and secession from the Federation. In June, another Dominion Party MP, Dr Ahrn Palley, had attacked his party's ineffectual opposition and had resigned to form his own party, the Southern Rhodesia Party, which gave its support to the Federation. Now at the congress Stockil's successor as leader, S. E. Aitken-Cade, was ousted by the more right-wing William Harper. And while the Dominion Party seemed to be moving even further to the right, the Central Africa Party of Garfield Todd was moving further to the left, and ended the year calling for a new franchise and an immediate end to all racial discrimination. Thus the opposition parties in the colony were divided and in the subsequent year were to continue to present a bewildering sequence of fragmentation and realignment, and an almost amoeba-like ability to split and reproduce at both Federal and territorial level. That, plus the Conservative victory in the British election, seemed to augur well for Whitehead's government in Southern Rhodesia, and its new Governor, whose political sympathies – such as they were – had traditionally lain with the United Party. But as the *Central African Examiner* commented, the days were in fact long past when 'the players were divided into those who believed "Huggie" was the country's hope and those who were sure he would be its downfall'.[303] 1960 was to show that the players, the playing field, the tactics and the umpire (if umpire the British government was) had changed out of all recognition.

'At the beginning of 1960', wrote Anthony Low, 'British newspapers and the British Labour Party dubbed 1960 "Africa Year". Subsequent events soon justified that description.'[304] Harold Macmillan's now famous 'wind of change' speech in Cape Town in February was followed by example after example of change and upheaval throughout the continent. The Sharpeville massacre in South Africa in March was followed in April by the attempted assassination of Hendrick Verwoerd, the South African Prime Minister. At the Commonwealth Conference less than a month later, Macmillan 'used all his skills to prevent the Commonwealth from breaking up and to keep South Africa within it',[305] but before the year was out that country had voted, by a tiny majority, to become a republic, and its place within the Commonwealth was doomed. Meanwhile the changes were sweeping the rest of Africa. British rule in Somaliland ended in June, and in the same month the Congo gained its independence from Belgium. In July Ghana became a republic, and United Nations troops moved into the Congo. In September Julius Nyerere formed a government in Tanganyika, and Nigeria became a republic in the next month.

On 5 January, Harold Macmillan had set off on his six-week-long tour of the Commonwealth. In Lagos, on the 13th, he replied to a journalist's question by suggesting that 'the people of the two territories [N. Rhodesia and Nyasaland] will be given an opportunity to decide on whether the Federation is beneficial to them', which was not Welensky's understanding at all. Five days later he arrived, 'bland and unrepentant' as Welensky said, in Salisbury.[306] It was his first, and only, visit to the Federation. Henry Fairlie had just written about how 'in Nairobi an Englishman feels he is among his contemporaries. In Salisbury an Englishman rediscovers his grandparents.'[307] For Macmillan, fresh from Nigeria, to arrive at Salisbury was 'to enter a different world'.[308] Macmillan, antennae well-tuned to the nuances of style and history, noted that 'it still had a colonial atmosphere'.[309] Speaking to the Rhodesia National Affairs Association Macmillan was pleased that 'the audience applauded vigorously not only my expressions of support for the federation, but also the numerous passages in which I reaffirmed our duty towards the Africans and praised the concept of partnership'. He was particularly pleased to see partnership in action at the University College. 'What an answer this is to those critics who pounce so readily on anything to blame and pass by so conveniently anything that they might have to praise.'[310] Nevertheless he left the colony feeling that 'the European temper at Salisbury and elsewhere was volatile'.[311] The climax of his African tour was the speech to the parliamentarians at Cape Town, which the Salisbury daily reported initially in rather admiring terms, saying that Macmillan had 'once again performed the politically impossible ... avoiding giving offence to those present and at the same time [he] pleased the British Labour Party'.[312] It was in fact a speech that had indeed been carefully worked upon, and it is likely that Humphrey's Etonian friends, Alec Home and John Maud, had some part in its composition.[313] At the core of this, Macmillan's most famous speech, were these words:

> Ever since the break-up of the Roman Empire one of the constant facts of political life in Europe has been the emergence of independent nations ... Today the same thing is happening in Africa, and the most striking of all the impressions I have formed since I left London a month ago is of the strength of this African national consciousness. In different places it takes different forms, but it is happening everywhere. The wind of change is blowing through this continent, and, whether we like it or not, this growth of national consciousness is a political fact. We must all accept it as a fact, and our national policies must take account of it.[314]

Later, the full impact of the speech sank in. Both the Federal and Southern Rhodesian governments were unhappy about the direction British policy seemed to be taking – bending with the wind of change. There was pressure from Britain for the release of Hastings Banda, still held in prison at Gwelo. The new man at the Colonial Office (after October 1959) was Iain Macleod, whom Doris Lessing's brother was not alone in branding a 'communist'.[315] Macleod had responsibility for two of the three territories of the Federation.

So there were fears about the arrival of a Monckton Commission which seemed to them, even before it had collected any evidence, predisposed to the break-up of the Federation. Welensky determined to visit London and have it out with Macmillan before the Commissioners arrived.[316] Then in what was locally regarded as a 'surprise development', it was announced that the Commonwealth Secretary, Lord Home, would fly to Salisbury for talks with Sir Roy and Sir Edgar.[317]

Humphrey's old friend arrived in February 1960, to try to calm the fears of the Federal Cabinet as to the government's attitude to the Monckton Commission. It was during this visit that he attended – unnoticed by the press – the 'largest multi-racial gathering seen in Salisbury'.[318] Some 20,000 people gathered at the show grounds to hear Billy Graham, the American evangelist. 'It was', Home records, 'a brilliant exposition and an unforgettable message.'[319] The message he himself delivered, as he left Salisbury a few days later, dealt with more transient matters. They were matters, however, which loomed much larger in the thinking of most Rhodesian whites. 'I want to reaffirm,' he said, 'that we believe in federation and we want to see how it can best be made to work for the benefit of all its peoples and find a solution which is acceptable to all its peoples, and that is our intention so I hope there will be no doubt about that.'[320] That seemed to be a message of some comfort and hope.

However, it was evident that the wind of change would blow through Southern Rhodesia once the Monckton Commission had reported. Would it propose the end of Federation? If so, what was the future for the whites not only in Nyasaland, where there were few, and in Northern Rhodesia, where there were many more, but in Southern Rhodesia, where they formed a very significant sector of the population. 'Africa Year' was going to be significant for the whites and the blacks in Rhodesia. The report of the Monckton Commission – whatever its conclusions – would ensure that. But before the report appeared, the colony experienced for the first time the kind of disturbances they had as yet only read about.

7   The End of Federation

Humphrey wore his full dress uniform as Governor for the first time in April 1960. When he held his first investiture at Governor's Lodge. A local newspaper carried a picture of the Governor in his finery, and wearing his OBE. Alongside him was Canon Sagonda, also wearing his newly awarded OBE. Sagonda was one of the first Africans to be ordained in the Anglican Church, and had been a mission priest in remote areas since 1923.[321] Humphrey donned the uniform again to greet the Queen Mother in May, and then in June to open parliament for the first time. There were two main thrusts in the speech from the throne. One was the statement that 'talks with the British Government on the removal of the remaining reservations in the constitution were due to be resumed "on a wider basis" in late September or October'.[322] This was a theme which was becoming dominant in white political debate in the colony. Whatever the outcome of the Monckton Commission, there was the urgent need to review Southern Rhodesia's own constitution, in the hope that dominion status, for the colony or for the Federation, might be attained. The other thrust of the speech dwelled upon the legislative achievements and aims with regard to African advancement, particularly in industry, in education, in housing and in land ownership. Within a week however an African nationalist leader was telling a British newspaper that it was a 'waste of time' fighting for such 'small things'; instead, he proclaimed, 'we now feel we should get control of the Government itself'.[323] The speaker, Michael Mawema, President of the National Democratic Party (NDP), was arrested on 19 July, along with its Treasurer, Sketchley Samkange, and a branch chairman, Leopold Takawira.

Rioting broke out in Salisbury's African township the next morning, and half the city's African workforce failed to turn up for work. Protest marches were attempted, the police used tear-gas, and all processions were banned. Whitehead asked for federal troops – a battalion of the Rhodesian African Rifles (RAR) – and their prompt arrival ensured that things returned to normal on the following day: and the government was able to point to this as proof that the work stoppages had been a result of intimidation, which the presence of troops ensured could not continue. On 24 July, however, more serious rioting broke out in Bulawayo when an NDP meeting was banned. Looting and car-stoning ensued, and the police used tear gas. The RAR battalion was dispatched to support the police. Most Africans stayed away from work on the following day, and rioting continued. It took until the 27th for the situation to return to normal, by which time thirteen Africans had been shot dead, six by police and seven by Europeans defending lives or property. The press, European and African, united in its sorrow that, for the first time in the twentieth century, Southern Rhodesians had died as a result of police action, and there was perhaps a new 'realisation that a gulf of ignorance yawns between the country's European and African inhabitants'.[324] Hardwicke Holderness, Garfield Todd's supporter and founder of the Inter-racial Association, pointed out that on only five occasions since the colony received responsible government had there been 'actual or alleged African disturbances'.[325] Now, he claimed, 'a lot of re-thinking has to be done and a lot of re-educating of the European public, and a lot of reform achieved, very quickly – if indeed it is not already too late'. Roy Welensky, well-used to troubles in the other parts of the Federation, allowed himself a 'certain satisfaction that Whitehead's "holier than thou" attitude had received a set back'.[326]

It was not the Governor's job to make political decisions but he could act on a humanitarian basis. Sir Humphrey spoke on the radio, and his words were directed at both Africans and Europeans.[327] 'I am sure', he began, 'that all of you are dismayed and angry at the happenings of the past few days, particularly those in the Bulawayo African Townships – dismayed that many people, decent law-abiding people, have lost everything that they have spent their lives working for, in the disturbances there, and are angry at those responsible.' He warned of overreaction: 'I believe we must be careful that any feelings of anger do not overshadow our outlook, particularly in these days when clear thinking has never been so essential in Africa.' He pleaded for a continuation of the progress which he had dwelt upon in the Speech from the Throne: 'Those who have looted and rioted will be dealt with by due process of law; our concern is to see that this disturbance does not check the progress which is being made by the people of this country. You need only look back five or ten years to appreciate the great strides forward we have made: such progress could only have been achieved against a background of everyone co-operating together.' He then picked up the point about the gulf of ignorance between black and white: 'We must keep it that way, and I am convinced that the only way we can do this is for you and I to take more interest in each other's problems and make a real effort to solve them. To do this we have to cultivate a much deeper understanding of the other person's point of view.' That was as far as a governor could go. The broadcast concluded with an appeal for donations to a 'Governor's Fund' to 'help those who have suffered material loss in Bulawayo'. The response was good, from companies, schools and individuals. In all, the Fund received £26,026 in such donations; the Federal government contributed £10,000 and the territorial government made the total up to £67,100.[328]

But the Governor's plea for tolerance and understanding was soon overtaken by events. On 26 July Garfield Todd, President of the Central Africa Party, and now firmly in the 'radical' camp, joined forces with Joshua Nkomo, International Director of the NDP who had escaped arrest by being out of the country. Together they delivered a letter to the Commonwealth Relations Office calling on Her Majesty's government to suspend the Southern Rhodesian constitution and to intervene with adequate armed force to ensure a peaceful transition to majority rule.[329] 'Needless to say', the British High Commissioner in Salisbury reported to London, 'Todd's action has brought his reputation to an all-time low with the majority of Europeans here.'[330] A few days later – on 30 July – Sir Edgar Whitehead went on the radio to give his answer. 'We will not', he proclaimed, 'be driven to try to put the clock back because there have been disorders, nor will we be driven to making changes in the opposite direction, which we believe will be harmful to all races.'[331] Whitehead's delicate balancing act was undermined, however, by further disturbances. There was a series of strikes in September and October, and both the Prime Minister and his Minister for Irrigation and Land (Stumbles) suffered the indignity of having to retreat from platforms to escape heckling or worse: Whitehead's car was stoned as he made his escape from the African township of Highfield; Stumbles was shouted down at Gwelo by Europeans and Coloureds who wanted to take the law into their own hands to suppress the disorders. The government's reply was a clutch of further repressive legislation. First announced on the radio by the Prime Minister on 13 October, he followed this up two days later by a visit to Governor's Lodge, to obtain from Sir Humphrey an Order banning for a month all public meetings in urban areas, except those held for religious, cultural or sporting purposes. Whitehead returned a month later to have the order renewed.

Meanwhile the government introduced into the Assembly the Vagrancy Bill. The Minister responsible claimed the new legislation would provide means to deal with vagrants that were based on the colony's experience, particularly of 'rehabilitation', rather than on the English Elizabethan poor law. Seeking to reassure sceptics the Minister, Abrahamson, declared that he would 'have the guts enough to resign from this Government at the first sign of misuse of this measure'.[332] An Emergency Powers Bill was introduced which proposed wide powers for the Governor to declare a state of emergency in the colony for the 'quite preposterous' (as one opponent in the House called it) period of six months. These two bills passed quickly. Far more controversial was the third measure, the Law and Order (Maintenance) Bill. Its severity drew protests from the heads of all the churches, and even in the amended form in which it went forward, it was unacceptable to many. The Minister stressed that the Bill was 'non-racial',[333] but it was certainly draconian. It severely curtailed the right of public assembly, made statutory savage sentences for riotous behaviour, and gave the Minister the power to detain people without trial. Taken alongside the other security measures, it completed a package of acts which 'all but eliminated the notion of the rule of law within Rhodesia'.[334] The Chief Justice of the Federation could not stomach it. Sir Robert Tredgold, who was a liberal (he had spoken at the inauguration of the Inter-racial Association) now felt his own position was untenable. The Bill, if it became law, was 'not intended to be invoked in times of national peril. It was to become part of the ordinary law of the land'.[335] He let it be known that he would resign if it was passed. He even contemplated entering politics to fight the Bill, a move resisted by Whitehead and Welensky on the grounds that, as the latter wrote to Tredgold, 'nothing was more certain to ensure a Dominion Party victory than your return to politics'.[336] Privately, Welensky was glad to see the Chief Justice go. As he reported to Duncan Sandys, 'we have had the embarrassment for several months of the Chief Justice of the federation being involved in political manoeuvring'.[337] Nevertheless, his resignation could not but weaken the causes for which Welensky, and more notably Whitehead, had stood. The Bill became law and Tredgold resigned, to the delight of Guy Clutton-Brock, the white radical (and the only white to have been detained under existing emergency powers) who told Sir Robert that his resignation statement was 'the most encouraging thing that has happened in Central Africa for a long time'.[338] Few saw it that way.[339] The temperature in the colony soared metaphorically and physically. It was what was known as 'suicide month' when the heat built up and the rains were expected but had not yet come. It was an inauspicious moment for the publication of the Monckton Report.

A NEW CONSTITUTION

The Federation of Rhodesia and Nyasaland had come into being in September 1953. Exactly seven years later, its death knell was sounded – or so it seemed to Roy Welensky when he saw the advance copy of the Monckton Report. 'Its mere publication', he wrote to Iain Macleod, 'will make the continuation of federation virtually impossible.'[340] On 7 October 1960 the Southern Rhodesia Assembly adjourned, to reassemble after the formal publication of the Report, which had meanwhile been 'sprouting leaks like a perished garden hosepipe'.[341] On 18 October, the same day that the Assembly gave the Emergency Powers Bill its first reading, MPs began their consideration of the Report. There was disquiet on all sides in the House, and many agreed with the Federal Prime Minister's assessment that 'the Commission had approached its task not from the point of view of what was right, or best for all the peoples of the Federation, but of the most that could be done to appease African nationalism'.[342] The main fears on all sides focused on the rush to extend the franchise, and the door that had been opened for the northern territories to secede. However, the Report was only a guideline and a background to the Federal Review Conference which opened in London on 5 December. It adjourned after only twelve days. The focus would now shift to the territorial conferences.

The Southern Rhodesian conference opened on 16 January 1961, attended by all parties, including Nkomo and Sithole for the NDP. On 7 February, Duncan Sandys, the Commonwealth Secretary, and Whitehead signed their agreement to the proposals: it seemed to be a significant breakthrough. There would be progress towards majority rule, changes to the hated system of land tenure, and a justiciable Bill of Rights.[343] The situation in Northern Rhodesia was quite different: ' fierce battle was joined and continued to rage for many months',[344] and it was becoming very evident that the interests of the two colonies were to be served by very different policies, and by very different men – Welensky and Whitehead – who, as the year progressed, demonstrated 'considerable mutual suspicion'.[345] For Whitehead, and for white liberals and white conservatives alike in Southern Rhodesia, the future development of the colony was more important than the continued existence of the Federation. Welensky's priorities were obviously different, and he was increasingly beleaguered, convinced that Iain Macleod, if not the British government as a whole, had determined to compel the peoples of Northern Rhodesia 'to submit' to the rule of Kaunda's party.[346]

In May, Whitehead held a conference in Salisbury of all the main parties who had agreed to the proposed new constitution for Southern Rhodesia. The NDP leaders, Nkomo and Sithole, staged a walk-out, on the grounds that the government refused to lift a ban on political meetings in the tribal areas. It is unclear whether, as Alport suggests, Nkomo was under pressure from extremist elements to act tough, or whether he really thought he could thereby pressure Whitehead into further concessions. The fact is that, once again, Rhodesia experienced a decisive moment, perhaps not unlike that 'lost chance' of 1958 when Todd was ousted. One young *Rhodesia Herald* reporter looked back on the walk-out a quarter of a century later and mused: 'It was the last chance there was then for a multi-racial Shangri-la in Central Africa ... the much-maligned whites ... turned sane for a moment and voted yes to Edgar's constitution. Yes, history must show that we crazy whites of Shangri-la once voted for African majority rule.'[347] This is something of an exaggeration. No one knew how long it would be before there was African majority rule: that would depend upon the speed of African social and educational advancement, which ultimately would be determined by the white government. In fact the arguments that raged then and subsequently around the new constitution could prove what the speaker wanted them to prove. Whitehead's broadcast statement at the beginning of the referendum campaign is typical. 'Southern Rhodesia will, of course', he said, 'not have achieved complete independence in the international sense, but the United Kingdom participation in our internal affairs will have ceased.'[348] Hence the voter could think he was supporting a move to virtual independence. Subsequently, there was room for critics to claim that the British government had so altered the original White Paper proposals when the Southern Rhodesia Bill was being debated at Westminster that it now had 'increased powers to alter the Legislature and Executive of Rhodesia'.[349] What is certain is that, as Robert Blake points out, 'Southern Rhodesia could not legally break off her connexion with Britain unless Britain agreed.'[350] Humphrey Gibbs, reading through the White Papers published in June which summarised the proposed constitutional arrangements, could feel that in practice, and despite the long sections dealing with the Governor, they would make little difference to his role.

In July the mainly European electorate voted for the proposed constitution by 66 per cent to 34 per cent. Despite the fact that an NDP-organised alternative 'referendum' among Africans resulted in total rejection of the new constitution, the result was encouraging for Whitehead. He could point to intimidation in African areas, and was determined to press ahead with the changes. On 8 August, in his Speech from the Throne, the Governor spelled out the government's commitment to a new constitution and a renewed thrust to remove discrimination.

Despite the 'very satisfactory outcome' of the referendum, the campaign itself, as Welensky noted, exhibited 'bitterness', 'racial hatreds' and 'personal vendettas', though he thought 'the public were the best behaved I've ever known'.[351] Whitehead faced opposition from a whole range of white leaders. Ian Smith, Welensky's Chief Whip in the United Federal Party (UFP), resigned from the party, because he saw the Federation was doomed and did not trust the new constitutional proposals as the sure way forward for Southern Rhodesia. The leader of the Dominion Party, Winston Field, opposed because the proposals were too liberal; Sir Robert Tredgold opposed because they were too conservative. The NDP under Nkomo were holding out for a settlement more akin to that which was now on the cards for

Northern Rhodesia. Garfield Todd launched a new campaign – the New Africa
Party – backed by one MP, Dr Ahrn Palley, with a programme that looked
very much like Whitehead's, only more so. But for the remainder of 1961,
and in 1962, Whitehead pushed forward his 'Build a Nation' campaign, and
he seemed to become more liberal. Perhaps it was this development which
so encouraged Oliver Lyttelton, who had been much involved in the
construction of the Federation. Writing his memoirs at this time, and now
ennobled as Lord Chandos, he felt able to express the hope that 'the present
controversies over the Federation should not lead anyone to despair of a multiracial society being the eventual issue', but, he continued 'many convulsions
are likely to shake this adolescent state'.[352] They were not long in coming.
In January 1962 Whitehead announced his plan 'to have abolished all
discriminatory legislation by the end of this year'.[353] The Judges Report
recommended 'the goal of common primary and secondary schools',[354]
while the school of which Sir Humphrey had just become Chairman of the
Board began its first steps towards becoming multiracial.[355] But the most
radical aspect of the changes which were unfolding in early 1962 was the
proposed repeal of the Land Apportionment Act. The Report of the Select
Committee on the Resettlement of Natives (the Quinton Report) had been
published in August 1960, and advocated the repeal of the Act. This became
part of Whitehead's strategy. He was backed up by no less a figure than Lord
Malvern who stated publicly in February 1962 that 'I have always regarded
the Land Apportionment Act as a temporary measure. I have further regarded
the removal of this law as a matter of timing.'[356]

But Whitehead was not dealing merely with a European population which
needed cajoling; nor indeed merely with African chiefs, who tended to be
compliant and indeed reactionary. He was faced with increasing violence
among the nationalists who, seeing the way the wind was blowing in the other
two territories, had stepped up their campaign of violence. And, as happened
in South Africa twenty years later, they nourished a youth wing which was
even more violent. 'When will Sir Edgar Whitehead move against the thugs
and hooligans who are making life unbearable for everybody who does not
believe as they do?', asked the moderately liberal *Herald*.[357] On 7 December
1961 the police had opened fire on rioters in Salisbury, and two days later
the NDP was banned, only to be replaced a week later by the Zimbabwe
African People's Union, again led by Nkomo. During 1962 Nkomo took the
nationalist case to the world, and was given a hearing at the United Nations.
Harold Macmillan was not best pleased: 'A group of countries, of which
Poland is one, is to enquire into liberty in Southern Rhodesia!'[358] Nkomo's
triumphant return to Salisbury in July led to further militancy and violence,
and the government proposed yet more legislation to deal with it. The Church

leaders in August begged the Prime Minister 'to arrange immediately for a private conference to which representative delegates of all the political parties of the land are invited, for the purpose of breaking the deadlock of opposition which so gravely threatens the country and all its peoples'.[359] Whitehead nevertheless pushed ahead with his own plans: on the one hand, amendments to the Unlawful Organisations and Law and Order (Maintenance) Acts, and on the other, his stumping the country trying to sell his 'Build a Nation' Campaign. But as Sir Robert Tredgold noted, 'The liberal talk alienated the white electorate. The tough action embittered the African majority.'[360] Hence – as one observer put it – the 'tragic paradox' that a great reforming ministry 'should have received, and in a sense deserved, a reputation for being illiberal'.[361]

THE ELECTION OF DECEMBER 1962

While Sir Edgar Whitehead took his 'Build a Nation' and 'Claim a Vote' campaign round the country, a new British Department was set up to handle the affairs of Central Africa. Its head, and First Secretary of State, was R. A. Butler. Macmillan had appointed Lord Alport as a heavyweight High Commissioner to the Federation early in 1961, but he now felt that yet more weight was required. On 9 March 1962 Butler agreed to undertake the task, and after 'an initial burst of derision', the appointment was well received, and Macmillan noted with satisfaction that 'Welensky, Whitehead, Banda and even Kaunda seem pleased'.[362] Welensky, privately, was sceptical, and as he told Butler – and later put in writing – 'I was convinced that he did it in the hope that it would break you'.[363] Butler was concerned mainly with the orderly transfer of power in the northern territories, and the prospects for continuing the federal experiment in some form or other. For Whitehead, the future of the Federation was of less importance than the transformation of Southern Rhodesia which – he believed – would lead to its independence within the Commonwealth.

The 'Build a Nation' campaign has been called 'a shambles from beginning to end'.[364] Hopes for a large enrolment of African voters were not fulfilled, as the nationalists actively discouraged any such support for the 1961 Constitution. Among the European electorate too, subversive forces were at work. Whitehead's Intelligence Chief confided in his diary (6 May 1962) that on returning from leave he discovered that the outgoing Commissioner of Police, B. G. Spurling, had 'been using his farewell visits to Police Stations throughout the country to address our now considerable Police Reserve [30,000 whites with an influence over all their families] – warning them that if Sir Edgar Whitehead's government is returned to power this will be the end of Rhodesia'.[365] As polling day drew nearer the Prime Minister seemed to become yet more radical. In 1960 October ('suicide month') had not been the best time for Rhodesian whites to read the Monckton Report. Now, in 1962, it was not the best time for them to read that of Whitehead's assurance to the UN Trusteeship Committee that there would be an African majority in the electorate within fifteen years. And he followed that up on the eve of the election by predicting that there would be an African in the new Cabinet, and more in the future. All this may have failed to secure more African voters, but it was grist to the mill of the Rhodesia Front (RF).

This was a new party, fighting its first election. It had been formed by Ian Smith, who had resigned from the UFP over the new constitution and by 'Boss' Lilford, an extremely wealthy farmer. They could see that the parliamentary opposition to the UFP – in the shape of the Dominion Party – was ineffectual. They approached the former leader of the Dominion Party at federal level, Winston Field. He was an establishment figure – the sort of man who would naturally have supported the UFP in the past. He was also a wealthy farmer, and had been educated at an English public school. He was no racist. 'He didn't want to take it on', his wife later recorded, for 'he was not really a political animal.'[366] But he was a solid, trustworthy figure: he was in fact the perfect choice for the new party, even though 'nearly everyone else in the new party was to the right of him'.[367] He campaigned for the slowing down of the pace of change in the colony. His supporters went further. One poster showed the legs of a black child and a white child against a school background, with the caption 'Rhodesia is not ready for this' – exactly the same poster was adopted by the ultra-right-wing Conservative Party in the 1987 election in South Africa, when it too feared the changes that were in train, modest though they may look in retrospect.

As the election drew close, the British High Commissioner in Salisbury, while hedging his bets in his dispatches to London, 'was pretty sure that Whitehead would win'.[368] But Welensky told Butler: 'He has as much chance of being elected as a snowball in Beira.'[369] The result was decisive: the RF took thirty-five seats to the UFP's twenty-nine. It was not an overwhelming victory in the style the old United Party had enjoyed at most elections since the 1920s, but it was conclusive. Again there were those who regarded this moment as the decisive one, 'the end of the moderate liberal experiment'.[370] The Intelligence Chief, Ken Flower, watching the results come in on 14 December, agreed with the army commander, Major-General Anderson, 'that Southern Rhodesia, as we knew it, had ended'.[371] Josiah Chinamano, African headmaster and prominent nationalist, told the National Affairs Association that the gates of communication between the races had been closed: 'They have been closed in that we now believe in the battle of white versus black.'[372]

Whitehead saw the Governor and took his leave. Neither has left a record of the occasion, but it must have been a melancholy one. The two men, so different in temperament, shared much: they had both been in Rhodesia for some thirty-three years; they had a similar background and education, and interest in farming. They shared a modestly liberal vision for the future of their county. Winston Field, who was not too dissimilar in background and beliefs, became Prime Minister. His Cabinet was derided by one newspaper as 'by no means an inspiring list'.[373] For the Governor, who greeted his new ministers at Governor's Lodge on Monday 17 December, the personalities in the new Cabinet were to have an importance as yet unthought of. The finance portfolio was taken over by Ian Smith, 'and one feels constrained to ask why this farmer's boy is considered suitable for the most complicated and technical office in the government'.[374] At least this comment was made at the time; perhaps Lord Alport's similar criticism had the benefit of hindsight, when he remembered seeing Smith 'looking somewhat blankly at the columns of figures provided by his Treasury officials and giving the impression that they would have made just as much sense to him if he had held the pages upside down'.[375] The Minister of Justice was Clifford Dupont, an Englishman (educated at Bishop Stortford College) who had emigrated to the colony in 1948, and was later to become the 'Officer Administering the Government' when Sir Humphrey was 'deposed' at UDI. The Duke of Montrose, an Old Etonian who preferred to be called Lord Graham, took over the agriculture portfolio. William Harper, for irrigation and roads, had been described on becoming leader of the Dominion Party in 1959 as 'of the extreme DP right wing'.[376] Jack Howman, Minister of Internal Affairs, from an old Rhodesian family, remained loyal to his Prime Minister and resigned when Field was ousted. He was brought back in by Smith soon afterwards, and was the one Cabinet Minister to accompany Smith to the *Tiger* talks with Harold Wilson in 1966. Ian McLean, labour and social welfare, ended up fifteen years later as a member of the Rhodesia Action Party, a segregationist breakaway group from the RF.

FEDERATION ENDED

Harold Macmillan contemplated the new situation and confided in his diary: 'The election in S. Rhodesia is, on the face of it, a retrograde and reactionary vote. But it may really simplify the situation for Butler since none of the three Provincial Governments is now in favour of the Federation.'[377] March 1963 'was in fact the end of the Federation'.[378] Field visited London and was told that Southern Rhodesia would not be granted its independence unless it implemented the policies which had been defeated in the December election. Welensky and his delegation saw Butler on the morning of 29 March, prior to a luncheon with the Prime Minister. The First Secretary of State – 'looking wan and grey and ill' – informed the Federal delegates that the decision had been taken. Any territory would be allowed to secede from the Federation and a conference, preferably in Africa, would convene to work out the details of any future relationship between the territories. Welensky's response was to announce that they would not be lunching with the Prime Minister: 'I cannot accept the hospitality of a man who has betrayed me and my country.'[379] For Greenfield, standing next to Welensky, it was evident that Britain had 'lost the will to govern in Africa'.[380]

For Welensky, that was in effect the end of the story, and he scarcely mentions the conference to dissolve the Federation. It was eventually arranged to take place at Victoria Falls, in the same hotel that in 1936 had hosted the informal conference out of which grew the federal scheme. For Field, the fight was just beginning. On the day that Welensky refused to lunch with Macmillan, Winston Field wrote to the Prime Minister stating that 'the Southern Rhodesian Government will not attend the Conference unless we receive in writing from you an acceptable undertaking that Southern Rhodesia will receive its independence concurrently with the date on which either Northern Rhodesia or Nyasaland is allowed to secede, whichever is first'.[381] The Governor-General of the Federation, Lord Dalhousie, who was about to end his term of office, wrote to Butler soon afterwards painting a gloomy picture of the situation in Salisbury where there was 'in many quarters an anti-British tide surging around, which one can't at present see either time or diplomacy calming in any way'.[382] He suggested also that his successor should be 'an acting governor-general only'. Thus it was that the final obsequies for the Federation were to be performed by the Governor of Southern Rhodesia.

Macmillan and his ministers were already under siege at home. General de Gaulle had given his resounding '*Non*' to Britain's entry into the Common Market in January; in February the first outlines appeared of the story which was rapidly becoming the 'Profumo Scandal'. Wider issues of world peace – Macmillan's relationship with the new US President John Kennedy, and his plans for a Moscow summit and a test-ban treaty – also loomed large in the mind of the British Prime Minister. In Central Africa, the enormously complex business of winding up the Federation, and reallocating federal resources, dominated government activity in the middle of the year. Field was still maintaining that 'the Southern Rhodesian Government insists upon the principle of its independence being agreed to before the process of breaking up the Federation is put in hand officially'.[383] Welensky supported him publicly, claiming that Field's aim 'is exactly what mine was four years ago and what was Sir Edgar's aim during his period of office as Prime Minister – to achieve independence for Southern Rhodesia'.[384]

Much controversy surrounds the decision by Field to attend the dissolution conference of the Federation, and around the negotiations between the Southern Rhodesian and British governments, which took place in June, first in London and then in the two days preceding the conference. The historian of the Federation writes that 'Welensky could not forgive him [Field] for throwing away the card of non-attendance at the Victoria Falls, and time has proved that it was a cardinal error'.[385] However, it must also be said that Field's attendance ensured that his country was a party to arrangements which – particularly in terms of the transfer of military material to Southern Rhodesia – were beneficial. But both Field and Smith were to claim that Butler had promised independence for Southern Rhodesia, and that Field's attendance was predicated upon that – unwritten – promise. Butler is adamant that he did not give any such undertaking. Thirty years later, Smith was still rejecting any suggestion that the misconception may have arisen because new, inexperienced, Southern Rhodesian ministers had spoken a different language from that of the agile-minded, silken British Secretary of State.[386] Whatever the reason, the Southern Rhodesians felt they had been betrayed and they were bitter. So too was Roy Welensky, but for different reasons. The Federation which he had done most to create, and which he had led, was ended. There was another ending too, which as he mused many years later, was at the root of it all: 'what I failed to recognise was that the Empire had come to an end'.[387] For the Speaker of the Federal parliament, Sir Ian Wilson, the bitterness was just as deep. To one British minister he wrote that 'there is nothing left in my life but the most utter contempt for the actions of the Macmillan government'.[388] To Macmillan's successor as prime minister he wrote at length of the 'great hurt, the deep resentment and the bitter feelings of contempt and disgust' which he felt for the government which had betrayed them.[389] For him, and for other Europeans in the Federation, it was an inglorious end. Had they known of it, they would have quoted with approval Baden Powell's advice to the young: 'don't be disgraced like the young Romans who lost the Empire of their forefathers by being wishy-washy slackers without any go or patriotism in them'.[390] For the officials in London, there was the worry as to how Southern Rhodesia would now develop, and concern about 'a possible unilateral bid for independence' began to grow.[391]

It fell to Sir Humphrey Gibbs, as Acting Governor-General, to preside at the last meeting of the Federal Assembly in Salisbury on 10 December 1963. It was, as the Bishop of Mashonaland recorded in his diary, 'a grave occasion'.[392] In the speech of prorogation, Gibbs detailed the achievements of the Federation, in health care and education; in the economy, and in the development of a non-racial civil service. But whatever its achievements, the dream of a multiracial society had not yet been achieved. It remained to be seen whether the colony of which Sir Humphrey Gibbs was Governor would strive to continue that experiment, or shift instead towards the racial policies of its southern neighbour. As Acting Governor-General he had one last duty to perform. On the final day of the Federation – the last day of 1963 – he received Roy Welensky and his Cabinet at Government House, when they came to bid their last farewells. They departed leaving Humphrey 'feeling a bit gloomy'.[393] The gloom was to deepen in the following year.

8   Prelude to UDI

THE GOVERNOR

In and around 1960 – 'Africa Year' – there was a deluge of books published in Britain, examining the problems and possibilities facing Britain in Africa, and more especially in Central Africa. Only one made any mention of Sir Humphrey Gibbs, who, like the constitutional monarch whom he represented, was not expected to give voice to any personal political views. T. R. M. Creighton, in a book published in 1960 on Southern Rhodesia and the Federation, pointed out that: 'The Governor of Southern Rhodesia retains the theoretical right, as representative of the Sovereign, to veto any legislation, more especially if it discriminates between the races, and to submit it to the Westminster parliament, but this right has not been used once in thirty-six years.' In a footnote he added: 'Britain has too few levers in this part of the world and this one should not be forgotten; though the appointment in July 1959 of a Southern Rhodesian, Mr H. V. Gibbs (now Sir Humphrey Gibbs), to succeed Vice Admiral Sir Peveril Barton Reiby Wallop William-Powlett makes it less likely than ever that a difference of opinion between Governor and legislature will arise.'[394] Even though this was written before the creation of the 1961 Constitution, it was a prediction that turned out to be widely off the mark. Nevertheless the question does arise: how did Humphrey Gibbs view the events which we have had to examine in some detail for the years 1962 and 1963? He was not a political animal – that is why he gave up politics after his brief spell as a member of the Legislative Assembly. Nor was he a man to discuss politics; his preference was for farming or sport.

Musing on the situation he found in the colony towards the end of 1961, Lord Alport summarised the state of liberal opinion as he found it.[395] A 'One Nation' Tory, he described how, 'If it were possible to find a basis of race relations which was equally acceptable to black and white, Rhodesia could be about the most stable and prosperous country in the whole of Africa.' But the battle of slogans between Europeans and their 'safeguarding of civilised standards' and Africans with their 'one man, one vote' reduced the 'already slim' prospects of success, as did issues like discrimination, lack of firm and generous leadership.

There were some who realised the facts of the situation clearly – the Governor of Southern Rhodesia, Sir Humphrey Gibbs, a man of high integrity as well as outstanding charm; Sir Robert Tredgold who had a great and justified reputation for liberal ideas, but was cursed with a faulty political judgement; industrialists, educationalists and most of the top newspapermen as well as the leaders of the various Christian denominations – all were acutely aware of what was needed and what was at stake. Unhappily they did not possess the ruthlessness necessary to force public opinion in their direction, or the opportunity and power to bridge the chasm of suspicion and animosity which divided black from white.

Alport published his memoir before UDI was declared, so his words carry a certain weight. Certainly what he wrote was true of the Governor, whose instincts were sane and liberal, but whose position put him above politics.

Humphrey Gibbs was not only the Governor of the colony; he was also Chairman of the Board of Governors of Peterhouse, the school with which he had been associated since its inception in 1953. In this context, his own personal views emerge. In 1962 a large chapel had been built at the school, and discussions were in train as to the decoration on the east wall behind the altar. In a rare letter – rare in the sense that few have survived, even if they ever existed – in December 1962, Humphrey expressed his own views and feelings to the Rector (headmaster) of the school:

> My idea was to depict a young Christ blessing school children of all races and showing children both at play (team spirit) and at work, possibly in a science room: the idea being to stress that at school one learns how to live a Christian life, learning to keep oneself fit, and to mix with everyone irrespective of race or position, and in the science room to make the best use for Christianity of the brains one has been given by the Almighty.[396]

In this letter, Humphrey also referred to the proposal to take Africans into the school, which had been decided upon in November.[397] 'The sooner we can do something the better', he wrote. This, it must be remembered, was during the election campaign which had featured the black and white legs poster that appealed to the deepest prejudices of Rhodesian Front (RF) voters. But the school had already been given a shunt in the right direction when the Bishop of Mashonaland had declared that 'the boys now at Peterhouse were going to enter an adult world where the entrenched superiority of the European, legalised segregation and land apportionment would no longer exist'.[398] His comments were reported on the BBC and given wide coverage in the local newspapers. The raising of funds to enable black boys to enter the school was an essential prerequisite. A private approach to Rio Tinto, Anglo-American and other large companies was delayed until early in 1963, so that the dust raised by the bitter election campaign might have subsided. The approach was successful. Sufficient funds had been promised to ensure that suitable African candidates for entry could receive large bursaries. A further delay came in the middle of the year, when it had been intended to use Speech Day to announce the new departure. However, in the context of the unsettled political climate, it was decided that since it had 'become apparent that on account of his official position, and possible political implications arising therefrom, it would not be possible for H. E. to be present if an announcement of any kind on this matter was to be made'.[399] Sir Humphrey attended Speech Day, spoke about the Christian nature of the education the school was offering, and no mention was made of the new departure.[400] Soon afterwards, however, the announcement was made that Peterhouse would take African boys, and the other independent schools in Rhodesia would follow suit; and that the funding which Snell had arranged would be placed in a trust fund for the use of any of the independent schools.[401]

This was a cause of great satisfaction to Humphrey – and no doubt also to his cousin's son, John Michael Gibbs. Humphrey's relationship with him and his work also reveals something of the Governor's own attitudes. J. M. Gibbs had been teaching at Cyrene Mission and in 1960 became the Principal of a new non-racial venture in Salisbury which in September 1962 took over the property by which it became well-known – Ranche House College. Its history has been written in a book aptly called *Laboratory for Peace*, and its aim, as the Principal said, was 'to produce a group of more informed, tolerant and effective citizens'.[402] John Michael Gibbs had to retire through ill-health in 1963, but Sir Humphrey and Lady Gibbs remained 'among those who never doubted the value of the college's work and who were prepared to give Ranche House their active support'.[403]

As Governor, Sir Humphrey had to remain above politics; but this did not prevent him from having opinions, or from seeking – as he had learnt from the Barings – to influence the society in which he lived from his position of prestige, if not power. When he spoke to a farming and conservation conference in 1960, he applied his belief – non-politically but none the less positively – in an area dear to his own heart. He said, 'It is in the farming sphere perhaps more than in any other that men of whatever colour or creed can meet on common ground to discuss common problems and create a spirit of friendship and understanding.'[404] The tragedy of 1964 and 1965 was to be that such a statement could no longer be regarded as non-political, and the audience to which it had been addressed was becoming more and more disenchanted with that liberal point of view.

THE FALL OF FIELD

In January 1964, the Federation no longer existed. Sir Humphrey now had to deal only with one Prime Minister, Winston Field, a man with whom he could talk. As Bill Bernard had reported to Butler, Field was 'more liberal than many UFP', but his 'difficulties lie in the men (or many of them) in his cabinet'.[405] It came as a shock therefore when in early February the Governor read Field's draft Speech from the Throne.[406] The background to the speech highlights the sense of urgency which the Prime Minister now felt. Events to the north of the Zambezi were ominous. In mid-January, a coup in Zanzibar took place just five weeks after the Duke of Edinburgh had been there representing the Queen at the independence celebrations. And, closer to home, on 22 January Kenneth Kaunda became the first President of Zambia. It wasn't only events north of the Zambezi. On the government's own doorstep, rioting in the Salisbury townships led the *Rhodesian Herald* to comment that 'rightly or wrongly, the feeling is abroad in the townships that the Government is not doing enough to enforce the law and order which is a primary duty of any Government'.[407] Field felt his own position weakening. His visit to London in January had advanced the cause of Southern Rhodesian independence not one bit. Or had it? Southern Rhodesian politicians had found R. A. Butler difficult to deal with at the Victoria Falls conference, and continued to claim that they had been misled – that Field had attended that conference on the understanding that the British government would grant independence. Ian Smith was still claiming, in the 1990s, that this had been the case, and still refusing to accept either Butler's own categorical denials,[408] or the more likely explanation that there was a unbridgeable gulf in understanding and language between the gnomic utterances of the donnish Butler, and the blunt talk from the plain-speaking Rhodesian farmers.[409] Now a similar misunderstanding appears to have arisen. Hugh Beadle, the Chief Justice, recorded the outcome of Field's visit to London:

> He said at his last meeting with Mr R. A. Butler ... at which Evan Campbell [Southern Rhodesia's High Commissioner in London] was present, Lord Butler [*sic*] had implied that it would be embarrassing for Britain to give Rhodesia independence, but if Rhodesia took it herself, it might get Britain off the hook, and arrangements might perhaps be made for the Queen still to be our Queen. We found this incredible, but Field then produced the note which Campbell had made at the time to support him. The note certainly supported all Field said, i.e. that Butler was almost encouraging Rhodesia to take UDI as the best way out.[410]

Evan Campbell was an unlikely person to play the role of Sir Nevile Henderson to Field's Neville Chamberlain. Yet there is a claim that he further encouraged Field to hope, by reporting that 'his assessment was that Home, if returned to power with a big majority at the coming election, would find a way to grant independence to Rhodesia within two years'.[411] It was clear however, when he presented Duncan Sandys on 7 February with a further demand for a public British commitment to Rhodesian independence, that there was to be no progress before the British general election; 'My reception was to say the least of it cool', wrote Campbell.[412]

It must have been at this point, when Field had returned from a short holiday in the Cape to learn that no progress had been made, that the draft Speech from the Throne was shown to Sir Humphrey. If – as Beadle claims – it was then toned down, the original must have been meaty indeed, for the Governor was required, on 25 February, to announce from the throne that:

> It is now plain that the British Government are not prepared to be brought to any conclusion [about independence] except on the most extravagant terms, not because of misgivings about my Government's competence and ability to govern in the interests of the country or the logic and rightness of my Ministers' case, but because they wish to placate at all costs those members of the Commonwealth who have declared openly their hostility to my Government and my country.[413]

The leaders of the churches in Rhodesia were sufficiently worried by these words to organise a delegation to see the Prime Minister and express their concern about the rumours of UDI which were flying around.[414] But even before the Speech from the Throne had been delivered, the British Cabinet had met, on 18 February, to discuss the growing crisis in Rhodesia, and to consider what alternatives were open to the government in the event of a unilateral declaration of independence.[415] It noted the 'grave difficulty' which would face the Governor were he to be presented with a Bill declaring independence, given the constitutional convention that 'requires him to assent to a Bill if so advised by the Southern Rhodesia Ministers'. Beadle claims that having had sight of the original 'Speech from the Throne' he and the Governor had cabled London asking for instructions in the event of UDI. The response was that in such a case 'the Governor should not resign but should carry on with the existing UDI government'. He went on to claim – and this cannot be verified or otherwise from the public records – that: 'It added a caveat, however, because it said, "We think in the circumstances ... it would be advisable is the Governor did not attend the UDI celebrations".'[416] However, a subsequent letter from Sir Alec Douglas-Home to Sir Humphrey admitted that this was to be disregarded, as it was merely advice from officials, and had never been considered by the British government.

The Governor's main concern in March was not an impending UDI, but the position of his Prime Minister, a matter also discussed by the British Cabinet on 18 February. It feared that 'the right wing of [Field's] party were intending to supplant him as Prime Minister if he did not bring back an assurance of independence on terms acceptable to them'. In the same month, Ken Flower, the head of the Rhodesian secret service, reported to the Governor that there was a plot to oust Field, but – as he records the conversation – Sir Humphrey already knew and had tried to stiffen Field's determination to resist, or to go to the country and seek a fresh mandate.[417] Field, however, was unwilling to resist the pressure, which came to a head on Thursday 2 April, when the Rhodesian Front caucus met and decided to ask for their leader's resignation. This decision was conveyed to Field on Friday. At the Cabinet meeting on the subsequent Wednesday, the request was officially presented. Field agreed, but before an official announcement could be made, the news leaked in the press on Saturday 12 April. Kenneth Young records that the Governor made one final effort to keep Field at his post, as they watched combined Army and Air Force exercises. 'Winston, why don't you fight them', said the Governor. 'No, it is all over now', replied Field.[418] On Monday 14 April he formally handed over his letter of resignation. A few days later he wrote to the Governor saying, 'I have derived great comfort from the knowledge that I could discuss any problem with you at any time and I took full advantage of this as you know. There could be no more pleasant relationship.'[419] For the Governor, things had changed dramatically. There was to be no such relationship with the man who now occupied the office of Prime Minister – Ian Douglas Smith. As British diplomats saw it, he had been brought to power by a 'palace revolt' and 'Right-wing in outlook himself, was at the same time the prisoner of the Right-wing of his party'.[420] Humphrey was worried by these developments. He wrote to Alec Douglas-Home asking for guidance. What action should he take in the event of a UDI? Should he indeed resign now, or should he 'see this thing through'? The reply was clear. Alec told Humphrey: 'you, as Governor, would be justified in taking any measures which are open to you to secure respect for the Constitution'. Moreover, he wrote, 'we here have complete confidence in you and feel that, at this critical moment, it is most important that you should continue to occupy this key position. I hope, therefore, that you will put out of your mind any thought of resigning ... '.[421]

NEW GOVERNMENTS IN LONDON AND SALISBURY

On 7 June, Ian Smith declared that he was 'naturally extremely disappointed' that he had not been invited to attend the Commonwealth Prime Ministers Conference. Of course his country was a colony, and thus had no 'right' to attend the conference, though it had become used to being accorded nominal dominion status, especially during the long premiership of Huggins. Now its exclusion seemed symbolic of the growing isolation of Southern Rhodesia. Other powerful symbolism was at work in neighbouring South Africa, where on 12 June Nelson Mandela was sentenced to life imprisonment. Thirty-one years later he was to appear triumphantly at the Commonwealth Heads of Government meeting, leading his country back into the Commonwealth. Rhodesia's own place in the Commonwealth was meanwhile increasingly in doubt as the new Prime Minister put his stamp on the government of the country, as if to show how wrong the press had been in claiming that 'by no stretch of the imagination could the title of national leader be bestowed on any member of the present Cabinet'.[422] On 26 August the Zimbabwe African People's Union (ZAPU) and Zimbabwe African National Union (ZANU) were banned. On 2 September Smith was in London meeting with Home and Sandys and returning with 'confidence in an all-party solution negotiated with Britain by Christmas'.[423] The British High Commission in Salisbury reported that the Rhodesian government had 'sedulously fostered' the impression that 'a bargain was arrived at during Smith's talks in London'.[424] In addition, Smith's position on his return was given a huge boost when Sir Roy Welensky – re-entering politics to fight Smith – was defeated by 1079 votes to 633 by Clifford Dupont in the Arundel by-election. A few weeks later, on the eve of the British general election, Smith felt confident enough to announce to the British government that he was proceeding with his own test of Rhodesian opinion. He would canvass white opinion via a referendum. He would also test African pinion by calling an indaba of chiefs, a move denounced by Selwyn Lloyd on his last day in office in a stern warning to Smith that the British government would not accept the outcome as a valid test of African opinion. The indaba nevertheless went ahead on 22 October, resulting in the backing which Smith had anticipated. Two days later he dismissed the head of the Army, General Anderson, who was known to be an outspoken opponent of UDI. The High Commissioner in Salisbury, warned in advance of this move, was concerned that it could precipitate the Governor's resignation.[425]

In London, meanwhile, on 16 October, Harold Wilson had become Prime Minister, with an overall majority of just five. That same day, the British High Commissioner in Salisbury reported to London on 'the Governor's growing exclusion from [the] constitutional right to be kept in touch with Government business', and warned of his growing feeling that 'he had no alternative but to resign and in so doing warn people ... of [the] grave consequences of UDI'. The message however added that the Governor 'felt he could not take [the] step of resigning without ascertaining first that his resignation would be accepted by The Queen'.[426] Humphrey had gone so far as to draft a letter of resignation. On 23 October, just a week after Harold Wilson had become Prime Minister, and the day before Anderson's dismissal was announced, the Governor received a message from London assuring him that 'the New Government here is prepared to back him with no less firmness than the previous one'.[427] Shortly afterwards, a personal message from Wilson to the Governor pressed him strongly to 'put on one side any thought of resigning'. The reason was quite clear: 'Your personal authority and the respect you inspire are bound to carry great weight; your action at the right time could, I believe, be decisive.'[428] The British government had few cards to play; Wilson was anxious not to throw away this one.

The Rhodesian problem was now the responsibility of a new Commonwealth Secretary, Arthur Bottomley. He reinforced the Sandys message and suggested that he visit Salisbury after he attended the Zambian independence celebrations on 26 October. This offer was refused, since it contained the proviso that the Secretary of State would wish to see African nationalist leaders. On 23 October Smith turned down an offer from Wilson of a meeting in London. In parliament, he talked of Rhodesia (the official name of the country now that Northern Rhodesia was independent as Zambia) being 'driven to a unilateral declaration of independence' by the British government.[429] The next day, British ministers were considering the problem, deciding that 'we must be ready, in the event of the Governor being arrested, to appoint another Governor'.[430] By 6 November, the Cabinet's working party on Rhodesia had abandoned that proposal.[431] Smith seemed to have turned off the heat. He had got what he wanted from the chiefs in the October indaba. Now he declared that a 'yes' vote in the referendum would not be regarded as 'a mandate to declare independence unilaterally'. And the Legislative Assembly passed a motion that was emollient: 'That the House takes note of the attitude of the British Government towards the independence issue, and rejects any policy leading to a unilateral declaration of independence based on the result of the referendum on November 5.'[432] The referendum result, with a 60 per cent turnout of the electorate, was 58,000 saying 'yes' and 6000 saying 'no' to independence on the basis of the 1961 Constitution. Now, while the heat had gone out of the crisis, there was merely stalemate.

In January 1965 the death of Sir Winston Churchill seemed to mark another moment in the passing of the era of British greatness and imperial might. Churchill was a great hero in Rhodesia. A boys' school in Salisbury proudly bore (and bears) his name. Ian Smith 'admired Winston Churchill above all others', and was not alone in feeling that he 'had not fought in Churchill's war, and Churchill had not led that war, to promote black majority rule or any kind of black mischief'.[433] Churchill was now dead; a man who had passed his preliminary examination to Sandhurst in the year that the pioneer column claimed Southern Rhodesia for the Crown (which was the year before his father claimed that his horse had been nobbled at a race meeting in Salisbury).[434] Churchill's passing was marked in Salisbury by 'a magnificent service in the Cathedral attended by the Governor, Cabinet Ministers, Judges etc.'[435] – perhaps the last great 'establishment' occasion in Rhodesia when the great and the good could feel a part of the British tradition of which they had been so proud, and could recall again the dark days of 1939 and 1940 when the colony had played its part in the defence of the empire. It also gave an opportunity for a breaking of the stalemate. Harold Wilson knew that Ian Smith planned to visit London for the funeral. The Queen intended to hold a reception for 'the greatest assembly of the world's leaders, and recent leaders, ever gathered together'.[436] Smith was invited, and Wilson decided to take him back to Downing Street for talks. Wilson claims that Smith simply failed to attend the reception, had to be sought out, and eventually arrived and 'stammered out his excuses to the Queen'.[437] Smith's biographer avers that the invitation arrived late, and that this was another of the 'political pinpricks' to which he and Rhodesia were subjected.[438] Wilson writes that when the meeting did take place Smith was 'extremely difficult, extremely sour and not a little offensive'. Another of Smith's biographers suggests that 'the meeting appeared to be a success'.[439] Certainly the deadlock was broken with an agreement that the Commonwealth Secretary and the Lord Chancellor should visit Salisbury in the near future. It was to be the first of many ministerial and official visits which the Governor was to host in the years ahead.

LAST MONTHS OF LEGALITY

In late February and early March 1965, Bottomley and Gardiner (the Lord Chancellor) were in Rhodesia. The main outcome was a formal statement of the British government's position, called the Five Principles (to which a sixth was later added). These are worth considering in full:

(i) The principle and intention of unimpeded progress to majority rule, already enshrined in the 1961 Constitution, would have to be maintained and guaranteed.

(ii)   There would also have to be guarantees against retrogressive amendment of the Constitution.

(iii) There would have to be immediate improvement in the political status of the African population.

(iv)   There would have to be progress towards ending racial discrimination.

(v)   The British Government would need to be satisfied that any basis proposed for independence was acceptable to the people of Rhodesia as a whole.[440]

The British ministers were encouraged by the personal and private statements by Smith that he was not averse to some 'blocking mechanism', whereby the non-European members of the Legislature might have a veto over any legislation which might contravene any of the first four of the Five Principles. Thus the belief was further encouraged that perhaps Smith was more 'moderate' than some members of his own Cabinet, and that 'Ian Smith needs time to outwit his right wing'.[441] This was a vain hope, though one that was to reappear throughout the 1960s and 1970s.

The Governor and his wife were given some respite from the pressures of official entertaining by the presence at Government House of Sir Charles Ponsonby, Humphrey's brother-in-law, whose business interests in Africa gave him an excuse for an extended stay in Rhodesia in late February and early March. Ponsonby was President of the Royal Africa Society, and it was to this body that Evan Campbell made a significant speech in April. He was coming to the end of his tour of duty as Rhodesian High Commissioner in London. Perhaps this speech helped ensure that he would not be invited to stay at his post. It would have made sense if he had stayed on, at this time when continuity and stability were paramount. Having told his London audience that 'virtual independence is not an adequate substitute for sovereign independence', and while complaining of the 'humiliating rebuff' when Rhodesia's Prime Minister was excluded from the last and the forthcoming Commonwealth Prime Ministers' Conference, he went on to make a bold assertion. He stated that 'Black Rhodesians would be in a majority on the voters' roll within the next decade, but the transition to majority rule can be achieved peacefully only if it is permitted to pursue its course without outside interference.'[442] By the time of his departure, the British impression was that he had 'shown much less eagerness than formerly to keep himself closely informed of progress in the talks with Mr Smith'.[443] Perhaps this was not simply because his own departure was imminent. Since the Rhodesian referendum he had perhaps seen that he was increasingly out of sympathy with his own government's policies. Indeed Harold Wilson reckoned, after a leave-taking of 'only ten minutes', that although Campbell had been unforthcoming, 'he would himself be a force on the side of moderation in Salisbury'.[444] That would not be true of his successor. Just after Campbell's speech to the Royal Africa Society, the Rhodesian Minister of External Affairs, Clifford Dupont (a well-known 'hard-liner') approached Brigadier Alexander Skeen in the Salisbury Club and sounded him out as a possible successor to Campbell. Skeen was a keen RF supporter, and one of the ex-Indian Army immigrants to Rhodesia who had settled in Burma Valley near Umtali, and had gained themselves the nickname, 'the Bengal Chancers'. London thought this replacement for Campbell was 'quite acceptable to us'. He was in place in London in July. Two 'moderates' in key positions had now been displaced: General Anderson the previous October, and now Campbell from London. But the Rhodesian Prime Minister had an even more significant move to make. He called a general election.

Or rather, Ian Smith asked the Governor for a dissolution. Humphrey turned to the Chief Justice for advice. Could he refuse a dissolution?[445] Beadle felt that if no one else could form a government, and if Smith had the full backing of his caucus, a dissolution could not be refused. But could someone else form an administration? The relatively new and inexperienced leader of the Rhodesia Party (formerly the United Federal Party – the 'establishment' party), David Butler, was sent for, as was Mr Smith. Robert Blake avers that it was a mistake for the Governor and the Chief Justice not to have seen Butler on his own, but rather to ask him, in Smith's presence, if he could form a government, which he declined to try to do. Had he been seen on his own, says Blake, he might have reflected on the situation and entered into negotiations. He could then have formed a government which, although it might have gone down to defeat in the House, could at least have fought a subsequent election on the clear grounds of opposition to UDI. This is a doubtful scenario. Only two days after the meeting at Government House, Butler was reported in the press as conceding that there was 'no ready belief in the country that it would be likely for us to form a government'. At any rate, it seemed clear that there was no alternative but for the Governor to grant a dissolution, and the meeting ended, rather dramatically, at midnight, with Smith claiming relief as he had already sent the dissolution proclamation to the printers. A few days later, the Governor received a message from the chargé d'affaires of India that the forthcoming election was seen by his government as a prelude to UDI, and therefore the mission was being closed forthwith. Humphrey hoped that Mr Gaind would speak in the same terms to Smith, but he refused. He did however speak to the British High Commissioner who told him: 'You are making a mistake – there won't be a UDI.'[446]

Ian Smith opened his election campaign, as reported in the British press, with the declaration that 'it is our intention to try to negotiate independence. If, in the end, we find we can make no progress, and the negotiations end in deadlock, then we must face up to the question of assuming our independence.'[447] That report was published with a picture of a youthful looking Smith addressing an election meeting under a large Union Jack. The election result was an overwhelming victory for his party, which won all the 'white' 'A' roll seats. Only one white (Dr Ahrn Palley) was in opposition sitting as an independent, and ironically with, for the first time, an African as official leader of the opposition. The opposition amounted to ten Africans elected on the 'B' roll, four African independents, and Palley – who was to become the 'lone spokesman for the conscience of the European opposition, a role then comparable to that of Mrs Helen Suzman in the South African Parliament'.[448] Sadly, unlike Mrs Suzman, Palley was something of a maverick. He had only recently been a member of the Dominion Party, and he never had the network of British, national and international contacts which helped give that redoubtable woman so much of her impact. The electoral propaganda had succeeded to the extent that in contested seats, Smith's party polled 28,165 votes to the Rhodesian Party's 6377. Thus in this election, far more than in that of 1962, the Rhodesian Front became 'the apotheosis of white populism in Southern Rhodesia'.[449] As Bob Williams, a leading member of the Rhodesia Constitutional Association (which replaced the Rhodesia Party) was to put it a few years later, 'if you are anti-Rhodesian Front you are anti-Rhodesia'.[450] And by declaring that 'UDI is not an issue at this election',[451] Smith was not so much being mendacious as cleverly casting the RF as the national party. This policy succeeded, and Smith and his colleagues had 'effectively created an atmosphere in which the election appeared not to be a party contest but a test of support for the government in its negotiations with Great Britain'.[452] The old liberal establishment had had many 'last chances'. It had none left. It was a full year since the British High Commissioner had reported to London that the opposition was 'supine' and 'appear to be modelling their conduct on that of Brer Rabbit'.[453] Now, as then, 'liberal' individuals existed. Their voices were to be heard during and after UDI. But they had no political clout. In a sense, on the political scene, the Governor was on his own, whereas in the past, friends, colleagues and old acquaintances – the establishment – had been part of the political and social milieu in which he moved.

Humphrey's own personal affairs provided some happy moments. In April, during the election campaign, his third grandchild – Arabella – was born in Salisbury. On 1 July John Pestell joined him at Government House as Comptroller – for a three-year secondment which stretched, as Humphrey's own appointment was to do, well beyond the prescribed limit. In August Humphrey was at Peterhouse for Speech Day, listening with some pleasure to Robert Birley, the headmaster of his old school. Birley had recently retired from Eton and was visiting Professor of Education at Witwatersrand University, in South Africa, where he and his wife were outspoken in their liberal views, made friends with Winnie Mandela, and shot secret film of protests against apartheid at St George's Cathedral in Cape Town.[454] Birley had already visited Peterhouse and had spoken to the boys. This was his more formal visit, and he spoke of 'loyalty'. It cannot have escaped many of his hearers that a test of 'loyalty' would soon occur in Rhodesia. The whole occasion was full of such resonances. Birley had been up at Oxford in the early 1920s, as had Fred Snell, the Rector of Peterhouse. Though neither could remotely be called a socialist (despite Birley's sobriquet 'Red Robert') both had experienced an Oxford with its focus on 'the social and political crusades of the time'.[455] Both viewed with deep suspicion any moves which would take Rhodesia down the fateful road South Africa had been travelling since at least 1949. Sharing the platform with Birley and Snell and the Governor was Bob Williams, Chairman of the school's Executive Committee. An 'outstanding sportsman with a body like a wrestler's and a nice streak of childish hankering in his nature for chivalry and the high life',[456] Williams was a leading light in the Rhodesian Constitutional Association, which took over from the defunct Rhodesia Party as a focus for liberal opposition to the RF. It was. in effect, the voice of the old United Party establishment. The leading Speech Day prize-winner was Tim Peech, the head boy, who was to be killed in the late 1970s during the dying days of the illegal regime, out in the bush trying to make contact with the guerrillas. Here was a little cameo of the 'liberal' side of Rhodesia which outsiders seldom saw. But in the Rhodesia of mid-1965, they represented a minority view.

The next day, Sir Humphrey hosted a Fair in the grounds of Government House, when over £4000 was raised for the school. On the same day, letters were sent out over Humphrey's signature, raising funds for the country's 'Winston Churchill Thanksgiving and Memorial Fund'. So the traditional work of the Governor continued. But the serious business of politics continued to impinge. In July Humphrey hosted Cledwyn Hughes on his abortive visit for talks with the Rhodesian government. In September, as a member of the Legislative Assembly reported to Sir Edgar Whitehead who was in Britain, the country appeared 'to be on the brink of something or other – perhaps UDI and there are masses of rumours flying about. It is rather unsettling.'[457] As the heat built up and Rhodesia entered the hottest time of the year, the 'suicide month' of October, so too – just as in 1960 and in 1962 – the political temperature soared.

9 The Unilateral Declaration of Independence

COLLISION COURSE

On 2 October 1965, Sir Humphrey Gibbs was the guest of honour at Presentation Day at University College of Rhodesia and Nyasaland. The climate in that multiracial institution was not good. Several incidents had recently soured the atmosphere. There had been an Education Department circular which demanded that students in receipt of grants should sign a pledge which would debar them from any political activity. There had been protests in the Students Union about any students taking part in the City of Salisbury's seventy-fifth anniversary celebrations, on the grounds that 'the progress celebrated has been essentially material and not in the field of race relations'.[458] There had also been racial tension as a result of the voting for the Rag Queen, with accusations of vote-rigging, with the split along racial lines. Against this background, the Governor arrived, and as he rose to speak, about one hundred African students and half a dozen Europeans rose silently, and in an orderly procession left the building. The Students Union president, a young Englishman named John Taylor, was aghast, and assumed that the reason was that the 'puerile' (his word) demonstration arose from a misunderstanding, a failure 'to distinguish between the Governor and Government'. A letter of apology was sent to the Governor a week later, but the debate that raged meanwhile within the College highlighted the problems and the passions of the time. Liberal Europeans assumed that the Africans had failed to understand that the Governor was in fact the last hope of liberal opinion, the representative of the Crown, and not a party to Rhodesian Front (RF) policy. African students argued that the Governor had failed to speak out against the threat of UDI, and was in fact the mouthpiece of a British government which had failed to act against a racist regime. It was a sombre prelude to a debate which was soon to rage on the national and international scene.

A few days later, at 8.30 a.m. on 8 October, the Governor, his Comptroller, the British High Commissioner and the Chief Justice gathered at Government House. A message was read out from the Lord Chancellor, intimating that he did 'not see how it can be considered treasonable for judges to remain in office' in the event of a UDI.[459] It was the Chief Justice's duty to pass this message on to the judges, which he did by reading it aloud to them in his office, emphasising its confidentiality, but in such a loud voice that Judge Quenet interrupted and asked why he did not read it out from the window to ensure that the Minister didn't miss any of it. It was a light moment at a time when the judges were seriously considering their position. They were divided, as was everyone else, as to whether UDI would take place or not. Judge MacDonald wanted them to issue a public statement making their position clear that they would regard UDI as an illegal act, and thus stiffen resistance to it in advance among servants of the Crown – the civil service and armed forces in particular.[460] The others had their way in insisting that any statement by the judges would be an unwarranted interference by the judiciary in the political process. In fact, the politicians had not yet made a decision. A meeting of the country's Security Council was held on 19 October. Ken Flower, Director of the Central Intelligence Organisation (CIO), has made public the top-secret minutes of this meeting.[461] Flower had a remarkable career. He set up the CIO at the behest of Winston Field, though as a result of an initiative by Sir Edgar Whitehead. He ran it for Field and Smith, for Muzorewa and for Mugabe. Flower saw himself as non-political, though with a bias against the 'cowboy element' in the RF, as he and General Anderson dubbed it as they watched the results of the 1962 election together. He was against UDI. That is what one might expect him to say in retrospect, but the fact that Sir Humphrey Gibbs, in the Foreword to Flower's book, *Serving Secretly*, spoke of 'my friend Ken Flower', and his dedication to 'the service of our country' lends credibility to his claim. At the meeting on 19 October Flower spoke of the difficulty he had in assessing the impact of a possible UDI 'without knowledge of the political exchanges at the highest levels'. The Prime Minister intervened to assert that 'massive support for Rhodesia existed in the United Kingdom', and the government might have to act while this was the case. If UDI were to be declared, a necessary prerequisite would be the introduction of emergency regulations, to forestall any attempt by Britain to undermine the regime. Smith had only just returned from a further round of fruitless talks in London, and was perhaps beguiled by the reaction to his television appearance on ITV. The shouts of 'Good old Smithy' he encountered thereafter seemed to stiffen his resolve.

In the interval between Smith's return from London on 12 October and the Security Council meeting on the 19th, there had been a great deal of activity in Britain and Rhodesia. In Britain there was an expectation of an imminent announcement of UDI. The Prime Minister was receiving worrying information about the Governor: that he was ill; that he might resign; that force might be used against him. At a Cabinet meeting on 7 October Barbara Castle had noted reports that the Governor 'appears to be pretty jittery'. She had been worried that Wilson might fudge the issue and sell the Africans short, so she was delighted when he announced, 'If there is a UDI there is no Government: we take over.'[462] All this prompted Wilson to revive the plan for an alternative Governor, and the name he came up with was Lord Mountbatten. He had recently retired from the new post of Chief of the Defence Staff. His war record and service in India were well-known. Labour leaders felt he was more sympathetic to their cause than most of the establishment. And his royal connection would carry weight in Rhodesia. Wilson flew to Balmoral to see the Queen: Mountbatten's closeness to the royal family made this necessary. It was during the Conservative Party conference at Brighton. The Conservatives, now out of power after thirteen years, were not amused: 'We've just sung the Queen: he is seeing her.'[463] The Mountbatten plan was given a provisional go-ahead by the Queen.[464] While the reasons for Mr Wilson's flight to Balmoral were not made public, and there was speculation that he might wish to call an election, the newspapers came close to identifying the focus. The focus was the Governor. The Rhodesian papers carried reports that Gibbs might be asked to 'assume to the extent of his abilities full responsibility for the future government of Rhodesia'.[465] At the same time it was noted that the Commonwealth Office had made clear that the Governor had received no new instructions, as 'he could not authorise any unconstitutional or illegal action and he therefore did not have to be instructed'. Two days later, Roy Welensky was writing to Lady Gibbs, highlighting a word he wanted to use about Humphrey – 'steadfast' – 'I think it describes Humphrey's qualities more than any other I can think of.'[466] Within the subsequent two or three weeks, that quality was to be put to the test to the full.

While Wilson was at Balmoral, a deputation from the Confederation of British Industries (CBI) had landed at Salisbury. The delegation, led by the Chairman of the CBI, attended morning service at the Cathedral on Sunday 17 October. The Governor and the Prime Minister were both there also. They had lunch at Government House with Sir Humphrey, his Comptroller John Pestell, and Evan Campbell. Getting to see Ian Smith was not so easy; they had been trying to do so since their arrival on the 15th. On Monday 18 October they finally succeeded, finding him 'tired and ill and worn down'.[467] They impressed upon him the devastating economic consequences for Rhodesia of any unilateral declaration of independence. While Smith had been prepared – in the end – to see the CBI men, he had at the same time rejected a proposal by Mr Wilson that he should receive a Commonwealth delegation led by Sir Robert Menzies. It was in proposing this mission and speaking on television that Harold Wilson had made his famous plea: 'Prime Minister, think again.'

Now that all options seemed to be closed, Wilson made a last bid. He would himself fly to Salisbury.

The British Prime Minister arrived at Salisbury airport on 25 October. It was very hot. He and his party drove to Government House through streets lined mainly with Africans. On his arrival he handed the Governor a letter from the Queen in her own handwriting; he 'read it gravely, much affected'.[468] Mr Smith later also received a handwritten letter from the Queen. It concluded, 'I should be glad if you would accept My good wishes and convey them to all the peoples in your country, whose welfare and happiness I have very closely at heart.' It had been drafted and redrafted to emphasise the 'all'.[469] Smith was brandishing this letter the next night at a civic banquet, claiming that 'the arrival of the British Prime Minister has spiked my guns'. The royal letter was to find its way onto the pages of the newspapers, and the public had a rare glimpse of the Queen's handwriting: it was even subjected to the scrutiny of a 'scientific graphologist'.[470] Sir Humphrey regarded his letter as moving message of support. For the Rhodesian Premier, his letter was to be regarded as yet another instance of the perfidious British government using the Queen for its own ends.

That night, Wilson dined at Government House. He sat between Sir Hugh Beadle and Lady Gibbs. The Chief Justice, who had read out the Lord Chancellor's letter in stentorian tones to the judges a fortnight before, was to play a major role in the unfolding crisis. Beadle was a Rhodesian, a small man with a huge appetite for big-game hunting, and his voice had a 'bucolic "country" ring not always associated with the bench'.[471] He had a weak back, and had the appearance of a 1930s gentleman: a disgruntled Harold Nicholson perhaps. He had been an MP from 1939 to 1950 and had held the education, health and justice portfolios under Huggins. He had been a judge since 1950 and Chief Justice since 1961. Aiden Crawley, former Conservative MP and broadcaster, who had sat with him on the Monckton Commission in 1960, reckoned that Beadle had started the inquiry 'as a radical advocate of white supremacy' but had then modified his views 'to a remarkable extent in the light of experience'[472] – one wonders whether Crawley had managed to get this information over to the Prime Minister. Certainly Wilson was interested in his dinner partner. Beadle was after all the person who would take over as acting Governor should Sir Humphrey become incapable – through illness or imposed restriction – of fulfilling his role. Wilson was later to change his mind entirely about Beadle, but for the moment these two men – so unalike in background and interests – perhaps found common ground in their Oxford experience. Wilson was a keen Oxonian; Beadle was soon to be elected to an Honorary Fellowship at his old college, where he had been a Rhodes Scholar in the early 1930s. After dinner, Wilson and his party had a long talk with the Governor and the Chief Justice, who 'appeared more optimistic than I had expected', as Wilson later wrote.[473] Wilson was pleased to discover, when he met Smith next morning, that there were grounds for Beadle's optimism. The Rhodesian leaders 'seemed more relaxed, and, on the whole, slightly more friendly'.[474] Perhaps this was simply because they were on home ground. But as the day wore one, the greater bonhomie and even optimism which Wilson might have felt began to vanish as a succession of visitors, from the white liberal Ahrn Palley to the veteran statesman Roy Welensky, impressed upon the British Prime Minister the intransigence of the RF, and the impossibility of accommodating their demands within a settlement acceptable to the majority. Things went from bad to worse the next day, Wednesday 27 October. Ironically it was the day on which Smith sent a reply to the Queen's letter – in his own handwriting – assuring her that her 'Rhodesian Government will do all in its power to succeed in finding a solution to the current difficulties'.[475] It cannot have looked that way to the British Prime Minister. Wilson saw Joshua Nkomo in the morning: he had been brought up from his detention centre. There was a row when Wilson discovered that the veteran nationalists had not been fed. After meeting Ndabaningi Sithole in the afternoon, Wilson asked him if he had eaten, and discovered he had been given neither breakfast nor lunch. Mr Wilson described in detail what happened when he heard this news:

> It was at this point, for the first time in my life, I totally lost my temper to the point where I was out of control. This was the first time I had ever known what 'seeing red' could mean. On going in to harangue the Governor, I was unable to see him because of red flashes before my eyes. I made it clear that I was not having this treatment of the Africans by the Rhodesian Government and their police. I told the Governor that the African leaders had come at my invitation and they were to be treated in a civilised manner ... I told the Governor that if in half an hour from the time I was speaking Sithole and his colleagues were not sitting down to a three-course meal, the menu of which I had personally approved and which would be supervised by my own staff – then I would take a hand.[476]

He brandished his wallet at the Governor and threatened to lead his staff into Salisbury and personally buy up sufficient food to feed the visitors – thereby letting the world's journalists and photographers know precisely how the Rhodesian government treated its Africans. Not long afterwards, the meal was on the table. Sir Humphrey himself never referred to this incident, and kept no record of it. But, like the demonstration at the University College in the previous month, it highlighted his own awkward position. Cast constitutionally in the role as the man in the middle, he may well have determined at that point to ensure that he was seen not as a representative of the British government, but as the Queen's Representative in Rhodesia. That was a principle the Governor was to stick by in the difficult months and years ahead. And while it preserved his freedom of action as a 'neutral' go-between for Wilson and Smith, it was nevertheless a delicate balancing act, and one that was open to misinterpretation by friends and enemies alike.

The next day Government House was the setting for further meetings. Thirty chiefs dressed in their regalia were followed by Anglican Bishops and other Church leaders. A further meeting with Smith – at the High Commissioner's residence – followed. Wilson again had a feeling that Smith 'was to some extent a prisoner of some of the extreme right'.[477] That evening the British Prime Minister had the opportunity to see some of the 'extreme right' in action, during a dinner party at Smith's house. The discussions which Wilson anticipated having with Cabinet members after dinner when the ladies withdrew never materialised. Instead a series of witty stories ended with a particularly prurient one by the Duke of Montrose, one of Smith's right-wingers. Known locally as Lord Graham, he was a farmer and at this stage Minister of Agriculture. Presumably because of his title, he was often spoken of as a possible 'Regent' in Rhodesia should UDI take place. Graham's story involved acting it out with an obscene dance on the table.[478] This did not go down well with Wilson. His comment at the end – 'I see ... now I understand what qualifications you have to have to become Regent of Rhodesia' – may, Wilson later claimed, have dished Graham's chances of filling such a role. Rhodesia's High Commissioner in London, Brigadier Skeen, who was a loyal RF man, attended the dinner and published his account of it before Harold Wilson produced his. Skeen's version was that 'it was a most friendly and convivial affair, at which everyone enjoyed himself'. It seemed to him the 'kith and kin' argument in action. Was he blind, or was he simply rewriting history?[479]

Further talks between Wilson and Smith the next day were inconclusive, but the suggestion of a Royal Commission to report on the problem was seen as a possible way forward. It could perhaps be chaired by Sir Hugh Beadle, and with a majority of Rhodesians on it. So some of Mr Wilson's party, including the Commonwealth Secretary, were to stay in Salisbury over the weekend to work out details. Wilson drove to Salisbury airport on Saturday morning; the last poster he saw being brandished on the route declared 'Home Rule for Scotland'. The mild amusement caused by this was dispelled at the airport. The Governor himself had turned up to see the Prime Minister off. He did so, as Wilson himself later recorded, with tears in his eyes.[480] There would have been reason for tears. The British Prime Minister had scarcely any cards left. But he had one. This he threw away later that evening, in his broadcast to the British people.

The broadcast has to be seen against a background of the Prime Minister's domestic concerns. He was worried about 'the delicate state of the pound'.[481] It was the run on sterling, rather than military weakness, that had foiled Britain's intervention at Suez just a decade previously. He was concerned about his own small parliamentary majority, which was just four. While his own left wing – and in the Cabinet, Castle and Callaghan represented this view – would tolerate no sell-out to Smith, he knew that the kith-and-kin argument would hold sway with some of his own back-benchers. Indeed his majority might vanish if MPs like Desmond Donnelly and Reginald Paget teamed up with the Conservatives.[482] And while the Conservative leadership was prepared to support a fairly tough stand against Smith, they could not rally all their troops to support immediate majority rule, or any suggestion of military intervention. There was a populist appeal in Gerald Nabarro's declaration that 'Rhodesians are British to the core and among the most loyal of all Her Majesty's subjects'.[483] And of course the grandest of the Tory grandees, the Marquess of Salisbury, was outspoken in his support for Smith. His own long family association with the colony was symbolised in Rhodesia's capital, named after his great-grandfather, and the capital's central area laid out in the shape of the Union Jack – Cecil Square – bore his family name. It was a connection that was to continue and was tragically sealed in blood when in 1977 his second son died in Rhodesia's bush war.[484]

Harold Wilson, the consummate politician, was all too aware of his own limited room for manoeuvre as he flew back from Salisbury and prepared to address the nation on 30 October. He himself makes no mention in his memoirs of the content of that broadcast, when he said:

> If there are those in this country who are thinking in terms of a thunderbolt, hurtling through the sky and destroying their enemy, a thunderbolt in the shape of the Royal Air Force, let me say that this thunderbolt will not be coming.[485]

Thus, as Ken Flower put it, 'did Wilson throw away what little advantage he had'.[486] Why did he do it? The background was an intervention by – of all people – the Archbishop of Canterbury. Michael Ramsey was a liberal, indeed 'a Liberal politician at the heart, and he was always a Liberal on what he took to be moral grounds', as his biographer records.[487] Ramsey had already written to Wilson on 10 October, backing the use of force if all else failed. On 18 October he joined with the Baptist E. A. Payne of the British Council of Churches to telegram Smith begging him to refrain from UDI. On 26–27 October, while Wilson was in Salisbury, the British Council of

Churches met in Aberdeen, and by a majority of sixty to five resolved that UDI must be resolutely opposed. Ramsey thought this did not go far enough, and he declared:

> It is not for us as Christian Churches to give the government military advice as to what is practical or possible. That is not our function. But if the British government thought it was practical to use force for the protection of the rights of the majority of the Rhodesian people, then I think that as Christians we have to say that it will be right to use force to that end.

Thus Ramsey found himself, as his biographer says, 'at the centre of the windiest political storm endured by an Archbishop of Canterbury since the revolution of 1688'. Wilson received from Ramsey what Kenneth Young calls a 'foolish and indeed impertinent message'[488] on 27 October, and it was publicised in the press at the same time. A few in Rhodesia welcomed it, notably Bishop Skelton of Matabeleland. But for most Christians there, it was an unwelcome intervention, and the response by some hundred was to threaten to burn their Bibles and send the ashes to Lambeth Palace. In Britain, the Archbishop had the whole-hearted support of the Liberals, and of some of Wilson's left-wingers. But he was opposed by a whole range of Christian opinion, from pacifists on the one hand to establishment Christians on the other. Humphrey's predecessor as Governor wrote apoplectically of 'our rather donnish and doddery [he was sixty-one] old Archbishop', and concluded that 'it almost turns one away from the Christian Church!'[489]

Wilson could hardly rely for support upon an Archbishop when it came to the use of force, and he felt, with his small parliamentary majority, that there was no parliamentary consensus for such a policy. Nor, indeed, was there any national consensus. There was however no risk of a Curragh Mutiny. The forces of the Crown would do as they were told. It was probably a myth that British troops would not fire on their kith and kin. Lord Callaghan, at the time Wilson's beleaguered Chancellor of the Exchequer, thought with hindsight that 'we should have used whatever means were necessary to apprehend and arrest Mr Smith and his followers'.[490] Britain had used the weapon of military intervention over the previous decade: at Suez in 1956, Oman in 1957, Jordan in 1958, Kuwait in 1961, Cyprus in 1963, East Africa in 1964 and Malaysia from 1963 to 1966. The historian of these interventions applauds 'Wilson's wise decision not to intervene in Rhodesia with military force', and asserts that 'other instruments for the projection of power and influence had to be adopted'.[491] It is surely the case that these 'other instruments' – from negotiations to economic sanctions – were the only viable way forward for a British Prime Minister with a tiny majority, who knew perfectly well that there was no obvious alternative government in the wings in Rhodesia. Barbara Castle's urging of 'Direct Rule'[492] seems rather less convincing in the light of the subsequent twenty and more years of direct rule in Ulster which give the lie to belief in direct rule as a panacea, when it is not backed by a consensus among those ruled, and where it is undermined by the armed opposition of even a small minority.

For the Governor, certainly, the Wilson broadcast came as a relief. But just as appeasement in the 1930s may have sent the wrong message to Hitler, so Smith was beguiled by Wilson's words, announcing to his Cabinet that 'Rhodesia's position today was stronger than it had been before Mr Wilson's arrival.'[493]

ELEVEN DAYS IN NOVEMBER

At the Cabinet meeting on 1 November, when Smith expressed this feeling of confidence, the decision was taken which would effectively usher in UDI. Assuming that the current negotiations came to nought, 'it would be the right tactics, in the event of the Rhodesian Government having to take the extreme step, first to introduce a general state of emergency and thereafter to let the impact recede before taking the next step'. Two days later, at 6.00 p.m. on Wednesday 3 November, the Prime Minister arrived at Government House bearing a Proclamation of a state of emergency. This was supported by an affidavit from Barfoot, the Commissioner of Police, setting out his 'deep apprehension over the future security of the country' because of a build-up of trained terrorists and materiel in Zambia and Tanzania.[494] The Governor was well aware that the country was in fact 'quieter than it had been for months'. He was also aware, no doubt armed with information from Ken Flower, that any declaration of UDI would most probably be preceded by a Proclamation of a state of emergency. Gibbs asked for, and was given by Smith 'a complete denial that this Proclamation had anything to do with a UDI'. Many years later, and despite the evidence in the Cabinet Minutes of 1 November, Ian Smith was still asserting 'with an absolutely clear conscience' that the Proclamation was unrelated to UDI.[495] Thus reassured – though it is difficult to see what option would have been open to him even had he not been – the Governor signed.[496] He assumed, as was normal, that the state of emergency would exist from the moment of his signature. He did not – and again this was normal – add the date himself; that was normally done by his staff. But the Prime Minister quickly departed with the undated papers. Next day the Comptroller, John Pestell, contacted the Prime Minister's secretary to ask two questions. Why had no notice appeared in the press or on the radio? And would Mr Thompson bring the papers back to Government House so that the details could be recorded, as was normal? Pestell was astonished to be told that the Proclamation was, on the Prime Minister's orders, locked away in the safe. Pestell knew this was irregular, and confirmed with the Governor that no agreement had been reached regarding keeping the Proclamation in cold storage. Ken Flower reassured the Governor, in a personal interview that morning, that no UDI was yet on the cards, and he assumed that a further Proclamation would be produced, to be signed and dated in due course. So even the Director of the CIO was unaware that events were proceeding with great rapidity. Flower was not privy to the latest message from Wilson to Smith the previous day, which in Smith's eyes had scuppered any hope of the Royal Commission proposals offering an acceptable way forward. Pestell phoned the Cabinet Secretary the next morning (Friday 5 November) to chase the matter up further. At 11.00 a.m. the Prime Minister, pleading pressure of business, apologised for the delay, and reassured the Governor that the Proclamation would be published forthwith. It gave the government wide powers of censorship and arrest, but led to no immediate panic: no police reservists or territorials were called up. Then on Sunday a further breakthrough occurred. Harold Wilson proposed that Sir Hugh Beadle should visit London, so that a plan could be worked out for an acceptable Royal Commission. Wilson noted that 'we have both expressed our full confidence in him'.[497] Sir Hugh's clothes suitable for an autumnal trip were in Bulawayo, and Smith laid on an RRAF aircraft to collect them, though meanwhile he made no response to Wilson's invitation, merely noting that the views of the two governments seemed irreconcilable.[498] At the same time, the whole Rhodesian Cabinet signed a letter to the Queen – Montrose heading the list of signatories – assuring 'Your Majesty that whatever happens there will still be found among all Rhodesians that same loyalty and devotion to the Crown which have guided and sustained us since our country was founded.'[499]

On Tuesday morning (9 November) Sir Hugh arrived in London. He was whisked into London in a car provided by the Commonwealth Office. Before setting off on a round of meetings with the Prime Ministers and other ministers, he called at Rhodesia House. Andrew Skeen, the Rhodesian High Commissioner, warned him to be careful, because 'not for nothing was Britain called "Perfidious Albion"'.[500] But Beadle's mission was a sideshow. The Rhodesian Cabinet's message of loyalty to the Queen arrived by diplomatic bag the next day. It was Skeen's task to deliver it to the Palace. There was no mechanism for this. The message had to go through the Commonwealth Relations Office. Skeen impatiently awaited a reply, which was forthcoming later that evening. It came in the form of a message from the Commonwealth Relations Office, for onward transmission by the

Governor, expressing the Queen's confidence 'that all her Rhodesian peoples on whose behalf the message speaks will demonstrate their loyalty by continuing to act in a constitutional manner'.[501] This attempt to contact the Queen highlighted for Skeen something which – curiously – he appears not to have appreciated up until that point: 'that loyalty to the Crown was a constitutional formula, quite separate from loyalty to the Queen's person, and in fact was no more than loyalty to the ruling party in England at the time'.[502] He claims he was later able to use this experience to ease the 'mind and conscience' of Rhodesians who felt a conflict of loyalties.

In Salisbury, meanwhile, the same issue was being debated at Government House. At 8.00 p.m. that evening the Governor spoke to Ken Flower, and asked him whether rather than waiting upon events he should appeal to the Chiefs of Staff. Flower went off to take soundings. Later that evening, the Queen's reply to her Rhodesian Ministers' loyal address came through, and was delivered to the Prime Minister. It thanked them for their assurances of loyalty, and expressed the hope that they would continue to act in a constitutional manner. At the same time, Harold Wilson was trying to contact Ian Smith by phone. He got through to him around 5.00 a.m. (London time) on the 11th, and spent an hour discussing the situation which the Rhodesian premier suggested had 'gone too far'. He ended the conversation with the words, 'I am grateful to you for taking all this trouble.' Given the time difference between London and Salisbury, Smith was able to report the content of the call to his Cabinet, who had already taken the decision to declare UDI. The Phoenix Room near the Cabinet Room was already set out for a signing ceremony, and the Proclamation had already been printed. At the eleventh hour of the eleventh month, UDI was declared. Twelve men signed the document. Photographs were taken and the nation was told to stand by for an important announcement at lunchtime.

While Smith was in conversation with Wilson, Ken Flower reported to Government House – shortly after 8.00 a.m. on the morning of Thursday 11 November. He reported that Putterill, the Army chief, was solid in his loyalty to the Governor as his Commander-in-Chief, though he felt that while his senior officers felt the same, the white rank and file were solidly RF. Hawkins, of the RRAF, was loyal, but he too felt that his men could not be relied upon to act against the government. Barfoot, the Police Commissioner, was however a Smith man. It seemed that the only options which the Governor had were to resign or to wait upon events. Events unfolded quickly. Immediately after the signing, the Prime Minister arrived at Government House, accompanied by Clifford Dupont. It was 11.30 a.m. When they entered Sir Humphrey said, 'This is it, is it?'[503] The Governor rehearsed the old arguments: that Smith had no mandate to take – as opposed to negotiate

– independence; that such an act would be immoral and unconstitutional; that at the very least the Prime Minister should await the arrival of the Chief Justice, who was at that very moment on his way back from London. But of course the die was already cast. Clifford Dupont later recalled that the Governor then asked the Prime Minister if he wanted him to resign. Smith's response was, 'Well, Sir, it is up to you whether you resign, but it would facilitate matters.' Humphrey's rejoinder was (and these 'were his actual words', says Dupont), 'Well, if I was to resign, I suppose I could go back to my farm and see if I can get some more milk out of my cows.'[504] This seems highly unlikely. He may well have asked if they wanted him to resign; and he may well have said that were he to resign he would happily go back to the farm to his cows. But in his own recollections, he noted that he told his Prime Minister he was not going to resign. George Rudland, another member of Smith's Cabinet, was asked ten years later whether he thought the Governor had been intending to throw in the towel and move out, and his response shows a greater understanding than Dupont: 'No', said Rudland, 'he's a very honest, very sincere man and I think his loyalty to the Queen was something that was so bred in him that he couldn't get away from it.'[505] That rings true. The interview ended with the Governor instructing his ministers that they no longer held office under the Crown. *De jure*, but not *de facto*, they were dismissed. Ian Smith makes no mention of this dismissal in his memoirs (and in an interview with the author, denied that it happened). It seems inconceivable that Sir Humphrey would not have carried out his duty to dismiss the Rhodesian Ministers in the Queen's name, as he had been commanded to do. He himself had no doubts thereafter that he had clearly done so, as his subsequent (censored) press statement made clear.

Ian Smith left Government House to record his broadcast to the nation. At 1.15 p.m. his long radio statement began. It sought to justify the action taken by the government, and announced the existence of a new constitution to replace the 1962 one. He ended with these words: 'We have struck a blow for the preservation of justice, civilization and Christianity, and in the spirit of this belief we have this day assumed our sovereign independence. God bless you all.' Hugh Beadle heard the news in Lusaka airport. By then Ian Smith had retired to bed with a cold.

In the afternoon, the Governor summoned the press, 'a very courageous band of men', as Harold Wilson called them, 'standing up, as they had fearlessly done, for the highest traditions of their profession'.[506] Having been told that the Governor was to issue a statement, they had wanted to publish it in a special edition in the morning, believing that if this was done 'before the Prime Minister had made his announcement [it] would have a profound effect on public thinking'.[507] Gibbs would not permit this. He was probably right in view of his position. To have entered thus into the fray would have compromised his status as a constitutional figurehead. Now, however, censorship regulations were in force, so they abandoned their idea of a special edition, having been told that they could not print the Governor's statement. It was this:

> The Government has made an unconstitutional declaration of independence. I have received the following message from Her Majesty's Secretary of State for Commonwealth Relations:
>
> 'I have it in command from Her Majesty to inform you that it is Her Majesty's pleasure that, in the event of an unconstitutional declaration of independence, Mr Ian Smith and other persons holding office as Ministers of the Government of Southern Rhodesia and as Deputy Ministers cease to hold office. I am commanded by Her Majesty to instruct you in that event to convey Her Majesty's pleasure in this matter to Mr Smith, and otherwise publish it in such manner as you may deem fit.'
>
> In accordance with these instructions I have informed Mr Smith and his colleagues that they no longer hold office. I call on all citizens of Rhodesia to refrain from all acts which would further the objectives of the illegal authorities. Subject to that it is the duty of all citizens to maintain law and order in this country and to carry on with their normal tasks. This applies equally to the judiciary, the armed services, the police and public services.

While the Governor was making this statement, Harold Wilson was dictating the statement he would make in the House of Commons later that afternoon. It expressed much the same sentiments, and promised further details of the actions which were being taken to place Rhodesia in financial and economic quarantine. Mr Heath and Mr Grimond both gave their support, and all joined in agreeing that 'the thoughts and prayers of the whole House will be with the Governor and Lady Gibbs, not only in his capacity as representative of the Crown, but as a very great statesman who will go through a very, very difficult time'.[508] Those words were kind. They were hardly quite true. Humphrey Gibbs was no statesman. That was not his interest or talent. Yet the months and years ahead were to prove that he could be statesmanlike in his handing of an unprecedented situation.

One other event of that fateful day needs to be examined. When Sir Humphrey died, the *Guardian* obituary was written by Patrick Keatley, who had been a young correspondent in Salisbury at that time. The obituary contains a story which is important. He asserts that on the morning of the UDI broadcast four senior Army officers travelled, armed, to Government House. The senior officer among them spoke to the Governor: 'Sir, if you will provide us with a warrant for the arrest of Mr Smith as a rebel against the Queen, we will do our duty.' The Governor refused, and the soldiers left. 'This', says Keatley, 'was the fatal moment of hesitation.'[509] It may be that four officers visited the Governor. But he had already considered the possibility of that course of action. And, on the advice of the Director of the CIO, as we have seen, it had been rejected. There was no 'fatal moment of hesitation'. Indeed the unwisdom of such a move on the Governor's part is highlighted by a note made by Flower nine days later. As he reported to the Governor, 'several senior Army officers' had 'disclosed strong opposition on principle to government'. On the other hand, while before UDI 'at least 20 per cent' of the army were opposed to UDI, there had been slippage. Some had resigned, and some had reluctantly decided to go along with it; at any rate, his latest assessment was that 'probably ten per cent opposed'.[510] Certainly all this ties in with the advice which the British Government had received a full year before UDI. In October 1964 the British High Commissioner in Salisbury had reported that 'the senior Army officers would be loyal to him [the Governor] and probably, though less certainly, senior RRAF officers'. He felt that the position of the BSAP was 'more doubtful' and that the bulk of the force 'would probably support the Government'. Gloomily he concluded that 'it is quite impossible to predict in relation to many of the senior officers (with the exception of [the] army commander, who would be at the Governor's disposal) ... whether their loyalty to the Governor and opposition to an act of rebellion would extend to actively opposing it at the Governor's orders'.[511] From its own sources, the Ministry of Defence in London had reached the same conclusion, emphasising that it would be unwise to 'frame our course of action on the assumption that the Southern Rhodesian Armed Forces are sure to side actively and wholeheartedly with constitutional authority against Mr Smith'.[512]

BELEAGUERED GOVERNOR

Now that UDI had been declared, the Rhodesian government had to decide what to do about the Governor. The new constitution they had announced with UDI provided for the appointment of an Officer Administering the Government, who would become Governor-General on being appointed by the Queen on the advice of her Rhodesian ministers – something of an Alice in Wonderland scenario. Legally, there were now no Rhodesian ministers: the Governor had dismissed them. Nevertheless on 12 November, Smith, Dupont and Lardner-Burke visited Government House to persuade Sir

Humphrey to resign. How could they have misread their man so profoundly? The Governor told them he had no intention of resigning, nor of moving down to his farm. In this he was backed up by Beadle who gave clear advice that the Governor must stay in Government House, and that he would move in with him if necessary.[513] The Governor's only response to the visit by Smith was to urge the British government not to abandon the possibility of a negotiated settlement, to which Harold Wilson responded with a message that any negotiations must be conducted through the Governor.[514] This was a clever move, in that there was now good reason for the Smith regime to leave the Governor in place.

When Smith with his colleagues visited Government House again after the weekend, presumably to reinforce their suggestion that he should move out, the Governor showed them the message from the British Prime Minister, and it was agreed that the Chief Justice should liaise with Lardner-Burke on any proposals the regime might want to put to Britain. Nevertheless, two days later the Government House phone was cut off. Smith later claimed that this was a result of security service pressure, as they were worried about the British Government's direct access to the Governor.[515] Ken Flower, however, blames the government for this 'petty' action.[516] Further pressure was applied. Ian Smith made public reference to the removal of Sir Humphrey's 'trappings as Governor', and the police guard was removed from his gates. The Governor personally interviewed and protested to the Police Commissioner, Barfoot, who claimed he could do nothing without jeopardising his job, which he was not prepared to do. The illegal regime finally tried to put a constitutional gloss upon their moves against the Governor. In a letter to the Queen early in December, Ian Smith noted that the new constitution provided for the appointment of a Governor-General on the advice of her Rhodesian ministers. So, he proceeded, 'I humbly submit to Your Majesty on behalf of Your Majesty's Ministers of the Government of Rhodesia, the name of Clifford Walter Dupont, for appointment as Governor General.'[517] A speedy and chilly response was transmitted by the Commonwealth Relations Office, through the Governor: 'Her Majesty is not able to entertain purported advice of this kind, and has therefore been pleased to direct that no action should be taken upon it.'[518]

Captain Christopher Owen, the Governor's aide-de-camp, was ordered back to his regiment: he refused and resigned his commission to stay at Government House. That was a timely boost for the Governor's morale, as was the announcement of his being awarded the KCVO (Knight Commander of the Royal Victorian Order) on 18 November. On that same day, the plans for a visit by Mountbatten were proceeding further in London. They were proceeding too fast for the Prime Minister's principal private secretary,

Derek Mitchell, who was anxious 'to restrain Lord Mountbatten from rushing to the aircraft before the necessary political authority had been obtained'.[519] Harold Wilson had talked to the Queen about the proposed Mountbatten visit during his weekly audience two days before. Mountbatten, with characteristic briskness, had already taken the matter in hand and had proceeded to spell out his requirements. An RAF Comet would be required, repainted to indicate that it was attached to The Queen's Flight. He would require a large contingent to travel with him, including 'four tall NCOs from the Life Guards' and a BBC television team. His son-in-law Lord Brabourne should accompany him, as should a member of Her Majesty's Household – preferably Sir Martin Charteris or Lord Plunket (whose brother, of course, lived in Rhodesia). The Queen had expressed her reluctance to allow a member of her household to accompany the party, and indeed in general stressed that 'there would have to be nothing slapdash about the mission since there would be a very considerable risk to the person of Lord Mountbatten'. Indeed the very fact that he was to undertake it involved her more personally than might be thought appropriate. A few days later, consideration was given to the purpose of such a visit.[520] It would sustain the Governor's morale. It would serve to ensure that communications with him were improved. It would 'disabuse Beadle of [his] present unrealistic political ideas' – an aspect which is interesting in the light of Beadle's rift with the Governor three years later. At this stage it merely underlined the fact that Beadle in his advice to the Governor was more anxious to set up talks between Salisbury and London than was the Prime Minister, who had stated publicly there could be no parleying with the illegal regime. But a further purpose of the visit would be to invest the Governor with his KCVO, a ceremonial and regal act which no doubt appealed to Lord Mountbatten. A week later, Harold Wilson called an afternoon meeting in 10 Downing Street. The Commonwealth Secretary attended, as did Humphrey's brother Geoffrey, who had been out to visit his brother and was able to give a first-hand account of how things were.[521] He was fairly upbeat. He encouraged the use of 'really tough sanctions' in order to 'get the whole business over quickly'. He was hopeful that Evan Campbell – whom the Prime Minister had hoped might be a voice for moderation, would emerge to oppose the regime forcefully, as he was 'raring for a fight'. Geoffrey confirmed what Wilson already knew: that while the higher ranks in the armed forces might be loyal, no one knew how securely that loyalty was felt in the lower ranks, nor in the police who were the strongest force of all. As far as the Mountbatten visit was concerned, Geoffrey may have delivered the *coup de grâce*. He suggested that 'Lord Mountbatten was not himself one of the most known members of the Royal Family', and said he 'hoped for someone "higher up"'. The Mountbatten Plan did not proceed. In fact, it had in a sense been overtaken by events.

On the day that Humphrey's KCVO was announced – just a week after UDI – late in the evening, Ian Smith visited Government House suggesting an approach to Wilson, which was duly transmitted through the residual British High Commission in Salisbury to the British government. Subsequently some clarification was sought by them, and duly sent. 'Nothing came of these exchanges.'[522] A week later, Richard Crossman was recording in his diary that 'The drama of the poor old Governor staying on in Government House has worn off.'[523] In fact the situation had changed subtly. As Ken Flower recorded in his diary on 20 November, it obviously suited Smith, if not some other RF leaders, 'for HE [His Excellency] to remain and provide the link with the UK'.[524] It was a contact Smith was to make use of frequently during the next four years: he visited Government House on at least fourteen occasions, secretly and at night. The clandestine nature of the visits suited him – he did not want to be seen to be consulting with the man he had 'deposed' as Governor. But it also suited the Governor, and the British government. On 7 December, Wilson assured his Cabinet that 'no one was negotiating with Smith'.[525] Crossman, however, reckoned that while 'Barbara needled Harold endlessly, trying to make him say on no account would we ever negotiate with the Smith regime', the Prime Minister had 'time after time wriggled out of repudiating the suggestion'.[526] On 17 December Britain stepped up its economic sanctions against Rhodesia. The initial ones, involving exchange controls and expulsion of Rhodesia from the sterling area, had 'struck Rhodesians as a damp squib'.[527] Now however, as Wilson reported to the Governor, events were 'moving rapidly to a climax', and Britain's plans for an oil embargo might be out-bid by UN action. Wilson was aware that the fragile cross-party consensus in the House of Commons was at risk. Humphrey Gibbs could only feel, as the first Christmas of UDI approached, that the gulf between Salisbury and London was as wide, or wider than ever. On Christmas Eve, Harold Wilson wrote to him assuring him that the 'British Government are prepared to try and negotiate a constitutional settlement through the Governor', and telling him that 'it will be increasingly important for us to keep in closest touch'.[528] So although Humphrey had written that nothing came of the 'exchanges' between himself and Smith, something had come of them. Both sides, both Smith and Wilson, regarded Humphrey as an intermediary. So it was in the interests of the illegal regime to leave the Governor in place, at least for the moment.

1. In Scotland for the grouse shooting: Humphrey's parents, Lord and Lady Hunsdon.

2. Edwardian boyhood: Humphrey Gibbs (left) and his brother, Geoffrey.

3. Colonial architecture: Government House in Salisbury, with the Governor's standard flying.

4. Full regalia: The Governor with tribal chiefs and Stan Morris, Secretary for Native Affairs.

5. The Art of the Possible: Greeting R. A. Butler during his visit to Rhodesia in 1963 when he promised (or didn't promise) dominion status for the colony.

6. The Commonwealth's longest-serving premier: at Government House with Huggie (Viscount Malvern) after his retirement.

7. Grasping the nettle: Harold Wilson (left), watched by the Governor, greets Ian Smith at Government House, October 1965, during a last face-to-face attempt to avert UDI.

8. Formal dinner while under siege: The Governor and Lady Gibbs with the Archbishop of Central Africa and the Bishops of Mashonaland and Matabeleland, March 1966.

9. Plain sailing? The Governor and the Chief Justice (Sir Hugh Beadle) aboard HMS *Tiger*, still hoping for a peaceful settlement.

10. The end of the road: Sir Humphrey Gibbs walking his dog in the aftermath of his resignation as Governor, June 1969.

10   Tensions and Talks

UNDER SIEGE

Life in Government House in the wake of UDI settled into a pattern. The initial fears that the Governor might be forcibly ejected, or even arrested, had subsided. Ian Smith went out of his way to issue a statement in which he 'denied that he had ordered the Army and Police Force to arrest the Governor and Chief Justice'.[529] Brigadier Skeen, the pro-Smith enthusiast and recently returned from London as Rhodesia's last High Commissioner there, published his account of UDI in 1966, and said of Sir Humphrey: 'It was hoped that in time the Rhodesian public would forget him, and this is what is happening.'[530] The regime certainly tried to play down his presence. All references to 'His Excellency' or 'The Governor' were censored. A series of measures added to the feeling that Government House was under siege. The first demand for rent arrived on the Governor's desk early in January.[531] A few days later there were claims (from sources at Government House) that the Governor's mail was being tampered with.[532] In early February an attempt was made by the Governor's Comptroller to have a phone connected to his cottage in the grounds of Government House, all the phones having been cut off just after UDI. But his request was refused unless he could give assurances that no one else would be allowed to use it: the Government obviously thought this was a devious plot to re-establish Government House contact with the outside world.[533] Towards the end of the month, without any warning, the Government House sign was removed. Next month, a policeman called with orders, signed by the Police Commissioner Barfoot, that the last three government employees – two orderlies and a batman – should return to general police duties. And early in March, the Governor's portrait was removed from the lobby of parliament, though it was not relegated completely, but was found a new home in the Members' Lounge.[534] This incident moved the right-wing Salisbury *Citizen*, in an echo of Brigadier Skeen's comment, to note that 'most Rhodesians have forgotten who Sir Humphrey Gibbs was'. But, the article went on to complain, 'couldn't we have gone into this removal business in one grand spring cleaning swoop some time ago and forgotten the whole matter?'[535]

    The early months of 1966 were also clouded by an outburst of speculation over the possible role the Governor might play in establishing an alternative government. This issue had first arisen in 1964 when Ian Smith came to power. Sir Hugh Beadle recorded that 'in the event of a UDI the Governor would appoint another government', and that 'considerable correspondence took place with the British government as to the form of the announcement to be made by the governor'.[536] The public records do indeed show a flurry of activity in London late in 1964. The question of 'treason' was investigated. What would be the nature of the 'treason' committed by the Southern Rhodesian government in the event of a UDI? The Attorney General's cautious conclusion was that UDI 'would in itself be unlikely to be held as an act of treason', but that 'any steps taken to give effect to it might well amount to treason'.[537] And there was discussion about the possibility of the arrest of the Governor and Chief Justice, and the consequent need 'to appoint another Governor and, if necessary, to establish him somewhere outside Rhodesia'.[538] However, Wilson agreed with Bottomley that no such plan of action should be set up.[539] Another aspect of the problem was also under consideration at the same time. What if the African Nationalists set up a 'government in exile' as a result of UDI? The Commonwealth Relations Office circulated all High Commissions in the Commonwealth pointing out to them that 'such a government would have no legal basis whatsoever'.[540] So the word was undoubtedly out that the British government had discussed – and possibly held – contingency plans. But they did not involve the setting up of an alternative government either outside Rhodesia or within it. The only faint trace of such a move might be seen to be when the Governor had interviewed David Butler, the opposition leader, when Ian Smith requested a dissolution.[541] But that had been open and above board. However, rumours abounded, as they tended to do in Salisbury at any time, but especially in the hot months towards the end of the year. At the time of UDI, the Governor received a letter from F. W. Fynn. He was the son of a former Prime Minister of Rhodesia, and his brother was a friend of Humphrey. He wrote:[542]

> I had a long discussion with my brother Robert shortly after he had seen you the other day and I would like to take this opportunity of saying how pleased I was to hear that you have shunned completely any attempt to allow yourself to be made the centre of a counter-rebellion. There is a certain amount of canvassing along these lines at present which I confess I deplore ... .

But the issue reached Cabinet level in London. At the end of November 1965 Barbara Castle records how she 'came across in my box a letter of 26 November from Kaunda to Harold ... it demanded financial help, British troops "to come and protect Kariba", and the granting of powers to Humphrey Gibbs to form a legal government in Rhodesia'.[543] Odd that this proposal should come from Kenneth Kaunda, who within a few months shocked Harold Wilson by calling Sir Humphrey 'a racialist'.[544] Nothing more was heard of this proposal, but the issue was raised again in early 1966. In late January, there was a report that the British Prime Minister might 'soon propose that Earl Mountbatten be appointed Governor of Rhodesia'. Perhaps this was a belated and partial leak of Wilson's Mountbatten initiative of the previous November. Or perhaps it was an attempt by the Rhodesian Front (RF) itself to stir up unsettling fears. This suspicion carries some weight, as the report was published in Salisbury in the right-wing *Citizen*.[545] The British press was quick to pick up the suggestion. The London *Telegraph*, in an editorial, averred that no British Governor, 'no matter how illustrious', could solve the Rhodesian problem.[546] It also discussed the role of Sir Humphrey himself, noting that 'an old-fashioned colonial role for the Governor ... is not possible'. Within a week, another story was hitting the headlines – the reports that Sir Humphrey 'may seek the Queen's permission to quit'.[547] The Governor's reaction was swift. Captain Owen, his aide-de-camp, described it: 'When His Excellency heard the report over the radio, he looked very surprised and said, "It's news to me".'[548]

But the issues of a Mountbatten Governorship, or rumours of the Governor's intention to resign, paled beside the next story which broke. On the day on which the denial about Humphrey's resignation was announced, the Minister of Law and Order, Desmond Lardner-Burke, declared in parliament in Salisbury that 'certain misguided individuals' had formed a 'shadow cabinet' with a view to overthrowing the regime. Described by London's *Sunday Telegraph* as 'the most respectable Fifth Column in the world',[549] the individuals were not actually named. The occasion of the announcement was a motion to extend the state of emergency for a further three months. The Minister stated that 'these people are trying to form themselves into a government so that they can take over if requested by Sir Humphrey Gibbs or Mr Wilson'. He warned that 'if they continue their nefarious works we will have no hesitation in dealing with them'.[550] The whole story may have been a diversionary tactic, or it may have had a vestige of truth in it. Tiny Rowland later claimed that in the wake of UDI, 'drawing together a wide group which included loyal army officers and members of Parliament, I had planned an alternative Cabinet which could be quickly installed'. The British reaction to this scheme, within a few days of UDI, was summed up by Sir Burke Trend, Secretary to the Cabinet, who told Rowland, 'Why don't you leave this little man Smith to us? He'll be gone in two or three months.'[551] Whether or not this plan leaked, who were these men? Who were these 'most respectable' individuals who might form an alternative government? Obvious anti-RF notables were being mentioned: Sir Roy Welensky, Evan Campbell, David Butler, General Jock Anderson, Sir Robert Tredgold and Sir Hugh Beadle. It is interesting to compare this list with later ones. At the time of the *Tiger* talks in December 1966, Mr Wilson presented Mr Smith with a list of possible Cabinet Ministers for an interim regime. The names mentioned at that time were Garfield Todd, Chad Chipunza, Sir John Caldicott (former Rhodesian and Federal Minister), F. C. Clements (Mayor of Salisbury in 1964), S. S. Sawyer (a former Federal and anti-RF politician) and Hardwicke Holderness (of the legal firm, Scanlen and Holderness) – so the list contained none of the names being bandied about in February 1966. In an undated list drawn up by Sir Robert Tredgold, probably at the end of the 1960s, two or three years after Wilson's, he made a note of 'men who would be useful in an interim government',[552] and he included Evan Campbell and Hardwicke Holderness. But his list otherwise was different from the previous two. He included Sir John Clayden (former Federal Chief Justice), Sir Henry McDowell (a director of Anglo-American and former Federal civil servant), Sir Charles Cumings (former Chief Justice of the Sudan and ex-director of the British South Africa Company), Sir Evelyn Hone (last Governor of Northern Rhodesia), John Pestell, Michael May (head of the legal firm, Scanlen and Holderness), Professor Sam Kaye (of the University College of Rhodesia)[553] – and Nathan Shamuyarira, who was later to become a minister in the Mugabe government. It is an interesting list in that it shows the extent of the 'great and good' who lived in Rhodesia and who were, more of less, liberal or mildly progressive. But all of these lists have something of an air of cloud cuckoo land about them. There was no 'shadow cabinet'. There was no possibility of an alternative government taking over, nor of the RF being willing to share power with a man like Garfield Todd. The absurdity of the rumours over the supposed 'shadow cabinet' is well-illustrated by the role in this whole affair of Mr George Brind. A former member of the RF who had resigned just before UDI, Brind claimed that he had seen the Governor, thus fuelling the feeling that Sir Humphrey was a contact man for malcontents. In fact, Brind had visited Government House and had left a note for the Governor who, as John Pestell reported, had not seen him and 'did not want to see him'.[554] The whole 'shadow cabinet' affair was based on rumour and innuendo, and the *Rhodesia Herald* put it down to some remarks made by a Rhodesian businessman to a South African journalist.[555] Nevertheless it helped to give further justification for Lardner-Burke's extension of the state of emergency, and also helped keep the temperature running high in the first few months of 1966. Other government actions had the same effect. Early in February the censorship laws were tightened, particularly aimed at removing the blank spaces from the newspapers – a ploy used by editors to show their readers just how extensively the censor's pencil was being wielded.[556] Equally calculated to stoke the fires was the report that powerful interests within the RF were pushing for a republic.[557] David Smith, the relatively moderate MP for the Marandellas constituency, went out of his way to assure his constituents that 'the day may come, but it must not be forced', and concluded that talk of declaring a republic was 'exactly what Mr Wilson wants, and we should not play into his hands'.[558]

For the Governor personally, more private worries were added to the public ones. There was hate mail. One correspondent, from Purley in Surrey, sent a picture of the Governor which had appeared in the British press, with a caption typed underneath: 'A stupid be-feathered clown and mountebank feebly clinging to office for the sake of the emoluments pertaining thereto.'[559] Such criticism, while obviously ludicrous and unjust, was, like all poison-pen letters, hurtful to receive. Even more worrying however was the telegram that arrived at Government House on 9 March. 'Your son has been kidnapped', it claimed, 'but he is no danger. His freedom depends on you. He will be released on condition that you meet Mr Ian Smith in the Meikles Hotel within 24 hours and discuss Rhodesia's problems with him. You must supply proof of this through local press.'[560] The story hit the press two days later, by which time it had become clear that it was merely a student prank. Kenneth Gibbs and Robert Smith were released within twenty-four hours as a result, it was reported, of 'official pressure', and the Students' Representative Council president described the affair as being 'in very bad taste'. Certainly it must have caused a moment of panic in the Gibbs and Smith households, and in the US it was taken seriously enough for the head of NBC to put through a call to Pretoria's Commissioner of Police, who had some difficulty in persuading him that it was just a prank.[561] It was perhaps fortunate for the Governor and his wife that both the Aldenhams and the Ponsonbys were staying in Government House during the early part of 1966, so there was family support on hand during a time of family worry. Soon after they departed, the Governor's morale was given a fillip when he became the first recipient of a new award by the Anglican Province of Central Africa. The Order of the Epiphany was instituted 'to give honour and express gratitude to members of the laity who have made outstanding contributions to the life of the people of our province'.[562] It was a brave gesture on the part of the Anglican Church in support of someone who had not only been a strong supporter of the Church, but was now a pariah. The Governor and Lady Gibbs hosted a dinner, after the presentation, attended by the Archbishop of Central Africa, the Bishop of Mashonaland, the Fynns, Sir Hugh Beadle and Captain Owen. As the port was passed round after dinner – in a decanter bearing the royal cipher – and as the Queen's health was drunk, the results were coming in of the British general election. 'From the first results declared', Harold Wilson wrote later, 'it became clear that we had been returned with a large majority.'[563] With a

majority of ninety-seven overall, Wilson could feel secure. But he was also
aware that 'the most urgent problem was Rhodesia'.[564]

TALKS ABOUT TALKS

To say that Government House was 'under siege' during the early months
of 1966 is to tell only part of the story. The Governor was not a prisoner.
He regularly went out to the Salisbury Club for a game of snooker. He had
taken soundings before showing his face there, and 'was assured that all would
be normal'.[565] On one memorable and uncomfortable occasion Humphrey
found himself in the lift with Clifford Dupont, his 'successor'; a nod of the
head was followed by silence during the short journey. Occasionally he went
out shooting on an estate near Salisbury, and increasingly towards the end
of 1966 – when there seemed to be the possibility of a political breakthrough
– he went to watch the national cricket team. And he regularly attended early
morning service at the cathedral. He never, however, spent a night away,
for fear of a takeover of Government House during his absence. He could
not know at this stage that he was therefore not to see his beloved Bonisa
again for another three years. While not a prisoner, he must at times have
felt like a hotel keeper. The number of visitors increased. Besides those locals
who called in to sign the visitors' book or to shake the Governor's hand, there
were the judges, the service chiefs and the Director of the Central Intelligence
Organisation who kept in touch. And there was a succession of visitors from
overseas who came for lunch or dinner, or just for talks. Sometimes they
stayed. Lady Eden famously commented that during the Suez crisis she had
felt that the Canal was running through her drawing room in 10 Downing
Street. Lady Gibbs must sometimes have felt that her house was the lobby
of the House of Commons. The first group to arrive, early in the new year,
represented quite a cross-section. One can imagine Sir Humphrey feeling
quite at home with the Conservative Member for Farnham, Sir Godfrey
Nicholson, a Wykehamist who was almost his exact contemporary. But
what must he have made of the other three? The maverick Labour MP
Reginald Paget was staying with Mr van der Byl, Smith's most flamboyant
– and decidedly right-wing – minister. Paget was, frankly, in support of Ian
Smith and did 'not believe that the sacrifice of Rhodesia to appease the
racialism of black Africa will succeed or is justified'. Such an opinion
coming from a Labour MP must have surprised the Governor, though they
found agreement in the belief that 'negotiations with Smith must start'.[566]
The other two MPs in this first delegation of 1966 were the Liberal Peter
Bessell and the Conservative Evelyn King. Bessell was already out of favour

with his party after his foolhardy attempt to get Jo Grimmond elected Speaker in the previous year, and of course was later to figure prominently, and none too honourably, in the Jeremy Thorpe saga.[567] King, a former Labour MP turned Tory, was sympathetic to Smith, and was later convinced that only 'Ian's ill-starred advisors' thwarted his reaching an agreement with Britain.[568]

Hard on their heels came another group of MPs, this time all Labour – David Ennals, Christopher Rowlands and Jeremy Bray. They had a fairly rough time at the hands of hecklers in Salisbury. Mr Rowlands was reported to have been 'kicked and punched'.[569] 'The three MPs were hardly able to say a word without being interrupted by screams of "Liar, liar", and "rotten swine".'[570] As the Governor was well aware, such incidents did nothing to advance the cause of moderate Rhodesian opinion in the eyes of the UK. Other visits, however, were less eventful. During the first three months of 1966, the Governor also met with the Hon Hugh Astor, the Deputy Chairman of *The Times* newspapers. Lord Dulverton and Sir Walter Coutts visited together: the former was to found a trust for the benefit of southern Africa, and the latter was an old Africa hand, ex-Governor of Uganda.

One of the most significant visitors early in 1966 was Selwyn Lloyd, who was about to end a period as Shadow Commonwealth spokesman. He was the most senior British politician to visit since UDI. He was briefed at a three-hour meeting with Sir Humphrey, refused the offer of a government car, and stayed at Meikles Hotel. In all he saw an astonishing 327 people. He felt – as he reported to Edward Heath – that his visit 'was doing quite a lot of good out here in letting everyone of every sort and kind of opinion blow off steam'.[571] But he also reported that 'The Governor and the High Commission are misinforming HMG. Although there will be a progressive decline in the economy it will be many months, perhaps years, before anything like an economic collapse will take place.' This was an odd interpretation of the information the Governor was sending back home: he was certainly not committed to a view that sanctions would work speedily. Perhaps Lloyd was basing his remarks on the upbeat message which Wilson tended to transmit on occasions, that sanctions were working and that 'on the expert advice available to him the cumulative effects of the economic and financial sanctions might well bring the rebellion to an end within a matter of weeks rather than months'.[572] There is no evidence that this was the message being transmitted from Government House. But Selwyn Lloyd's interpretation was curiously echoed later in the year by Brigadier Skeen, who wrote that 'the British Government was receiving false information through its sources in Salisbury ... The sort of people, belonging to what one might call the "old establishment" who used to be in touch with the British High Commission, were the same who belonged to what can be described as the "Government

House set".'[573] Philippa Berlyn, writing over a decade later, was the wife of Professor Christie, a lawyer who might himself have been described as being on the fringes of this set. Yet she, in her life of Ian Smith, also alluded to the same phenomenon: 'The British High Commissioner and the Government House set ... sent back a flow of information to Whitehall, much of it incorrect, as to the state of the economy, the reaction of the people and general business attitudes.'[574] I can find no evidence that – as far as the Governor was concerned – any such false and misleading information was channelled back to London.

In late January, the British Prime Minister formally stated that 'the Governor was authorised at any time to receive from the illegal regime any proposals about the means by which the rebellion might be brought to an end'.[575] Thus he was publicly acknowledging his statement to Humphrey a month earlier when he had written that the British government 'are prepared to try and negotiate a constitutional settlement through the Governor'.[576] Sir Humphrey accepted this role, but went further. He saw himself correctly as the one person who might persuade the two sides to open up channels of communication once again. By far the most important visitor for the Governor to receive would be someone who was an emissary from Harold Wilson, not one who – like Selwyn Lloyd – had been sent out by Edward Heath. There were press reports in mid-January that Arthur Bottomley would fly in to update the Governor on the Commonwealth Conference, and to negotiate aid for the drought-stricken areas of Rhodesia – aid that would be channelled through Sir Humphrey.[577] In fact, the proposed mission came to nought, because Smith was only prepared to receive the Commonwealth Secretary as a private citizen. Wilson reckoned that Smith was holding out, in the hope of a British general election which would unseat him.[578] Perhaps this is also what gave Smith the impetus to demand the withdrawal of the British High Commissioner. To sort this problem out, Duncan Watson, of the Commonwealth office, arrived to see the Governor on 15 March. Little progress was made in his attempts to open up talks with Ian Smith – still, presumably, lying low until the British election. The Governor however took the opportunity of sending back with Watson a note in which he wrote as one 'intensely loyal to Her Majesty' and 'also intensely loyal to Rhodesia'. He suggested that 'the main question at the present time is how to break the deadlock'. He ended by underlining the difficulty of his own position, and the fact that he had not seen 'Smith or any of his colleagues' for about three months. Watson finally departed, bearing this note, on 28 March. Weeks passed and the Governor heard nothing. Hennings, the new head of the residual mission and successor to Fingland, arrived, but no news came from London.

The Governor decided to set things moving. The situation was looking even bleaker in April, as the British government stepped up pressure on Rhodesia by moving to block the docking of the Portuguese tanker *Joanna V* at Beira, bearing oil destined for Rhodesia. And the Rhodesian government seemed determined to break the last links with Britain by closing the residual mission and sending home the newly arrived Hennings. So in a talk with Nick Cambitsis, Chairman of the Industrial Development Corporation, Humphrey made clear that he was willing to see Ian Smith at any time – knowing that Cambitsis' links with the regime were strong enough to ensure that the message got through. On the same day, John Pestell told the Governor that in chatting during golf with the ex-Federal Minister, Graylin, the message was coming through from him that talks must start soon.[579] In the same vein, Lord Bolton in a statement to the press declared that the Governor had told him 'that Britain and Rhodesia "should get round a table and talk"'.[580] Bolton was an old friend who had visited the Governor but had not been authorised to publicise their conversation. Ironically, the press on the same day – 16 April – carried reports of Ian Smith's decision finally to recall all diplomatic staff from London and ask the British to withdraw theirs from Salisbury. But on that day too the Governor at last had a reply from Harold Wilson: that talks could begin but only if and when Ian Smith made some approach, via the Governor. Two days later, Smith called at Government House in the early evening, and stayed for an hour. It must have been a strange meeting. The Queen's representative who had formally dismissed the Rhodesian Prime Minister three months earlier was now meeting the man who was still, quite obviously, the Prime Minister of a country which proclaimed loyalty to the Queen. Smith stated he was ready to open talks without preconditions. Two days later, Oliver Wright, Wilson's envoy, called on Sir Humphrey. A meeting was set up, and Smith called again at Government House on 23 April, to see Wright, Hennings, the Governor and the Chief Justice. The way was open for 'low-level' talks to begin in earnest.

On 27 April, in a 'surprise curtain-raiser to the debate on Rhodesia'[581] in the House of Commons, Harold Wilson announced that he had 'received a report from the Governor last week, at a time when, as it happens, my Private Secretary, Mr Oliver Wright, had just left by air for Pretoria to assist Her Majesty's Ambassador in his talks with the South African Government'.[582] The result had been that Wright had gone to Salisbury to consult with the Governor who had then 'arranged a meeting'. The Prime Minister concluded: 'In view of the importance of these talks the House will not expect me to say anything more.' Even Wilson's own Cabinet were unsure of the origins of the proposed informal talks. Barbara Castle was again suspicious: 'a worrying doubt: was it really Smith who took the initiative in approaching the Governor, or was it Smith responding to an overture by the Governor?'[583]

The new mood soon made itself felt. The next day, the British and Rhodesian governments halted the withdrawal plans for their diplomatic representatives. Within a week, the Rhodesian talks team had been announced: Gerald Clarke, Stan Morris and Cornelius Greenfield. It was a well-chosen team. Clarke, as Secretary to the Cabinet, had the ear of the Prime Minister. Morris had been a 'paternalistic but pragmatic' Secretary for African Affairs who had been dislodged from that position in the RF cleansing operation which had also removed Jock Anderson. Morris was now Chairman of the Public Services Board.[584] Greenfield had, like his brother Julian, served the Federation enthusiastically and was now the government's chief economic adviser. They flew to London on 7 May. That same day, Ian Smith announced to an audience of farmers at a fête near Harare that 'there has been a dramatic new development in our relations with Britain'.[585] And the Governor was 'quietly confident that the talks must succeed'.[586]

There was certainly now a more upbeat feel at Government House. Smith passed on via the Chief Justice his pleasure that the talks had started, and thanked him and the Governor for their part in bringing them about. Evan Campbell called to report that Smith's position in the caucus was looking shaky, and that there were moves to replace him with Lardner-Burke. This, if true, might have worked either way: to bring about a settlement which probably only Ian Smith could sell to the rank and file, or to precipitate an open split in the RF, which could lead to a hardening of attitudes. For the moment, however, the outlook was brighter than it had been since UDI. The Governor could even take some private pleasure from the report that the Churchill Trustees had had to adjourn their meeting, as some members refused to countenance the replacement of Sir Humphrey and John Pestell.

There was no dramatic breakthrough. The second session of talks opened in Salisbury in early June, and the Governor felt happier now that he was able to hear at first-hand how they were going. A gratifying 'sign of reconciliation' was the reconnecting of the Government House phones early in June. It may not have been the 'equivalent to the raising of the siege of Mafeking', the *Daily Telegraph* commented, but it 'raised the spirits of Government House and the British team of officials'.[587] So did the publication of an editorial in a South African newspaper the next day hailing Sir Humphrey, and predicting that the people of Rhodesia and Britain would 'one day appreciate the part he has played in preventing a deplorable situation deteriorating even further'. It concluded, 'A great patriot is Sir Humphrey.'[588]

The writer was Donald Woods, who himself was to gain fame when he made his stand against the apartheid regime in South Africa a decade later, inspiring the film *Cry Freedom*. The elation the Governor felt had its amusing side. Lady Gibbs was concerned by a 'strange noise' she heard in Government House. It turned out to be the Governor in his bath singing 'O what a beautiful morning'!

But the next few weeks were an anxious time. The Governor received mixed signals from the British team. One day the talks were 'near breakthrough'; on another they were making 'little progress', on another 'slow progress', and on another 'not complete deadlock'. *The Times* reported 'talks go unevenly',[589] while the *Daily Mail* declared that pressure from Verwoerd had stopped Smith halting the talks.[590] On 25 August, the British team flew home, on the grounds of 'provocation' by the Smith government in bringing a Constitutional Amendment Bill before the House, designed give the government greater emergency powers. In fact it was obvious that the talks must enter a limbo period, as the Commonwealth Conference was due to start soon. Oliver Wright wrote from Downing Street to assure the Governor – who respected him greatly – that 'we ought to be able to pull it off', though as he wryly put it, 'the next thing is to survive the Commonwealth Prime Ministers'.[591] On 30 August, Ian Smith asked the Governor for a 'top secret' meeting, at which he made it clear that he had not intended to provoke the British government, and that he wanted talks to restart. John Pestell recorded in his diary that the Chief Justice 'said that this was the first time he had seen Smith frightened'. The Governor reported these exchanges to Downing Street, which must have strengthened the Prime Minister's hand as he faced 'fierce arguments and profound disagreements'[592] with the Commonwealth leaders. Harold Wilson later recalled the pressure on Britain, the press leaks and the accusations of racialism, though eventually on 15 September the conference ended 'in an atmosphere of mutual friendship, cordiality and self-congratulations'.[593] The end result of the meetings was an agreed communiqué, which in effect gave Britain the clout to issue an ultimatum to Smith that the dispute must be settled by the end of the year. The Commonwealth leaders noted the stages whereby Britain proposed to end the rebellion. A legal government would 'be appointed by the Governor and [would] constitute a broadly based representative administration'. This interim administration would by negotiation with the British government come up with a constitutional settlement on the basis of the six principles. These settlement proposals would have to be submitted to all the peoples of Rhodesia, and the British government would have to be satisfied that this test of opinion was 'fair and free and would be acceptable to the general world community'.[594] Thus the British Prime Minister had won for Ian Smith 'a three months' respite to end the rebellion and resume negotiations for independence under defined conditions, but without mandatory sanctions'.[595] Already, before the conference broke up, Sir Morrice James of the Commonwealth Office had reported to the Governor in Salisbury, with plans soon to be set in motion for the visit of a Cabinet Minister. The talks were to move into higher gear.

And events moved swiftly. Herbert Bowden, Commonwealth Secretary, and Sir Elwyn Jones, the Attorney General, arrived in Salisbury on 19 September. The fiction had to be maintained that this visit implied no recognition of the illegal regime. As Bowden told reporters before take-off: 'While we are in Rhodesia we hope to see a great many people, leaders of opinion and if Mr Smith, who is a leader of opinion, wishes to come along and talk about the position, we shall discuss it with him.' However, he added that he was going to see Sir Humphrey, as representing the Crown in Rhodesia: 'I am going out to see him. If I do nothing else except thank him for all he has done in the last 10 months, this visit will have been worthwhile.'[596] The visit lasted a week. It was not immediately obvious that it had been worthwhile. Bowden left saying that the talks were not over, but that he 'would not hazard a guess about a settlement'.[597] The Governor was confident that things were now moving, and that some progress – and possibly a further British visit – would take place before 11 November, the first anniversary of UDI.

On the aeroplane with the British party were Lady Gibbs and her secretary Belle Baxter. Her son Nigel had been taken ill in Belfast, where he was working at Gallagher's tobacco factory, and was in hospital with suspected TB. The Governor's eldest son Jeremy, and his wife Alison, moved into Government House to keep the Governor company. Lady Gibbs was away for most of October, and was able to report back that Nigel was making good progress. While in Belfast, she stayed with the Prime Minister of Northern Ireland, Terence O'Neill, who had gone to Eton about five years after Humphrey left, and with the same housemaster. He described Molly as 'one of the most charming people I have met'.[598] He too was 'under siege'. Only a few months earlier, as he records, he had lunch with Harold Wilson at Downing Street: '"I suppose", said the Prime Minister, "Northern Ireland is rather like Rhodesia". "Maybe it is", I replied, "but I do not intend to be the Garfield Todd of Northern Ireland."'[599] The dinner conversation must have been interesting for Molly. There were many in Northern Ireland who felt an affinity with the white Rhodesians: 'both the Rhodesians and the Ulstermen had "primitive natives" to deal with; in Rhodesia cannibals believed in the throwing of bones, while in Ulster "the Irish scum" believed in the throwing of holy water'.[600] The dinner conversation also prompted a suggestion by

O'Neill that 'the Queen Mother, with her fantastic charm', might have a role to play in settling UDI. Molly was taken by the idea, and O'Neill subsequently approached Harold Wilson, and again in the New Year suggested to him that the Queen Mother, who was recovering from an operation, 'might be invited out to recuperate in Rhodesia'. His suggestion, not surprisingly, came to nothing.[601] He was to survive as Prime Minister until April 1969 – so Sir Humphrey outlasted him in office. In perhaps his most famous speech, O'Neill warned the 'so-called Loyalists who talk of independence from Britain' that UDI would be disastrous for the province.[602] As he spoke, he must have remembered his dinner conversation with Molly, and the chats he must have had with Nigel, who spent Christmas 1966 with the O'Neill family after coming out of hospital.

While Lady Gibbs was dining with the Prime Minister of Northern Ireland at Stormont, and taking tea with the Queen at Buckingham Palace, Sir Humphrey was entertaining Sir Morrice James from the Commonwealth Office, and putting in several appearances at the cricket grounds for Rhodesia's matches against the Transvaal. By the beginning of November, Lady Gibbs had returned home but there seemed to be no progress in getting a further round of talks at ministerial level. Sir Humphrey was now anxious that no ministerial visit should take place before the anniversary of UDI, but he put pressure on Wilson to send out a representative as soon as possible thereafter. In the event the anniversary passed off without incident. A few days later, Smith informed the Chief Justice that he was anxious to meet Bowden again, and this was passed on to Hennings on 19 November. On the 23rd, Wilson announced in the Commons that Bowden would return to Salisbury, and the next day in Cabinet explained he had had to spring this announcement without informing his colleagues, because it was going to leak. The usual opposition in Cabinet was met by Wilson with the argument that there was 'grave danger' of the Governor resigning, which would mean that 'we should be on the spot'. Barbara Castle again recorded her distaste at the 'pathetic telegrams' from the Governor being used as a weapon by Wilson.[603] In fact there had been masses of rumours flying round Salisbury towards the end of October that the Governor was on the brink of resigning. These seemed to owe more to the usual gossip machine, and the height of the 'suicide month' of October when rumour grew in the oppressive heat, than to any solid information. Certainly none emanated from Government House; John Pestell wrote in his diary that the rumours were 'quite untrue'. However, the content of the Governor's telegrams to London certainly gave the Cabinet pause for thought. Richard Crossman, when he read them later, admitted that they brought home to him 'what a disadvantage it would be if [the Governor] resigned on the ground that we hadn't genuinely tried to reach a settlement'.[604]

THE *TIGER* TALKS

On 4 November the Rhodesian government published a reply to the British government, indicating their desire 'to invite the Secretary of State to come to Salisbury with full powers to reach final agreement on the settlement'.[605] Herbert Bowden arrived in Salisbury on Saturday 26 November for what were, as a local newspaper realistically dubbed them, 'eleventh hour talks'.[606] The deadline laid down at the Commonwealth Prime Ministers Conference was fast approaching. As if to signal the urgency felt on both sides, Bowden drove straight to dinner at Government House, and saw Ian Smith the next day. On the following morning, Bowden accompanied Sir Humphrey and Lady Gibbs to early morning Communion at the Cathedral. He was on the plane again for London by lunchtime that day. He reported to the Cabinet on Tuesday, suggesting a 'neutral venue' for full-blown talks. On the same day, Sir Morrice James arrived in Salisbury to outline the plans for the summit. The dramatic venue was soon revealed: a destroyer riding at anchor off Gibraltar. On the first day in December, Sir Humphrey left Government House, accompanied by Sir Hugh Beadle and John Pestell. They boarded the Comet which had brought Sir Morrice out to Salisbury, and with him and Ian Smith they occupied the VIP section of the aircraft, along with Group Captain Merryman of RAF Transport Command who was responsible for the travel arrangements. The rest of the Rhodesian government party, sitting aft, were John Howman (Minister of Information), Sir Cornelius Greenfield, Stan Morris, Gerald Clarke, plus some officials and secretaries. The plane stopped at Luanda for refuelling, and then flew to Ascension Island. Here the party split up, with the Government House group flying on in a Britannia, and the rest an hour later in a second. The ten-hour flight ended for the Governor just after midnight, when they touched down at Gibraltar to be met by the Governor, and transferred to a launch to be taken out to HMS *Tiger*. The rough ride, and the manhandling from the launch to the cruiser, must have been particularly painful for Sir Hugh, who was wearing a harness because of his back trouble. In the dark and wet, they were met on board by a distinguished welcoming party, including the Prime Minister, the Commonwealth Secretary, the Attorney General, the Secretary to the Cabinet and others. The Governor and Sir Hugh were taken down to the Prime Minister's cabin for a brief discussion before retiring to bed and leaving Wilson to chat briefly with Smith and Howman who had now come on board. It had been a long and exhausting day.

It was in fact later that same day – at about 10.45 a.m. on Friday 2 December – that the first session of talks began. They did not finally break up until after midnight, by which time Wilson had angrily told the Governor and Chief Justice that Smith was claiming he had no power to settle. Yet he had specifically assured Sir Morrice James that he would come to the talks with plenipotentiary powers. The Governor reckoned this was merely Smithian 'brinkmanship'. But the talks did not go well the next day, and instead of breaking up in early evening, they went on into the night. At around 11.00 p.m. the Governor and Chief Justice were called to Wilson's cabin. He told them that Smith would not accept the agreed document, and that he demanded to right to take it back and get Cabinet concurrence in Salisbury. 'They were devastated', Mr Wilson later recorded.[607] He also recorded his surprise that the Chief Justice seemed willing to envisage some further compromise on the part of the British. Harold Wilson had good reason later to doubt Beadle's 'loyalty', so perhaps it was hindsight that made him add at this point in his narrative: 'I regret that I was moved to say, of Sir Hugh, that I could not understand how any man could have a slipped disc whom Providence had failed to provide with a backbone.'

All that remained for the Governor to do was to append his signature, under 'signed in my presence', to a covering note which was to accompany the '*Tiger* Plan'. It read:

> The attached document was worked out by the British Prime Minister and Mr Smith on HMS *Tiger* off Gibraltar on 2/3 December 1966.
>
> It is without commitment on either side and both sides will decide by 12 noon Salisbury time on Monday, 5th December, 1966, whether it is accepted in its entirety.[608]

It was signed by Harold Wilson and Ian Smith, and dated 4 December 1966, since it was now after midnight. Very shortly afterwards, the Governor and his party left HMS *Tiger*, and were taken to Gibraltar to be entertained to a drink at Admiral's House, while Smith's party separately travelled to their aircraft which took off. The Governor's party then joined their aircraft, drank a cup of tea, and retired for the night at around 3.00 a.m. The Governor's party joined Smith's at Ascension Island for the flight home. There was a stopover at Luanda, where the Governor and Chief Justice shared a table with Smith and Howman for dinner, and tried a final bit of persuasion.

Back in Salisbury, there was a tiny hiccup over protocol. Smith's secretary said that his Prime Minister and party should leave first by the front steps; Sir Humphrey and his party should then depart by the back steps. The Governor's secretary was having none of it, and pointed out that they were on an RAF plane, and the captain would certainly want to stick to the protocol observed when a Governor was on board. Sir Humphrey and his party left first, and the Governor and Chief Justice were whipped away by Kit Owen in his car. Smith had been met by most of his Cabinet colleagues at the airport, and they then went to Smith's house. What transpired is the matter of some debate. The *Sunday Times* pieced the story together and reported that Smith had been met with a hostile reception when he first, somewhat tentatively, presented the proposals to his colleagues that Sunday evening.[609] He proposed that they sleep on it and meet again the next morning. From 8.00 a.m. on Monday they worked on it, asking the British for an extension of the deadline. Wilson later thought that the extremists in the party brought pressure to bear; Lord Blake records an opinion that the Cabinet members came under pressure from their wives over the lunchbreak – 'The women are the real hard-liners.'[610] John Pestell records that he had picked up from various sources a move while the Prime Minister was in Gibraltar by right-wingers like Harper and Graham to unseat Smith should he give way. Pestell was not all that sanguine as they arrived back at Government House. He recorded in his diary – while the Cabinet were meeting across the road at the Prime Minister's house – 'In the frame of mind he is in I cannot see him trying to sell this to his cabinet at all.'

What were the *Tiger* proposals which were the subject of such intense debate? They were to figure so largely in discussions over subsequent months and years that it is important to understand what was involved. The basis for Rhodesia's future was to be the 1961 Constitution, with the franchise qualifications extended to ensure more African voters and members. Safeguards would be built in to ensure the rights of the minority would be guaranteed, and that there could be no going back in terms of the rights of the majority. But the crucial concession – if that is the word – on Wilson's part was that there would be no immediate shift to majority rule. Sir Edgar Whitehead, perhaps somewhat ruefully remembering his own plans for widening the franchise, reckoned that majority rule might be delayed until the next century.[611] The quid pro quo however, the face-saving formula on the British side, was that Smith must accept a period of 'return to legality' when the Governor would exercise more than usually extensive powers. He would appoint a new Cabinet which would have to be constructed so as to include Africans and some more liberal Europeans. It was this 'return to legality' aspect which was to cause most trouble.

News was awaited all next day. The Rhodesians asked for an extension of the deadline, which was granted. Maybe there was a Cabinet vote, with the result that the hard-liners won the day. It was later reckoned that five ministers voted for acceptance (Ian Smith, Dunlop, Howman, Arthur Smith, Wrathall) and eight voted against (Graham, Harper, Lardner-Burke, Mussett, Partridge, Rudland, Lance Smith, Van Heerden).[612] Whether this was true or not, we have as yet no way of knowing.

The news came through to Government House on Monday evening at 6.00 p.m. Lady Gibbs and Kit Owen were listening to local radio. In another room the Governor, Chief Justice and John Pestell were listening in to the BBC hoping for news, but Rhodesia was not mentioned. Then Kit Owen came through to report that the answer was 'no'. The Governor said nothing, but went through with Lady Gibbs to her study. The Chief Justice stood as if stricken, and Lady Beadle and his daughter had to assist him to his room. Shortly afterwards, Sir Humphrey and Lady Gibbs came into the reception hall where John Pestell was standing. 'John', said the Governor, 'this is going to be a long haul.'

11   A Long Haul

THE CLIMATE OF OPINION

The Central Intelligence Organisation (CI0) wrote an assessment of reactions to Sir Humphrey's position towards the end of 1966, and estimated that there were 'at least four different attitudes' towards his stand.[613] It is worth quoting in full:

(1)   It is believed in some circles that by remaining in his position as Governor he has merely served to divide the loyalties of Rhodesians. This seems to be the view of many back-benchers and other supporters of the Government, and it coincides with the view expressed to me some time ago by Brigadier Skeen, who also argued that Rhodesia should have cut every existing tie with Britain at the time of UDI. This same gentleman has made several public expressions to the effect that Sir Humphrey is a tool for Mr Wilson.

(2)   Another school maintains that, by remaining, Sir Humphrey has provided a rallying point for those who have confidence in Britain's ability to resolve the confrontation. To this extent these people are basically loyal to Britain (not necessarily HMG) but they would claim that loyalty to Britain is not inconsistent with loyalty to Rhodesia. They are not necessarily anti-Government, but most of them would appear to have been anti-UDI and some of them are opponents of Government.

(3)   The third school represents all political persuasions, and Mr Pestell has told me that it includes a number of strong Government supporters who have mentioned to him, or have indicated to Sir Humphrey, how disastrous it would be if Sir Humphrey were to leave his present position. They seem to appreciate that Sir Humphrey is a man of the highest integrity who has the true interests of Rhodesia at heart, and that he is providing the only real insurance against the possibility of extreme action being taken by the British Government. His presence is the best shield against the use of force; it prevents the British imposing direct rule through a British Governor; it keeps control within Rhodesian hands; and, whilst he remains, there is less possibility of Britain referring the Rhodesian issue to the United Nations and disclaiming responsibility for Rhodesia.

(4)   Insofar as it is possible to assess 'moderate African opinion', it appears that there is a substantial number of 'moderate Africans' who

are particularly interested in the stand taken by Sir Humphrey, and
that as long as he remains his 'opinion' is likely to remain 'moderate'.
Should Sir Humphrey go, it is possible that they would think this has
removed their sole hope for a just settlement.

This document bears all the hallmarks (as well as the personal pronoun)
of Ken Flower, the Director of the CIO. It was undoubtedly written to
convince Smith that the Governor still had a role to play. Although his
analysis was therefore directed to a particular object, it nevertheless
corresponds to a 'conventional wisdom' among whites then and later.[614] Ian
Hancock found that the whites reckoned there were three basic points of view
with regard to African advancement, and had been since the Second World
War. There were those who were 'white supremacists'; there were 'middle
of the roaders', and there were those whom he dubs 'the left'. Each of these
'groups' in fact contained a whole range of opinion. White supremacists might
include all of Smith's Cabinet, but Harper and Graham were reckoned to be
very hard-line, while Smith himself and certainly D. C. Smith were regarded
as more flexible. Among the 'left' were white radicals like Todd (after
1958), the RC Bishop Donal Lamont (who was eventually deported), and
the Cold Comfort Farm group around Guy Clutton-Brock. What of the
'middle of the roaders', among whom the Governor himself might have been
reckoned as one, certainly before he became Governor?

One of the problems is that UDI changed everything. It may well be true,
as Robert Tredgold's even more radical sister Barbara later claimed, 'that
at least 20% of the whites never bowed the knee to Baal'.[615] As one white
farmer's wife put it: 'there was a small but steadfast minority of the Rhodesians
who did not support Ian Smith's Rhodesian Front Party in its headlong
progress towards a declaration of independence, who had voted against the
party in the elections earlier in the year, and who saw the prospect of majority
rule as just and inevitable'.[616] But even among those who never voted for
the Rhodesian Front (RF), there was ambivalence after 1965. Geoff Ellman-
Brown, former Cabinet Minister (under Todd and Whitehead) and prominent
business man during the UDI period, claimed he never voted RF. But his
position, and that of many others, was well summed-up:

> His ambivalence was, in fact, typical of many well-placed and more
> liberal-minded businessmen who propped up the Smith government by
> successfully breaking the economic blockade. They knew that UDI was
> a mistake and a disaster, they knew that political change was inevitable
> and not wholly undesirable, yet they were also patriots who could not accept
> surrender in the economic war and who were, in the later 1970s, to resent
> and fear 'Marxist terrorism'.[617]

One English academic conducted a research programme in Marandellas in 1967. Despite the fact that the town – some fifty miles south-east of Salisbury – was home to a number of multiracial independent schools, the electorate in the area was regarded as right of centre. He found that in the year or two after UDI, white opinion had shifted, and he reckoned that while in November 1965 only just over half the electorate had approved of UDI, by mid-1967, in retrospect, 67.2 per cent claimed they had been in favour.[618] It was patriotic, by then, to support the government. It was difficult, in a country where the state controlled the broadcasting and censored the newspapers, to gain access to alternative points of view. 'Terrorist' incursions – especially by freedom fighters trained in the communist bloc – tended to underline the need for rallying to the government. Most whites who disapproved of Ian Smith disapproved also of the armed struggle by some black nationalists. As the farmer's wife who wrote of some whites seeing majority rule as just and inevitable also said, somewhat ruefully, 'no freedom fighter was going to stop and ask your politics before opening fire'.[619] The sharp rise in violence, which put white Rhodesia on a war footing, took place in the 1970s after the Governor had left office, but the beginnings of the fears and effects were being felt in the mid-1960s.

So could one be loyal to one's country and at the same time show loyalty to the Governor? This was a dilemma for many. Professor Christie, of the university's law department, exemplifies that dilemma. He wrote an article after the *Tiger* talks proclaiming that 'the Cabinet had no option but to reject the Working Document', but he went on to say that the objections on the Rhodesian side could have been overcome. He called for clarification by Britain so that 'we will know that whatever happens, the Governor will be a true Rhodesian of known honesty and ability'. That, he made plain, would be the case were Sir Humphrey to continue or (were he incapacitated) if his replacement were to be Chief Justice Beadle.[620] The dilemma was even more starkly put by Christie's wife, who wrote under the name Philippa Berlyn. She sympathised with the position the Governor found himself in. He had 'courage, courtesy, and above all, integrity', but 'he is also the fall guy for Harold Wilson'. The result for her was that 'there was no concrete way in which to demonstrate my sympathy. I could not even sign the visitors' book, since this would have been interpreted by Mr Wilson as my loyalty to him.'[621]

Signing the visitors' book took on a symbolic significance in the UDI years. It all started soon after the declaration of UDI. A picture appeared in the newspapers showing a woman signing the Governor's visiting book at the Tredgold Building in Bulawayo. Astonishingly, the picture passed the censors, as did the caption which informed readers that thirty people in all had signed the book, as opposed to fourteen who signed the Prime Minister's

Macro and Micro.

A cartoon by Kit Owen, Sir Humphrey's ADC (who shared his somewhat mischievous sense of humour) depicting the 'Officers Administering the Government' – the Queen's representative, tall and distinguished even if effectively powerless; the Smith appointee, small and insignificant (and later to be appointed 'President' of Rhodesia). *Reproduced by kind permission of Kit Owen* book.[622] Battle was joined more significantly however in June 1966 when more than a thousand people visited Government House on the Queen's Birthday to sign the visitors' book; details of this were censored in Rhodesia.[623] The Governor and his staff were joined by the British team who were in Salisbury for preliminary talks, and by members of the High Commission, for a small drinks party, when Sir Humphrey emotionally proposed the toast to The Queen. Concurrently a large party was being held by Dupont where the toast was to 'Her Majesty Queen Elizabeth II, Queen of Rhodesia'. Later that year Lord Malvern conceived the idea of positively encouraging people to express their admiration for the Governor's stand, and sent out a circular letter to that end. The result was that 1750 people called at Government House to sign the book (actually three separate books to cut down the queuing time); a further 1250 who could not personally get along wrote letters of support. In June 1966 however, far fewer people turned up to sign on the occasion of the Queen's Birthday. Just 900 people called to sign, and a few wrote or telephoned. John Pestell concluded that 'there is no doubt that a sort of lethargy has set in among the people, even those who do not support UDI'.[624] On the same occasion in 1968, the number had bounced back to over 3000, probably – as *The Times* noted – 'stimulated by the Government's decision officially to ignore the birthday', and also by the Government's propaganda to the effect that support for the Governor was support for Harold Wilson.[625] By then, censorship had been lifted and the 'Battle of the Books', as Salisbury's *Sunday Mail* called it, became known to the Rhodesian public at large. At Governor's Lodge, Dupont's officials took the precaution of removing each page after it was full, and never published the result, so the final tally was never known.[626] It was however clear that there was no erosion of Sir Humphrey's personal prestige and standing. Indeed in 1967 and 1968 it is unlikely that an observer, however biased, could have reported – as Douglas Reed did in 1966 – that Gibbs was 'the most unpopular man in Rhodesia' and that 'people wished he had resigned at the moment of Independence'.[627] But as Bishop Skelton of Matabeleland wrote in his diocesan magazine, the idea was all too prevalent that 'to be a loyal Rhodesian one has to support the political party on power, or as it is sometimes crudely put, to be "for Smith" and "against Wilson"'.[628] Bob Williams, Chairman of the Rhodesian Constitutional Association which was a rallying point for former United Party moderates and liberals, made the same point in his Chairman's Address in June 1967 when he complained that the all too common perception was 'that if you are anti-Rhodesian Front you are anti-Rhodesia', and likely to be branded a 'traitor'.[629]

So as time went on, while many Rhodesians were still prepared to praise the stand taken by the Governor, John Pestell was right to point to a 'lethargy' in 1967 among opponents of UDI. Those opponents had no political clout. They were living in a society increasingly dominated by the place-men and the emergency regulations of the Rhodesian Front. Sanctions, which were meant to bring the rebel government to its knees, had the opposite effect of rallying support for the country, and therefore for the government, among that group which had been most decisively opposed to UDI – the business community. And for that broader spectrum of opinion – the middle-of-the-road white liberals and moderates – the result was to emasculate them politically and perhaps even to bankrupt them morally. It became increasingly obvious that 'their opposition to the government was tempered by a patriotic concern for their beleaguered country and the objectives of preventing or ending UDI and of obtaining an internationally-recognised independence were given priority over attacking racial discrimination and supporting African political advancement'.[630]

THE 'RELUCTANT RIGHT-WINGER'

1966 had ended with the failure of the *Tiger* talks. It had, as Percy M'kudu the African MP put it, 'seen our country led into a dark forest of trouble'. He was gloomy about the prospects: 'as the New Year commences, there is nothing to indicate that we will soon find our way out into the open'.[631] The view from Government House was similar: 'things have been so dull and quiet', John Pestell recorded in his diary. The chance of a settlement had gone. Where could the Rhodesian government go from here?

A not unsympathetic biographer of Ian Smith wrote of how, 'during these months [the Prime Minister] gave every indication of being a reluctant right-winger, a man who had done his best but was now being pushed, against his natural inclinations, to take irrevocable steps'.[632] This was the impression among those who thought that he himself had been in favour of the *Tiger* settlement. It was also the impression he gave the Governor during the first of their evening meetings in the new year. They talked for some two hours. Smith indicated that he was in no hurry to declare a republic, despite right-wing pressure to do so; that he was considering lifting censorship and easing up on detention; that he was still willing to work on the basis of the *Tiger* proposals; and that 'he would like to head a more moderate centre party in the country'.[633] But in fact the whole drift of policy and mood in government and country seemed to be moving in a right-wing direction. A few days before his meeting with the Governor, Smith had been told forcibly by Putterill and

Hawkins, his Army and Air Force commanders, that they believed any moves to a republic would be harmful to the country, 'and in no foreseeable circumstances would we personally align ourselves with such a move'.[634] The CIO came up with similar views without even being asked, and these were forwarded to the Prime Minister 'as an indication', the Director later wrote, 'of the deep disappointment felt in official circles over the failure of the British and Rhodesian politicians to negotiate an independence settlement'.[635] These pressures were not known to the general public, but others were. The public soon became aware that the Prime Minister was under pressure from opposite extremes in the political spectrum. The failed talks were a starting point for Smith's critics. Opponents on the right circulated an anonymous document in mid-January criticising his attendance at the talks, and the non-implementation of right-wing policies, and it was held within the RF that the criticisms would be 'widely supported within the party'.[636] But from the opposite side came criticism that the government had not agreed to the *Tiger* constitution, and there was a call, probably originating in the business community, for a new party – provisionally called the 'Reconstruction Party'. The anonymous document which put forward this proposal was a follow-up to the call by Lord Malvern, at the end of 1966, for people to voice their support for acceptance of *Tiger*. That petition had attracted some 3600 signatures.[637]

There was gloom at Government House as January ended with the Prime Minister's speech to the reassembled parliament. He announced a constitutional commission, a review of censorship and of detention, but also commented that 'the door to negotiations with Britain was now fully slammed and locked'.[638] So while the more hopeful aspects which Smith had discussed with the Governor earlier in the month – regarding censorship and detention – were now on the political agenda, so too was signal that the government was more and more prepared to 'go it alone'.

Smith's position seemed to be strengthened in the subsequent months. His official RF candidate in a by-election won the seat against a strong bid by an independent 'right-right-wing candidate' in mid-February.[639] Lord Reay, speaking in the Lords, noted that 'the brief whisper of a more liberal attitude seemed to have died away'.[640] He was certainly correct as regards the possibility of a new political party. Those plans came to nothing. The RF began to discuss moves towards apartheid, and Wrathall, the Finance Minister, announced the ending of Commonwealth preferences. Ian Smith now felt confident enough to defend those who had signed the Malvern petition. One MP had declared in parliament, at the beginning of February, 'that the traitors in our midst' ought to be thrown out. The Prime Minister, at the end of February, commented that it was 'a little bit unfair to refer to them as traitors'. Indeed he went on to claim that many of them had signed in order to 'assist the Government'.

The Governor and his wife had at least some distraction during the early months of the year. The political climate was hardly encouraging, so it was a joy for them to have some congenial house guests. Early in the New Year, Sir Edmund Bacon and his wife came to stay at Government House. Soon afterwards, in mid-February, Sir Charles and Lady Ponsonby arrived, he on Beit Trust business. Before the end of the month, Lady Jean Rankin, Queen Elizabeth the Queen Mother's Lady-in-Waiting, also arrived to stay. So despite the gloominess of the political scene, there was some personal refreshment and diversion for Humphrey and Molly. There was a personal crisis in February. The Governor heard from the family firm – Antony Gibbs and Co. – that his request for a transfer of money to his son Nigel, whose stay in the UK had been prolonged when he contracted polio, had run into difficulties. The firm reported that they could not transfer money to Nigel 'as your account in our books is designated a United Kingdom Resident Account and that of Mr Nigel Gibbs is a Rhodesia Account [and] transfers cannot be effected from a United Kingdom Resident Account to a Rhodesia Account' without the Bank of England's permission.[641] The Governor asked the British High Commissioner in Salisbury to intercede, but it was not until early April that the Commonwealth Office was able to report that the transaction could go ahead.[642]

But meanwhile two events of enormous long-term significance had taken place, the results of which would not be known until 1968. At the end of January what was known as the 'Constitutional Case' opened in the High Court. This involved an appeal by Africans who had been sentenced for murder, but the appeal was to test the validity of the regime, and the final judgments which were handed down a year later were to isolate the Governor even further. Yet another long-term sequence of events began in late February with the appointment of the Constitutional Commission under Sam Whaley, which was charged with suggesting a new constitution, and was to report within a year. The full effect of these was not felt in 1967, but meanwhile other events seemed to indicate that the drift to the right was real enough. In April, a special RF Congress adopted a range of proposals which were right-wing, though perhaps not so right-wing as they might have been. The principle of land apportionment was upheld, and further European immigration was to be promoted. Government was to be 'kept permanently in responsible hands', though an amendment that it should be kept 'in European hands' was defeated. The loyalty oath to the Queen was dropped from the party's constitution, though delegates 'backed away from an all-out push for a republic after a "take-it-easy" talk from the Prime Minister'.[643] In the months following, proposals for enforcing segregation in residential areas, and in public amenities, and further moves by the Ministry of Education to inhibit multiracial sport and to limit the numbers of blacks which the non-racial independent schools could admit all suggested that Rhodesia was shifting to the right. A newspaper's leading article in the middle of the year called for further efforts to be made for a settlement, 'for on present trends unless something be done soon to counter the drift it will be too late, and Rhodesia will have passed the point of no return. Inaction favours extremists.'[644]

MORE TALKS ABOUT TALKS

The gloom engendered not so much by Smith's visit to Government House in early January, but by his subsequent statements in parliament later in the month, was not dispelled by the evident drift to the right during the first half of 1967. The gloom deepened when a letter was received from Herbert Bowden spelling out the British government's position, and indicating that there was little likelihood of further talks with the rebel regime.[645] This position was underlined in a letter from Viscount Head early in February. He had visited the Governor and Smith and had reported back to Wilson, Bowden, Heath and Maudling. None was optimistic about any resumption of talks.[646] Nor was the gloom dispelled by other visitors. Sir Robert Tredgold and Sir Roy Welensky both called during February, depressed about the prospects. More surprising was a secret visit by David Smith, the moderate RF MP for Marandellas, and the only one in regular 'Christmas card' contact with Government House. His assessment of the situation, which he gave to the Governor in the presence of the Chief Justice and of John Pestell, was comprehensive. He was worried about the economic situation, which was being neglected by the government. He felt that the right-wing drift was being tolerated by Smith 'to keep the wild men quiet'. He wanted the Governor to stay on until a settlement was reached, and he was hopeful that further negotiations might lead somewhere.[647] However, when Beadle tried to follow this approach up with Smith himself a few days later, he got nowhere. The Governor began to feel that neither the British nor the Rhodesian government was showing much interest in pursuing a solution. When parliament reassembled in Salisbury in April, the 'Speech from the Throne' contained no mention whatever of relations with Britain. On the same day, the British High Commissioner called at Government House on his return from London – but he came empty handed, apart from personal greetings from Wilson and Bowden to the Governor.

In May, Patrick Wall, the right-wing Conservative MP, wrote to *The Times* after returning from a visit to Rhodesia. He suggested that 'perhaps the key to this complicated situation lies once again in the hands of that great Rhodesian, Sir Humphrey Gibbs, who is alone in a position to persuade the British Government to break the present deadlock'.[648] A few days later, Sir Humphrey received, via diplomatic bag, a letter from Duncan Sandys in the same vein: perhaps the Governor could put some pressure on Wilson? Sir Humphrey took up the challenge in a letter to Herbert Bowden. Much of this letter was concerned with 'the welfare of loyal Rhodesians in the public service', and in particular the position of the judges. It ended, however, with a plea for new talks: 'Would it not be possible for you yourself to pay us a visit; you could say you wish to discuss future events with me. I know we could arrange for Smith to meet you here, and there is a fair chance you might break the deadlock.'[649] Even before Bowden replied, Harold Wilson informed the Commons on 13 June that Lord Alport was 'to pay a visit to Salisbury in a few days' time' – and at this point the Prime Minister was interrupted – 'for an exchange of views with the Governor'.[650] While committing himself to NIBMAR (no independence before majority rule), Wilson did make a conciliatory gesture. He suggested that 'if there were a substantial change in circumstances, we should be prepared to discuss the situation which arose with the rest of the Commonwealth, but there would have to be substantial and guaranteed change in circumstances'.[651] The Rhodesian press picked this up and interpreted it as a 'hint UK may back-track on majority rule'. [652] Alport, a 'notably liberal former Tory minister',[653] had been the last British High Commissioner to the Federation. He was described by Smith as 'quite an extraordinary choice' of envoy.[654] The *Sunday Mail*, however, reckoned that by sending any envoy Mr Wilson was making a concession, 'a climb-down however small'.[655]

Alport spent three weeks in Rhodesia. After his first meeting with Smith, he reported optimistically to the Governor. Thereafter, he was more subdued. After his departure on 13 July, Humphrey was left to wait for some response from London. Wilson had to be careful about his own left wing, in the Commons and in his Cabinet. Having had a verbal report from Alport, Wilson summoned Cabinet Ministers to Chequers on 22 July. Discussions were dominated by the government's economic problems. However over dinner Wilson broached the Rhodesian problem with two of his more left-wing ministers, Judith Hart and Barbara Castle. He admitted that 'Alport had nothing promising to report but was recommending the resumption of talks'. Castle could see no point in reopening talks. Wilson tried to play his 'Governor will resign' card. 'Damn the Governor', said Castle, 'Let him resign.'[656] That was not Wilson's intention however. He reported to the Commons after the weekend that having listened to Lord Alport he was 'authorising the Governor, to whose steadfastness and courage once again I would pay full tribute' to undertake further exploratory talks with Mr Smith.[657]

The news was welcomed in Rhodesia, and by the Governor himself who had received notice of Wilson's statement just before it was made. All were agreed that the *Tiger* proposals were a basis for discussion to begin.[658] For the Governor, the question was how to initiate the talks. He agreed with the British High Commissioner that Smith needed to see something further from London before any meeting should take place. This was forthcoming on 27 July when London sent a letter for transmission to Smith. There was a further delay because Smith had a bad cold and had cancelled his weekend engagements. However in the middle of the following week he called on the Governor, who had the impression that Smith wanted to settle the problem, though was confident that sanctions would not bring Rhodesia to heel. The Governor passed his report of this meeting back to London. Smith called again a week later, on 15 August, and again seemed to suggest that a settlement would be possible on the basis of the *Tiger* constitution, provided that an acceptable mode of 'return to legality' could be worked out. His comment that he did not envisage majority rule 'for a thousand years' was discouraging, as was his insistence that Dupont could not be sacrificed to achieve a settlement. The Governor duly passed a report on to London, recommending that talks should begin without any preconditions – that is, without insisting that the only offer on the table was again the *Tiger* constitution. Matters were not going to proceed with any speed, however. Late in August there was a Cabinet reshuffle in London: Bowden went to the Lords to be replaced by George Thomson. They couldn't decide at Government house whether this augured well or badly for future negotiations. They would have to wait to find out. Desmond Donnelly and Frank Tomney, two Labour MPs on yet another fact-finding mission, suggested to the Governor that Wilson was unlikely to make any further moves until after the end of September, by which time both his own and Smith's party conferences would be over.

So the month of September was to be a period of waiting. There was plenty of activity at Government House, since Nigel was being married at the Cathedral on 9 September. His bride was Barbara Paterson, daughter of Canon Paterson of Cyrene Mission near Bulawayo, on the board of which Humphrey had served for many years. That was to have been followed for the Governor by some happy days attending Yorkshire vs Rhodesia cricket matches, which were, however, cancelled, much to Humphrey's fury. He dashed off a letter to Thomson complaining about the British government's 'petty action'.[659] He than had to retire to bed with a chest infection, his first indisposition since UDI.

At the end of September Smith's party congress ended with 'a mild victory for RF moderates'.[660] There was some optimism in Salisbury that Smith, fresh from a Congress which had gone his way, now had a free hand to deal with new negotiations with Britain.[661] Similarly the Labour Party conference in Scarborough early in October ended with reports in the Rhodesian press which were optimistic that new moves were afoot, and it was reported that 'Sir Humphrey's request [for a minister to visit Salisbury] was, however, kept quiet until now until it could be seen how Mr Smith fared at his party conference.'[662] On the day that this report surfaced – 7 October – a letter was in fact received at Government House suggesting that Thomson would like to call 'for twenty four hours' on 8/9 November, as a stopover on a tour of African capitals.

In the event, the Secretary of State's visit was not quite so rushed as had been suggested. He arrived with a large party at noon on 8 November. For Humphrey, it was a relief to welcome a Cabinet Minister after the long haul since the *Tiger* talks, and particularly gratifying that he got on so well with George Thomson. While the Secretary of State was effecting introductions, there was a little incident which illustrates the oddity of the situation. The Governor was introduced to a young official named Tim Everard, who worked in the Foreign Office's (FO) Rhodesia sanctions department. Humphrey raised an eyebrow and asked if he was any relation of Lieutenant-Colonel Everard, the deputy to Dupont. The young man had to admit that it was his second cousin who was working for an illegal regime which his own FO department was working to bring down![663]

Ian Smith arrived at Government House that same day at 3.00 p.m. and stayed in all for four hours, meeting first alone with Thomson, and then in the presence of the Governor and Chief Justice. Further talks took place the next day at the Police Camp Officers Mess. That evening Thomson had a private drink at Smith's house, then flew out at midday on the 10th, partly in order to avoid being present for the 'independence' celebrations the next day. His report back to Wilson was 'sombre', but Mr Wilson had more important and pressing problems on his mind.

November was a bad month for the Labour government. Its standing in the opinion polls was poor. Its Vietnam policy was under attack, and the violence of the Governor Square protests outside the US Embassy in late October dented the image of a law-abiding society. Worse was to come. On 14 November Thomson found himself a member of the 'Tuesday Club', set up that Tuesday to supervise the package which would be arranged to tackle the Government's growing financial problems. On 18 November, after a week in which the Tuesday Club had many meetings and international speculation ran rife, James Callaghan announced the devaluation of sterling from US$2.80

to US$2.40. Patrick Cosgrave has written that this was a watershed moment, 'the moment when Wilson began to face up to the fact that the grand pretensions, both domestic and international, of British politicians could not be fulfilled'.[664] Little wonder that there is no mention in Harold Wilson's memoirs of the Thomson visit to Rhodesia. Little wonder that there was virtually no follow-up on Thomson's meetings. When Thomson did make reference in the Commons to the distance which separated the two sides, Ian Smith regarded it as a 'bombshell', a breach of an understanding that neither side would go public while negotiations were – however tenuously – still in progress.[665] The Governor refused to get too gloomy. At the end of November he enjoyed his outings to watch the Currie Cup cricket. In December he had the family arriving in force for the Christmas celebrations. Any further contacts between Britain and Rhodesia would have to wait until the New Year. Harold Wilson spent his Christmas at Chequers, aware that the New Year would bring – as its priority – the review of government expenditure and further decisions on the economy.

12 A State of Uncertainty

The Rhodesian Prime Minister's New Year message for 1968 declared that
Rhodesia could not keep on in the current state of uncertainty. The *Tiger*
talks had, just perhaps – and despite their failure – yielded up some possible
ways forward. But was Smith really intent upon following these up? Or was
he preparing Rhodesians for an ending to 'uncertainty' by the declaration
of a republic? Was Rhodesia going to move closer to South Africa by
adopting an apartheid policy? Certainly the Methodist Church thought so,
and made clear in a statement on 19 January that Rhodesia seemed to be going
down a fateful segregationist road.[666] On that same day, Harold Wilson was
speaking in the House of Commons in London, announcing his policy of
withdrawal from 'East of Suez'. One historian of empire has written: 'So
far as the end of the British Empire can be set at a definite point of time, it
was the afternoon of 19 January 1968' when Wilson 'announced the final
homecoming of the British legions'.[667] But Britain had not become 'a solely
European power'. The colonial and imperial responsibilities vested in the
Crown and the Privy Council – and with the British Prime Minister – were
a prominent part in the uncertainties of 1968 of which Ian Smith had spoken.
The New Year opened in an atmosphere of uncertainty, and continued that
way until it ended in yet another attempt to find a negotiated settlement. But
it began with a series of events and uncertainties which related to the
judiciary, and which would dramatically affect the position of the Governor.

The first months of 1968 were overshadowed by the consequences of a
murder that had taken place years before. In 1964 Petrus Oberholzer, an
Afrikaans farmer, had been driving to his home in the Eastern Highlands when
he was attacked and murdered by a group calling themselves the 'Crocodile
Gang'. A decade later such murders became almost commonplace in white
Rhodesia, but in the days before UDI, such an outrage was a rarity.[668] The
gang was hunted down and two men were arrested, tried, and sentenced to
death. Ten months later the remainder of the gang struck again, this time killing
a pro-government chief. One man was arrested, tried and sentenced to death.
All this happened before UDI. The men had been on 'death row' ever since.
In August 1967 the government announced that the death sentences would
be carried out. An application was lodged, and the case was heard in
September 1967 before Mr Justice Lewis. The point at issue now 'involved
the right of the authorities to execute a convicted criminal when not the

Governor but the Officer Administering the Government had decided not to exercise the prerogative of mercy'.[669] The judge based his conclusion on the decisions he himself – along with Mr Justice Goldin – had handed down in what has been called the 'Constitutional Case', then under appeal. He therefore stated that it was lawful to carry out the sentences, but granted leave to appeal, and a stay of execution.

The Constitutional Case had been brought in June 1966 as a test case, on behalf of detainees Madzimbamuto and Baron, the purpose being 'to challenge the validity of the state of emergency after UDI so as to obtain their release from detention'.[670] Madzimbamuto, a young African nationalist, had been detained shortly before UDI; Baron, a white Bulawayo lawyer, was detained on the day UDI was declared. The judgment was eagerly awaited not only because it would determine the immediate fate of the two men, but because it would rule on the validity of the regime. In the event Judges Lewis and Goldin declared that the 1965 Constitution 'is not the lawful constitution of this country, and the government of this country set up under it is not the lawful government'. This damning indictment of the Smith regime was tempered by the further declaration that 'it is, however, the only effective government of this country'.[671] Even though they had in fact therefore concluded by turning down the application for release by the detainees, Goldin later remembered how he and Lewis left the courthouse that morning saying to each other 'Let's run' and 'Let's pack up'. He was amazed to discover, later that day, that their judgment had in fact been welcomed by the regime. He remembered arriving at the Agricultural Show. 'I encountered several friends who astonished me with the news that Mr Smith declared the judgement as a victory, as it accorded what he described as "de facto recognition".' That was not however the last that was heard of the 'Constitutional Case'. Baron and Madzimbamuto appealed, and the case came before a full bench of five judges at the end of January 1967, 'the first time that the court had ever sat with more than the normal complement of three judges'.[672] The case dragged on for thirteen months, and the outcome was of only academic interest to one of the appellants, Leo Baron, who 'fell ill in prison, was allowed to leave for London and was broadcasting back to Rhodesia over the BBC while the court were still trying to decide the legality of his detention'.[673] On 29 January 1968 the appeal was upheld unanimously by the five judges, on the grounds that the Minister of Justice had exceeded his authority. But one of the judges involved, John Fieldsend, notes that there was 'no binding determination as to the true status of the government'. He himself had concluded that the government's actions were valid only in so far a they conformed to the 1961 Constitution 'and which were directed to and reasonably required for the ordinary orderly running of the country'.[674]

Three of the five judges did however find that the government was a *de facto* government, and these included the Chief Justice. His words were significant. He stated that '*de facto* governments ripen as a matter of course into *de jure* governments ... The dividing line between a *de jure* government and a *de facto* government in the present situation in Rhodesia today is an extremely narrow one ... .'[675] In reporting the case the London *Times* did not highlight this statement, as it might have done, and contented itself with commenting that 'the effect of today's judgements, apart from causing a change in the Government's machinery for preventive detention, seems to be to continue broadly to uphold the position which has prevailed in the courts since the first judgement in the test case delivered by Mr Justice Lewis in September 1966'.[676]

This was the position at the end of January 1968. But what did the Chief Justice's statement mean? Already, at the beginning of January, Pestell had confided in his diary that 'HE is a little worried about the CJ at the present time'.[677] And a few days later the worry was heightened by a visit from Roy Welensky, who wanted to know whether it was true that the Chief Justice had 'gone over' to the Rhodesian Front (RF). But Beadle had stood by him – and indeed lived with him – for over two years now. For a man of such straightforwardness and integrity as the Governor, it was both difficult and distasteful to have such doubts begin to grow in his mind. And it was difficult to dispel them. Sir Humphrey had not conversed over the dinner table at Government House about the details of the Constitutional Case, as it was *sub judice*. He expected that the Chief Justice would merely reaffirm the Goldin/Lewis declaration of the previous September that the government had to be regarded as *de facto*. He foresaw, in fact, an outcome much as *The Times* was to report it. Nevertheless there was a worry. It was partly mitigated a week later when he and the Chief Justice saw Ian Smith, who came to Government House one evening at his own request to discuss possible new proposals to the British Government. After that meeting, the Governor told Pestell that Beadle had fully supported him, 'and was very pleased at this after the doubts of the last few weeks'.[678] When the judgment of 29 January was announced, the Governor was again pleased – and relieved. There had been no statement in court that the Smith regime was the *de jure* government. Sir Robert Tredgold was less sanguine. He called on the Governor that afternoon and 'said that it could not be worse'.[679] While Sir Robert admitted that the judgment would be difficult for the man in the street to understand, he nevertheless thought that the Chief Justice had sold the pass, and should be asked to leave Government House. While the Governor may have disregarded this advice – Tredgold had a tendency to be gloomy – he must have been disconcerted when a few days later, Mr Justice Fieldsend called to offer his resignation. He had his resignation letter ready to hand over, but the Governor persuaded him to hold fire, in the hope that a political settlement would render it redundant. Fieldsend agreed to wait.[680] But Tredgold was back later that day. He was particularly worried that the Chief Justice's determination seemed to suggest that at some stage in the future he might be prepared to accept the full legality of the rebel regime. For that reason alone, Tredgold suggested, the succession to the Governorship should be reviewed. The 'dormant warrant' declared that if the governor were indisposed or unable to act, the Chief Justice would automatically become acting governor. This Tredgold thought should be changed. Sir Humphrey probably saw the wisdom of the suggestion, but was embarrassed at the thought of going behind the back of the man who had been, and indeed still was, his chief adviser. He agreed however that if Sir Robert felt strongly about it he should pass his thoughts on to the British government. This he agreed to do as he was due to see the British High Commissioner the next day. Sir Robert's other piece of advice – that the Chief Justice should be asked to leave Government House forthwith – was also embarrassing for the Governor, who felt that the time was not ripe yet for such a move.

The death sentence case and the Constitutional Case appeals were heard one after the other on Thursday 29 February. In the former, the condemned men's lawyers made a new plea: that it would constitute an inhuman or degrading punishment to carry out sentence of death after the two- or three-year delay. But the court concluded that 'the present government has the lawful right to ensure that death sentences properly imposed by this court are carried out'. The Chief Justice further declared that following the Constitutional Case decision, the government had 'the power to exercise all the powers relating to the prerogative of mercy which the Governor's Council exercised under section 49 of the 1961 Constitution'. However, a stay of execution was ordered to allow counsel to argue the right of appeal to the Privy Council. The right of appeal to the Privy Council – or to its judicial committee of usually 'five judges meeting in a room in a quiet corner of Downing Street'[681] – was another of those responsibilities left over from the height of empire. Immediately following the stay of execution, the Madzimbamuto application for leave to appeal to the Privy Council was heard, again by five judges. Lardner-Burke, the Minister of Justice, then stepped in and lodged an affidavit with the court to the effect that 'it is the deliberate and considered decision of the Government that it will not in any way recognise, enforce or give effect to any decision, judgement or order of any other court or tribunal which purports to be given on an appeal from a decision of this Honourable Court'. In the Madzimbamuto appeal case, the judges found that on technical grounds there was no right of appeal to the

Privy Council. They were not declaring that no right of appeal to the Privy Council existed in Rhodesia: simply that in this case, there was no basis for such an appeal, without the leave of the Privy Council. In the death sentence case however, which followed, no such technical determination could be made. So could the convicted men be given leave to appeal to the Privy Council, as was their right under the 1961 Constitution? The Chief Justice concluded that 'no judgement of the Judicial Committee of the Privy Council would be of any value inside this territory'. Fieldsend later wrote: 'The Chief Justice's reasons ... do not disclose any legal basis for the conclusion founded upon them. It is difficult to find in them any basis other than mere acceptance of the fact that nothing the Court could do would prevent the government from acting as it wished.'[682] Yet this was the same Chief Justice who had been resident in Government House for nearly two and a half years, in support of the Governor who was the Queen's representative in Rhodesia, and whose ultimate authority in the land they both by their stance had been upholding and proclaiming. Now, for practical reasons it would seem, the Chief Justice was denying the authority of the Queen's Privy Council. Was the authority of the Queen herself, by the same token, to be questioned?

That question was now to be posed, because for the condemned men, the only possibility now was to petition the Queen for mercy. With speed, this was set in motion, and at 9.00 p.m on Saturday 2 March the British High Commissioner called to tell the Governor that Her Majesty's Ministers in the UK had advised her to exercise her prerogative of mercy. The news that she had done so reached Government House after midnight, Hennings again calling personally with the news. The Sunday papers the next day were full of it.

These were difficult days for the Governor. On Friday he had been wondering whether he ought to have taken Tredgold's advice and asked the Chief Justice to leave. Now the problem was even greater. How would a court which existed under the Crown, with its judges exercising their functions under the authority of the Queen, react to the Queen's exercise of her prerogative of mercy? Fieldsend called on Saturday saying he would now resign, and promised to return the next day with a formal letter. He felt that the Chief Justice had in effect already abandoned the 1961 Constitution. Thus Sir Hugh no longer regarded himself as operating under a constitution granted by the Queen. Dendy Young came up from Bulawayo, 'hopping mad' about the Chief Justice's statement, and threatening to make a public statement. This was particularly significant, because Dendy Young had in the past been involved in politics as a segregationist right-winger. The next day Gibbs and Beadle met after church, and the Chief Justice fulminated about 'dragging the Queen into the political argument'.[683] Fieldsend called at

10.00 a.m. bringing his formal letter of resignation, and offering to be of any assistance to the Governor in the month or so that he remained in Rhodesia. When Fieldsend left, Gibbs and Pestell discussed the problem of the Chief Justice. The Governor then saw Beadle alone. It was a fairly calm discussion during which Beadle admitted that he had not for some time regarded himself as a judge under the 1961 Constitution, but his justification for having said nothing was that he could not fully accept the 1965 Constitution either. It was agreed that the Chief Justice and Lady Beadle should move out of Government House for Bulawayo on the following Saturday, ostensibly on the grounds that he would be filling the gap which Dendy Young appeared to be leaving. There the matter rested for the moment. During the course of that long Sunday, perhaps Sir Humphrey's mind turned again to the words of the Epistle he had heard in the cathedral that morning at Holy Communion: ' ... in all things approving ourselves as ministers of God, in much patience, in afflictions, in necessities, in distresses ... '.[684]

Later that Sunday Hennings called with a message from the Secretary of State, suggesting the Dormant Commission in Beadle's name should be withdrawn. Obviously Tredgold's suggestion had been quickly acted upon. Hennings also brought a message from Edward Heath to Ian Smith, urging the latter, whatever the merits of the case, to respect the exercise of the Queen's Prerogative. This message was delivered – secretly – to Smith on Monday morning. But the Court presided over by Beadle later that day rejected the bid to stay the executions on the basis of the Queen's clemency. On the next day the newspapers inside and outside Rhodesia carried the news of Beadle's statement that 'Her Majesty is quite powerless in this matter'. The Governor now resolved to act more quickly than he had earlier intended. Early on that Tuesday morning he summoned the Chief Justice and told him he must vacate Government House forthwith. Beadle said he could not understand what had changed, though it must have been obvious to him that the statement he made in court the previous day, with its dismissive reference to the Queen's Prerogative, must have been anathema to the Governor. Moreover the press comment at and since the weekend had heightened the tension and had revealed the very real rift between Governor and Chief Justice. Whether he was being disingenuous, or whether he was putting a brave face on it, is not clear. Perhaps when he recorded in his diary that he met 'cordially' with the Governor that evening at 5.00 p.m. to take his leave, he was being disingenuous.[685] But his description of the parting, which he penned to a friend a week later, smacks of special pleading or putting a brave face on the episode. He described how 'Humphrey and I thought it better if I returned to my residence in Bulawayo, as I am thoroughly fed up with the way the Wilson Government has behaved in this whole affair. However our parting was most amicable and I will naturally still give all the assistance I can to try and arrive at a settlement.'[686] In fact the parting of the ways was complete. There is no evidence that Sir Humphrey and Sir Hugh ever met again. They had an acerbic exchange of letters at the end of March, when the Chief Justice refused to return official papers to Government House, and never did so. In June Beadle asked to see the Governor, whose answer was that no useful purpose would be achieved by such a meeting. Humphrey was not a vindictive man, but his feelings about Beadle had not changed nearly a decade later when there were discussions about a Silver Jubilee presentation to the Queen from her Rhodesian Privy Councillors, of whom there were four – Gibbs, Welensky, Tredgold and Beadle. Humphrey wrote to Tredgold, 'I omit Hugh Beadle as I expect none of us would sign if his signature was included and I think we all feel he ought to have resigned as a Privy Councillor before now.'[687] Being the sort of man he was, this was the nearest to a public expression of displeasure that Humphrey Gibbs ever made about the affair. But he would probably have agreed with the English academic who wrote soon after the event that it was 'the failure of the members of the Rhodesian court to face up squarely to their responsibilities as the judicial upholders of the British Crown in Rhodesia that led to the sorry disarray to be found in the judgements in the constitutional case'.[688]

POLITICAL UNCERTAINTIES

Late in January Humphrey received the good news that Sir Alec Douglas-Home was to make a visit to Rhodesia. It was good news on a personal level, for they were old friends. But it was good news politically as well. Home was an old Africa hand, held in high respect in Rhodesia and beyond. 'The visit of a man of this calibre is welcome', declared the *Rhodesia Herald*, 'but wide-eyed optimism about the outcome might be out of place'.[689] Home and his wife arrived to stay at Government House late in February. He plunged into a busy round of talks, with Tredgold, Malvern, Field, black leaders, and representatives of the Forum and of the Rhodesian Constitutional Association. The meetings that really mattered, however, were those he held with Ian Smith, in the presence of Hugh Beadle. They met for one and a half hours at the Prime Minister's residence, and there was some optimism locally when a further meeting followed the next day at Government House.[690] Home's mission, as his biographer has suggested, was to impress upon Smith that 'time was running out' and perhaps even more importantly 'to underline the bi-partisan approach at the most senior level in Britain'.[691] While Home in private told Humphrey he thought Smith was a 'peasant',[692] outwardly there was some progress. Smith seemed to be prepared to open up discussions again with Thomson, for whom he appeared to have some respect. A *Tiger*-style settlement which would contain sufficient guarantees of movement towards majority rule was agreed as the basis for further discussions, and at his final press conference Sir Alec was able to say that 'he was taking back to London certain suggestions which could lead to a resumption of negotiations'.[693] For the Governor this was at least a glimmer of hope. For Humphrey himself there were more personal aspects to the visit. One was the letter which Sir Alec brought from the Queen, which in effect told him to 'stay put' even if the judicial decisions which were pending should go badly. And there was the fun, for both Humphrey and Molly, of chatting freely with old friends. Humphrey particularly enjoyed the moment when, sitting in the gardens of Government House, Sir Alec looked around him and said, 'Well, sanctions don't seem to be doing much harm to your roses, Humphrey.'[694]

The weeks after the Homes' departure – in early March – were dominated for Humphrey by the decisions of the judges and the departure of Beadle from Government House. There were other depressing aspects to cope with as well. A poll conducted by a Salisbury newspaper asked people if Rhodesia should become a republic: 1256 said 'yes', 884 said 'no'.[695] Even more depressing was the news that two soldiers – a white trooper and a black corporal – were killed in a skirmish with guerrillas. An English reporter in Salisbury reported back to London that 'Rhodesia today is at the dawn of its Vietnam'.[696] While the guerrilla war would not in fact escalate until some years later, it was a prescient comment. The Vietnam theme was taken up by Sir Roy Welensky, who turned upside down the usual anti-communist argument often heard in Rhodesia. While Smith supporters played on the idea that Rhodesia was a bulwark against further communist penetration of Africa, Sir Roy claimed that the fate of Australia, New Zealand, and Africa, all depended upon the outcome of the Vietnam War. All that Rhodesia could or should do for the moment was to negotiate with Britain – 'still Southern Africa's best friend' – for a settlement of the independence issue.[697] But no progress seemed to be taking place on the question of Anglo-Rhodesian relations. Jim Bottomley slipped into Salisbury at the end of March to brief the Governor and to sound him out on Smith's position. The Governor had had an hour-long meeting with the Prime Minister the previous evening, and found him calm, cordial, and willing to proceed on the basis of the *Tiger* proposals, at least if the 'return to legality' requirements were softened. A few days later, Michael Hamilton called. A Conservative MP (for Salisbury, Wiltshire), he was a son-in-law of Charles Ponsonby, and he brought with him a letter from Alec Douglas-Home with words of encouragement about the possibility of further negotiations, and the admonition to 'stick it out'.[698]

Humphrey was sticking it out in an increasingly confused political atmosphere in Rhodesia. The Whaley Commission on the constitution reported in April, and as one newspaper commented, 'one of the greatest attributes of the report they presented last week ... is that it has already been attacked from all sides'.[699] The Report opposed any immediate move towards republican status, and also rejected moves towards a South African-style apartheid system. Politically it suggested that the aim should be 'parity' between the races, achieved very gradually.[700] Smith showed himself in no hurry to act upon the report, and the reports the Governor received over the next few months seemed to underline the feeling that Rhodesia was in the midst of what one British newspaper called a 'winter of discontent'.[701] There were significant strains within the Rhodesian Front. Evan Campbell reported secretly to Humphrey in May that the party was making strenuous efforts to get him on board – efforts that he was resisting. More publicly the RF suffered the loss through resignation both of the right-winger, Harper, and also of its former leader, Winston Field. Ian Smith came under increasing pressure from the right-wing both inside the RF, and outside it. A new right-wing party calling itself the Rhodesia National Party was established with a firmly right wing agenda. To the left of the RF came a new challenge from a Centre Group, which was struggling to become a party and to sweep up members of Forum and of the Rhodesian Constitutional Association into one coherent opposition group. More immediate pressure on the Prime Minister came from the apolitical ARnI (Association of Rhodesian Industries) which at its conference in Bulawayo in May called for a negotiated settlement with Britain.

The Governor could only watch and wait. It was a curiously unsettling time. While Humphrey could hope that the Prime Minister would come under increasing pressure to negotiate a settlement, he was also aware that Smith needed to be in control if any such settlement were to be widely accepted within the RF and beyond. And other issues worried him. In May Sir Frederick Crawford had his British passport confiscated on a visit to the UK. Crawford was an ex-Governor of Uganda and a director of Anglo-American, with a tendency to give support both to Sir Humphrey and to the Smith regime. What annoyed Humphrey more than the confiscation was the way in which the Conservatives, and particularly Alec Home, used the issue as a stick to beat Harold Wilson. As with Smith, so with Harold Wilson: Humphrey was only too aware that a strong British Prime Minister was needed if a settlement was to be negotiated and accepted. In June John Pestell was recording that Home was 'a great disappointment' to the Governor. He was disappointed, even angry, with another British politician. Arthur Bottomley, Minister of Overseas Development and former Commonwealth Secretary, said during the debate on the Crawford affair that 'the Governor of Rhodesia appealed to me at the beginning to see that there was a full and effective application of economic sanctions'.[702] Humphrey was angry on a number of counts: first that his name should be mentioned in political debate. He felt strongly that the Governor's advice – like the Queen's – should remain confidential. Second, he was annoyed that this would transmit a wrong message to the illegal regime, as he had always worked to bring about a settlement rather than to bring it down. Fortunately the press in Rhodesia did not pick up this statement, and no damage was done.[703] Nor was any real damage caused, though it was an irritant, when two of Humphrey's predecessors as governor – William-Powlett and Kennedy – attended a party at Rhodesia House in London and were accused by Garfield Todd of giving 'comfort' to the illegal regime.[704] William-Powlett explained, perhaps somewhat naively, that the party had had 'no political significance' and that he 'would certainly do nothing to embarrass my friend Sir Humphrey Gibbs'.[705] Humphrey had more immediate worries. One was the issue of the dormant commission – who was to take over from him if he were incapacitated, as it could no longer be the Chief Justice? Humphrey considered the matter carefully in May, and was inclined to feel that Sir Robert Tredgold was not the right man, though Tredgold was prepared to have his name put forward. Humphrey felt, correctly, that he would be unacceptable to the Smith regime as a channel of communication with Britain. One day in June, Humphrey read about the appointment of a woman Governor (in Grenada) and came up with the idea that Molly might fit the bill. However, in August, finally, a more conventional solution was agreed upon when Sir Henry McDowell was approached and agreed to act if need be.

There were a few cheering moments during the uncertain and indeed somewhat bleak winter of 1968. In June, as usual, the 'Battle of the Books' was joined once more, when Malvern and Barrow wrote a circular letter calling for signatures in the visitors' book at Government House on the occasion of the Queen's official birthday. Sir Frederick Crawford soured the atmosphere somewhat by saying that he would not sign either book because it was simply a way of declaring one's political affiliation. Newson of the ARnI privately told Humphrey that he supported him but would not sign the book. Nevertheless the end result was over 3100 signatures, up from 900 the previous year; the Governor received 600 letters of support from those who could not get to Government House, up from 200 the previous year.[706] A parallel visitors' book at Dupont's residence was also opened, but as the pages were removed as soon as they filled, there was no way of knowing how many signatures it attracted, but it is to be supposed that the number fell far below those at Government House, as no capital was ever made out of it by the regime. Another cheering event for the Governor was the arrival of three brace of pheasants in August from his old friend Lord Bolton, who announced that as in previous years, the first birds of the season would be sent to Rhodesia.[707]

KNIGHT IN THE COLD

The journalist John Worrall, writing towards the end of Rhodesia's cold winter of 1968, focused on Humphrey, the 'Knight in the Cold'. The signatures in the Government House visitors' book, he wrote, had always been 'a sign of admiration for a dedicated man's stand'. This time round, he felt they were also expressing 'a wish for settlement of the conflict'.[708] Before the winter, Humphrey was 'still optimistic of a settlement this year'.[709] But no progress had been made during the winter of discontent. Humphrey met Ian Smith only once, and felt that no progress was on the horizon. He was unaware of developments taking place in Britain.

The Governor had last heard from the British Prime Minister in March, in the wake of the hangings which had led to the traumatic breach with the Chief Justice. Wilson, while telling his cabinet that Smith had now 'effectively slammed the door', assured the Governor that 'we shall be prepared to pick up the threads again as soon as we are satisfied that we are dealing with people who can be trusted to give effect to the spirit as well as to the letter of the six principles'.[710] Nothing that had happened since could be construed as providing any cause for satisfaction. But unknown to Humphrey, Wilson had called a meeting at Chequers in June. The House of Lords had recently and narrowly defeated a sanctions order, and Wilson in disgust had called off his all-party negotiations on reform of the upper house. Rhodesia was now creeping again to the top of his agenda. He writes of 'various reports reaching us from Rhodesia suggesting that they would be prepared to accept an honourable settlement'.[711] Hence the meeting at Chequers with Sir Max Aitken and Lord Goodman. Aitken, the newspaper proprietor and war-time colleague of Ian Smith, had strong links with the Conservative front bench. Goodman was Wilson's lawyer and 'fixer'. Wilson records with some relish how he told Sir Max that 'he thought he had said he would shortly be visiting Rhodesia', though it took some time for Aitken to realise he was being asked to become an emissary. Thus was a secret mission launched to open up the possibility of further talks. The Governor was not informed. The news broke when a *Daily Express* reporter talked to Peter Carter at the British Mission. Carter called on the Governor on 6 August to report that Sir Max was coming out 'on a business trip'. Humphrey heard from another source that he had been sent by Wilson as an emissary, but thought this was unlikely as he had not been consulted or informed directly. Slightly put out, he asked Carter to ensure that Aitken called upon him. The visit took place on 16 August, after Aitken had seen Smith. He and the Governor had a rather stilted conversation, and Humphrey learned very little, and ended up feeling 'rather peeved'.[712] He was not told the name of 'his lawyer' whom Aitken said he had brought with him, though Humphrey and Pestell assumed it must be Goodman. Humphrey learned more when he had a visit from Sir Roy Welensky a few days later. Sir Roy had seen Aitken just before the latter's visit to Government House on the 16th. Sir Max had been much more open with Welensky, explaining to him that the visit had been planned for some months (this was an exaggeration), and asserting that he had come at the request of Harold Wilson and not in connection with any pre-arranged business trip. He had managed to get Smith to agree to a meeting, probably at Gibraltar, on the negotiating basis of the Six Principles. Welensky agreed that Humphrey could share all this with his Comptroller, so when his visitor left, Humphrey called for Pestell, who records that the Governor 'was visibly shaken', and fortified with stiff drinks, they retired to the study to discuss the situation. Humphrey was delighted that talks were to reopen, but mystified as to why he had been left in the dark, and could only piece together the details by listening to various accounts.[713] It was a week later that formal notification arrived from London that there would be talks, though the Governor was still left wondering whether Wilson was desperately anxious to settle, or whether Smith was more anxious to settle than was apparent in Salisbury.

While no significant progress towards substantive talks could be expected before the RF and Labour Party Conferences – in early September and early October respectively – James Bottomley (a Commonwealth Office official) made a preliminary foray in mid-September, to assure Smith that the British government was anxious for a settlement, and was flexible in its interpretation of the Six Principles. Both Smith and Gibbs had hoped the visit would be secret, and that was agreed. However it leaked – a 'balls up' rather than an 'inspired leak', as Peter Carter put it.[714] Bottomley reported to the Governor in fairly optimistic tones, but when he left, Humphrey retreated to his bed with 'a tear in his eye' and feeling useless and sidelined.[715] A few days later he heard reports that Kenneth Kaunda had known of the visit, and seemed to know all the details of what had transpired, including the Governor's annoyance with Mr Wilson. How did he know? The Governor and his Comptroller conjectured that Tiny Rowland might be behind all this. Rowland was of course a close friend of Kaunda, and of Nkomo. A 'cool, buccaneering panjandrum criss-crossing Africa in his new Mystere Falcon jet',[716] Rowland was increasing his holdings in Africa to the extent that his profits jumped 97 per cent in 1968 alone. He had extensive contacts in southern Africa, and within the British establishment. He had called on the Governor on three occasions in the course of the year, the last being on 24 August. While Humphrey had not confided in him, Rowland was astute enough to read between the lines. No doubt he knew that the Governor was feeling marginalised. Certainly September ended with the Governor feeling very much the 'Knight in the Cold'.

However, there was some optimism growing in Salisbury that these talks might succeed. Both Smith and Wilson came out of their respective party conferences the stronger. Wilson even went so far as to praise Ian Smith for his 'considerable courage' in dealing with the extremists in the RF. In carrying a report on this unlikely development, the *Rhodesia Herald* concluded its 5 October leading article with the statement that 'the report of Mr Wilson's TV appearance gives the impression that he thinks circumstances in Rhodesia are more promising for negotiations than they were. Salisbury opinion agrees with him.' Many in Wilson's own Cabinet didn't. Richard Crossman reckoned that those who might have opposed any further meetings with Smith – such as himself, Barbara Castle, Tony Greenwood, Tony Benn and Jim Callaghan – had not been consulted. Those who had been consulted during conference week – Gerald Gardiner, Elwyn Jones, Fred Peart, Eddie Shackleton, Michael Stewart, George Thomson, Denis Healey, Tony Crosland and Roy Jenkins – were, Crossman confided to his diary, 'committed in advance to Harold's going if he wanted to go'.[717] For Harold Wilson, the politician, there was the added advantage that the talks would steal the thunder of the Conservatives, whose party conference was about to open, and who were thus left with little to say about Rhodesia. Their cry that talks should reopen had been answered. The newspapers would concentrate on the talks, and not on the Conservatives talking about talks.

Three days later, the Governor and Smith were on their way to Gibraltar. The arrangements that had been made for Smith's party reflected Wilson's determination that things should go well. Smith and his party were accorded the sort of accommodation to be expected by a head of government and his colleagues. They were housed in their own quarters on HMS *Kent*, which was moored alongside HMS *Fearless*, where the talks were to take place. Humphrey was put up by the Governor of Gibraltar. The talks, Harold Wilson later recalled, 'were more agreeable and freer from rancour than those held on board *Tiger*'.[718] For Humphrey, this was certainly the case. He and his Comptroller had time for some sight-seeing, as well as meals with the Governor and with the Admiral commanding in Gibraltar. It must have been a considerable relief to walk the streets freely, to visit museums, and to enjoy the autumn sunshine, without the tense late-night meetings which had heightened the drama on HMS *Tiger*. There was a minor drama when

Humphrey tried to change his Rhodesian currency at a local bank, and was refused sterling on the grounds that he was tendering an illegal currency![719] He had to make do instead – and as befitted a member of the Gibbs clan – with a guided tour of the bank. A rather more elevating experience took place on Sunday, when Humphrey read the lesson at matins in the cathedral. 'Comfort ye, comfort ye my people' were the opening words. They could hardly have been more appropriate.

There was comfort too in the fact that this time round, the British government set no deadline. Smith could return to Salisbury and continue to negotiate. Although the British ended the talks with the phrase 'no sell-out, no slamming the door', the concessions to the Smith regime were significant.[720] In effect, it would remain in power while a new constitution was introduced, though diluted by a minority of Africans. The 'humiliation' of the RF Cabinet having to surrender its powers to the Governor would therefore no longer be a stumbling block. It would be Harold Wilson who would have the problem of selling the 'no sell-out' agreement to the Commonwealth. Initial optimism ran high. One reporter, probing sources in London and Salisbury, even ventured beyond the settlement to predict that Humphrey would be offered the Garter and a peerage, 'possibly an earldom'.[721] Back in Salisbury however Humphrey soon found the optimism begin to drain away. Ian Smith talked openly in parliament about appeal to the Privy Council being a sticking point. Wilson was meanwhile comforted that there appeared to be a broad parliamentary consensus in favour of the Fearless proposals, even though they did not include a demand for NIBMAR, no independence before majority rule. The fact that Smith had achieved that much made some feel that 'there is always a danger of encouraging impossible demands from an Oliver Twist'.[722] Humphrey was anxious that the momentum should not be lost, and he supported Smith's request that George Thomson should visit Salisbury to work on the details. The timing was awkward, as the 'independence' celebrations were looming, and this year would include the raising of the new Rhodesian flag and the final hauling down of the Union Jack – a further break between Britain and Rhodesia. It was agreed that Thomson would arrive before the 11th, disappear briefly on the day, and return to resume negotiations thereafter. The results were hardly auspicious. Harold Wilson records eight points of disagreement, some of them quite new, which arose during the Smith–Thomson talks.[723] He writes of Thomson's report back to the Commons on 18 November as 'the end of a chapter'. Thomson spoke of having found the previous fortnight 'disappointing and saddening'.

On the next day, Ian Smith appeared on Rhodesian Television, and told the viewers that 'in case in the end we fail to agree, your Government is continuing its preparations for a long haul so that whatever happens we will sooner or later arrive at our destination'. The uncertainties of 1968 had been foreshadowed in Ian Smith's New Year message. They were still there, despite the *Fearless* talks and the British government's willingness to make concessions, as the year ended. When Michael Palliser, Harold Wilson's secretary, wrote to thank Molly Gibbs for her hospitality during the Thomson visit, he spoke of the happy fortnight he had spent at Government House. But, he continued 'I only wish the end could also have been happy and that we had not left you both to yet a further period of waiting and uncertainty.'[724]

13 Near the End of the Road[725]

LONG INCARCERATION

On 22 November 1968 Humphrey Gibbs celebrated his sixty-sixth birthday, and entered the tenth year of office as Governor. The Queen sent her best wishes,[726] and in conversation with her mother's Lady in Waiting, Lady Jean Rankin, expressed the hope that he 'could be extricated from his long and miserable incarceration'.[727] The December issue of *Illustrated Life Rhodesia* carried a long article on 'The Forgotten Rhodesian' for whom the previous month had been 'one of traumatic anniversaries', including of course the third anniversary of UDI. The article was by John Worrall (soon to be declared a prohibited immigrant), and was a timely reminder to Rhodesians that the Governor was still in place. The front cover of the magazine carried a large picture of Humphrey at a state opening of parliament, and a smaller recent one of him sitting on the verandah of Government House. Rhodesians who might have forgotten were vividly reminded of the Queen's representative in their midst.

But there was in that 'patrician villa', as Worrall called it, a sense of unease as the year drew to a close. While it had been a comfort to leave Gibraltar feeling that there was no deadline, there was also now a feeling that things were dragging on. John Pestell was concerned that Lady Gibbs went into a 'flat spin' when she heard that Ian Smith was to broadcast to the nation. Fearing lest he was going to slam the door and declare a republic, her reaction was uncharacteristic. In the event, it turned out that he was still 'pondering' on what road to take.[728] But Pestell was struck afresh by the 'tension' in the atmosphere. It wasn't helped by the drama when 'the "captains" of the economy emerged from behind the Forum'.[729] They determined to apply pressure on the government to settle on the basis of *Fearless*. First E. S. Newson on 27 November, and then Evan Campbell on 10 December, spoke out strongly against UDI, forecasting disaster for Rhodesia if no settlement were reached. These two, and in particular Campbell, were men whom the Governor trusted, and thought highly of; they were powerful men in the Rhodesian economy. It was a shot in the arm for the Governor. But the government's response was swift. Newson and Campbell were savaged by Ian Smith as 'mud-slinging critics' who, as he told the people of Rhodesia, would 'offer to sell your heritage for a mess of pottage, to abandon your independence, and then your country in exchange for some dazzling economic prize in the immediate future for which we and

160

those who follow will subsequently have to pay a prohibitive price'.[730] Such
was the ferocity of the attack that the *Herald* called it 'Government by
intimidation'. Such was the success of the tactic that no other captains of
industry came forward in support of Newson and Campbell. The plan – or
at least the expectation – had been that a succession of prominent captains
of industry speaking out in such terms would apply sufficient pressure to
encourage Smith to pick up the *Fearless* terms and settle on that basis. In
the event, the whole incident left the Governor feeling even more isolated
and hopeless. The one crumb of comfort offered by Smith was his mention
of a 'secret plan' which might lead to a settlement. But this was regarded
by Government House as a blind, and certainly neither at the time nor
subsequently were any details released. Indeed in the New Year Smith was
claiming that he had no new proposals to put to Britain.[731] To add to the gloom
was the newspaper report from London that the Governor read at about this
time which proclaimed that '[t]he gap is even wider'.[732] Humphrey would
have felt even more miserable had he been aware of a memorandum circulated
by the Secretary for Internal Affairs, Hostes Nicolle. He only caught sight
of it a month later.[733] Dated 5 December, it was circulated within the
Ministry, and to Provincial and District Commissioners, to put them in the
picture in the wake of the *Fearless* talks. In the language of a white supremacist
it talked about *Tiger* being a 'hyena' and *Fearless* being a 'jackal', the Privy
Council a 'witch doctor' and the aim being majority rule which would lead
to chaos.

Reading through a copy of the Nicolle memorandum was not a happy
start to 1969 for the Governor. Further blows fell in January. Christopher
Owen decided that he must leave Government House, and he went with
Humphrey's blessing to seek a new career in England; but he was not
replaced. Towards the end of the month, George Thomson was relieved of
his responsibility for the problem of Rhodesia, much to Humphrey's distress
for he had come to respect him enormously. Christopher Owen wrote from
London to say that the Commonwealth Office people were 'seething with
discontent' at the way Thomson had been removed.[734] Fortunately for
Humphrey there were happier days in January. He had a visit from Harry
Oppenheimer – the enormously powerful mogul of Southern African
industry, and chairman of the Anglo-American Corporation. Pestell and the
Governor found him to be a 'charming and modest man'.[735] On the day
following his visit to Government House he addressed the seventy-fifth
anniversary dinner of the Salisbury Chamber of Commerce, a gathering
attended by most of the Cabinet. He did what people like Ellman-Brown
had failed to do as a follow-up to the outspoken comments of Newson and
Campbell. He called for a settlement, as the dispute was damaging to the

economy and had gone on 'much too long for the good of race relations in this country'.[736] This came a few days after newspaper coverage of Selwyn Lloyd, newly arrived in Cape Town en route to Rhodesia. He had declared, in perhaps unconscious contradiction of the newspaper headline of the previous month, that 'the gap between Britain and Rhodesia had been narrowed by the *Fearless* talks'.[737] He was to add his voice to those of such right-wing Tories as Cyril Osborne and Patrick Wall who were encouraging Smith to settle while Labour was still in power. Julian Amery made the same plea while visiting in February. A general election would take place in Britain within the subsequent eighteen months. No doubt these Tories had no wish, if elected, to inherit the poisoned chalice. But there was more to it than that. They told their friends in Rhodesia, as Alec Douglas-Home had done years before, that it was easier for Labour to negotiate, make concessions, and be assured of carrying the settlement in the House of Commons than it would be for the Tories. And it was true that Wilson was still insisting that 'the *Fearless* proposals remain on the table'.[738] So despite the isolation and gloom at Government House, there were still some shafts of light. There were more to come. At the end of January the Aldenhams arrived for a month's stay. And later that month, the Prentice affair gave Humphrey some hope that all was not lost. Bob Prentice was a senior Army officer who had called on the Governor early in February to ask advice. He had been asked to accompany Dupont on a two-day tour of duty while the 'Officer Administering the Government' visited remote areas. Prentice felt that, as an aide-de-camp (ADC) to the Queen, he could not undertake such a duty. He, like his superior officer 'Sam' Putterill, had spent the previous three years doing his duty while trying to avoid any obvious conflict of loyalties. Now it seemed the crunch had come. Later on the same day, the Governor had a visit from Lieutenant-General Keith Coster, who had succeeded Putterill as Army commander in June 1968, and who was regarded as 'more pliant' from Smith's point of view than his predecessor had been.[739] Coster had not visited Government House since UDI. He now asked the Governor to ask Her Majesty to release Prentice from being an ADC. This Humphrey refused to do, and further suggested that the whole matter should be dumped on the Prime Minister's table, as Smith had always declared his loyalty to Her Majesty. Some days later, a message arrived at Government House by hand from Prentice, to say that the Dupont trip had been postponed, and when it happened he would not be required to be present. 'So, they climbed down', Pestell noted with satisfaction.[740] Not only a comfort to the people at Government House, this was a remarkable example of how some higher Army officers managed to live with a somewhat bizarre situation. Prentice, like Putterill, still regarded the

Governor as his Commander-in-Chief; Mr Dupont was a usurper. Their Commander-in-Chief, at the time of UDI and in the name of the Queen, had required public servants to stay at their posts. A few had resigned, unwilling to serve the new regime in any way at all. Some, like Prentice, managed to carry on with their jobs while there was – as they saw it – no obvious conflict of loyalties. It was a curious situation. But then so was the fact that names like the Royal Rhodesia Regiment and the Royal Rhodesian Air Force were still in use, and the Queen Mother was still Honorary Commissioner of the British South Africa Police, with its proud motto, *Pro Rege, Pro Lege, Pro Patria.*

While there was to be no showdown as yet, the potential for one was now on the horizon. The RF government released its plans for a new constitution on 16 February. The 'Yellow Paper' proposals which were the Rhodesian Front's (RF) riposte to the Whaley Report were ditched. In their place came sweeping proposals for entrenching 'government in the hands of civilized Rhodesians for all time'. A national parliament of sixty-six was envisaged, with fifty returned by Europeans, Asians and Coloureds. African representation would only increase as African contributions via income tax to the national exchequer increased. Provincial assemblies were also proposed, though Smith refused to give any more details than these broad outlines. As the *Sunday Mail* commented, 'It also appears that Mr Smith is getting less and less interested in reaching a settlement with Britain.'[741] A referendum was also promised, though the Governor was sceptical about this aspect, and advised London that the *Fearless* proposals, despite all, should be allowed to remain on the table. But Harold Wilson could be forgiven for stating in the Commons at the beginning of March that he was not hopeful of a settlement. 'I have not seen anything which remotely represents an acceptance of the *Fearless* terms', he said.[742] He had done his best at the Commonwealth Conference in January to hold out against demands for the reassertion of NIBMAR, and against renewed demands by some for the use of force. But the events in Rhodesia seemed to have a momentum of their own, and it was not going in the direction of a settlement. There were no more clandestine visits by Smith to Government House. There were only three communications from Salisbury to London as a follow-up to *Fearless* and the subsequent Thomson visit. On 23 January the regime asked for some clarification; on 13 February it listed eight points of difference between itself and the British government, and on 16 April it effectively drew a halt to negotiations since 'it now seems clear that the intransigent attitude of the British Government stands in the way of any agreement being reached'.[743] By the end of March Smith's Minister of Local Government and Housing was promising a new Land Act, to replace the Land Apportionment Act, which would allow for segregation within urban residential areas. Within a few days of this, the holding of a referendum on the new constitutional proposals was announced, and Ian Smith was stating publicly that Rhodesia had 'no option but to become a republic'.[744] It began to look as if Sir Humphrey's 'long and miserable incarceration' would soon end.

THE REFERENDUM

Everyone knew, after 3 April, that there would be a referendum. On 10 May the Governor wrote to the Queen setting out his thoughts about his position thereafter.[745] It was not until 21 May that it became clear just what Rhodesians would be called to vote for or against. Smith had outlined the proposed new constitution in February. In late May the details were published.[746] There was little change from the Smith outline, save that provincial assemblies were dropped, though there was provision for the introduction of provincial or regional councils 'as and when such delegation is considered to be appropriate'. The premise upon which the new constitution was constructed was that it would replace one that contained 'a number of objectionable features', these being 'that it provides for eventual African rule' and that 'it does not guarantee that government will be retained in responsible hands'. There would be a senate consisting of ten Europeans, ten African chiefs and three members appointed by the Head of State – who would no longer be the Queen or her representative. This new republican constitution would also make provision for protecting the land rights of Europeans and Africans, and would include a non-justiciable Declaration of Rights. When it finally came before parliament later in the year, Arhn Palley, the only white opposition member, attacked it as the inevitable outcome of taking UDI, the main reason for which was 'the halting of political advancement by the African population' and bringing to an end 'the experiment of multiracialism'.[747] At least now that the White Paper had been published, opposition could be mobilised.

But what opposition? The 'liberal' opposition had its focus in the Centre Party which had now existed for just a year. While John Worrall – before his deportation – was calling it a 'dynamic new voice in Rhodesia',[748] it never quite managed to unite the RF's opponents. The businessmen of the Forum did not emerge to back it whole-heartedly, perhaps put off by the Newson-Campbell debacle of December 1968. The members of the Rhodesian Constitutional Association – the successor to the old establishment party – had hung back from endorsing it. Part of the problem was its leader, Pat Bashford, temporarily appointed in August 1968. An outspoken Karoi farmer, he had an 'image' problem. The Centre Party commissioned a public relations firm to discover what the public attitude was, and found that while Smith had 'an exceptionally fine image', Bashford was widely regarded as 'devious, ineffective, unpopular, unreliable and not very acceptable'.[749] If the only thing that stood between the Governor and resignation was a victory of the 'no' vote in the referendum, it was obvious that he had no hope of continuing. The attempts by the Centre Party to replace Bashford failed. He was willing to stand down in favour of someone else – but no one else could be found. One can see again resonances with what was happening in Northern Ireland. In Rhodesia, the Governor could only watch as the 'liberal' opposition tried to mobilise its forces to oppose the hard-liners. In Northern Ireland, the Governor there could do nothing but accept the resignation of his 'liberal' Prime Minister, Terence O'Neill, who at the time of the Rhodesian referendum was replaced by someone more acceptable to the hard-liners of Ulster.[750]

In fact the 'no' vote propaganda during the weeks before the referendum attracted a remarkable degree of support from a wide range of people. Members of Forum and of the Rhodesian Constitutional Association either joined the Centre Party or supported its 'no' campaign. Lord Malvern and Sir Roy Welensky issued a joint statement condemning the proposed 'break with our past'.[751] Professor Dick Christie – a distinguished lawyer who was regarded at Government House as having given rather too much comfort to the illegal regime – declared the new constitution to be 'so unbalanced as to take Rhodesia clean out of the Western European tradition'.[752] The country's Roman Catholic bishops fiercely attacked the proposals as 'quite irreconcilable with God's law and [are] calculated to destroy every possibility of achieving the common good'.[753] In less fierce terms, 'Anglican and Protestant leaders alike rejected the new constitution'.[754] David Butler (almost always described as 'handsome and wealthy former Olympic yachtsman'[755]), who had been asked by the Governor if he would try to form a government back in 1965, came out for a 'no' vote, as did the respected and recently retired under secretary in the Ministry of Internal Affairs, John Foggin. But the most sensational attack on the government's proposals, and the one that attracted most of their counter-attack, was by Major General 'Sam' Putterill. He had retired in June 1968, and was now apple farming at Inyanga. 'I cannot sit back and see my country go headlong into this mess', he announced, and calling on his own military experience he declared that the new constitution would create 'fertile ground' for terrorism by 'creating disaffection between the races'.[756] Ian Smith attacked his 'despicable behaviour'.[757] Brigadier Dunlop, now Minister of Transport, was almost apoplectic when he demanded to know how such a man could 'virtually stab his country in the back'.[758] Bob Williams was again proved right: the current attitude was that 'if you are anti-Rhodesian Front you are anti-Rhodesia'.[759]

While the campaign raged, the Governor heard the news of the death of his eldest brother, Lord Aldenham, who had been staying with him just three months before. The title now passed to Humphrey's nephew, Antony.[760] He was, of course, unable to fly over for the funeral. Just a week after his bereavement, the Governor called a 'Council of State' at Government House, on Sunday 8 June. He had prepared a statement which had been cleared with the British government, and which he reluctantly felt he might have to make public. Those who assembled to advise him were Lord Malvern, Sir Roy Welensky, Sir Malcolm Barrow, Sir Henry McDowell, Sir Ian Wilson, 'Baffy' Dugmore and Dr Robert Fynn.[761] Two of the Governor's sons, Nigel and Tim, sat in, as did John Pestell, while Sir Robert Tredgold and Sir John Caldicott were unable to make it. The consensus was that the statement should be made public, so on the following Wednesday Humphrey faced journalists and photographers on the lawn of Government House. Having explained to them that he had given serious consideration to the question of whether he should make any statement at all, he went on:

As Her Majesty's representative in Rhodesia, I have no place in the political arena, and it is my intention to preserve the non-political role I have maintained since I was appointed Governor in 1959. Because of the gravity of the situation, and the speculation which I believe is current about my position, I have come to the conclusion that I would be failing in my duty to the people of Rhodesia if I did not make my position, as I see it, quite clear. To remain silent might be deemed unfair to those who will be giving thought to all aspects of the problems besetting the country. As I believe that my position may have some bearing on the future of this country, it is right that I should state what it is.

Shortly after UDI in November 1965, I said, and I quote: 'I hope and believe that if I continue in office as the Governor of Rhodesia, I may provide the link which will make a satisfactory settlement of the present position possible'. Since that time I have done everything in my power to bring about an honourable settlement, in the earnest belief, firstly – that an honourable settlement is in the best interests of the future well-being of our country, and, secondly – that the granting of legal independence to our country on reasonable terms, with all the benefits which would follow, is a negotiable possibility. It is the greatest disappointment to me that such a settlement has not been reached.

The electorate is now being asked to give a mandate for the declaration of a republic and the introduction of a Constitution which the leaders of the British political parties have said could not form the basis of a settlement with any Government in the United Kingdom. If enough of the electorate vote for these proposals for them to be put into effect, then leaving aside the legalities, the door to further negotiations will have been closed, and the electorate will have demonstrated their wish to break all ties with Her Majesty the Queen and with Britain.

In these circumstances it would in all probability be impossible for me to continue to be Governor of Rhodesia. I cannot predict what effect, if any, my going would have on the country's future: but it is possible that my departure, and the loss of what I stand for, could push us into even greater isolation from the rest of the world. I feel that I must draw attention to this possibility, not because of the great personal grief that I should feel, but because matters of profound importance to the country are now being considered, and I must not remain silent.

I earnestly pray that in coming to your decision you will have full regard to your obligations to the large numbers of unenfranchised Rhodesians who will have no voice to express their wishes.

It was the longest statement the Governor had issued to date, and the only one thus far to be printed in full in the local press.[762] The last sentence was about as close as the Governor came to becoming controversial. It was picked up by the Bishop of Mashonaland, who wrote a few days later to recount what his African clergy and laity were saying: 'If Sir Humphrey Gibbs goes, we are left to the hawks and the eagles.'[763] On that same day, Mindy Bacon arrived to provide some moral support, the more necessary since Molly had been unwell. On the 20 June the referendum was held. With an 85 per cent turnout by the overwhelmingly white electorate, 72.5 per cent said 'yes' to the new constitution, while 81 per cent voted for a republic. In an unholy alliance, extreme right-wingers joined with the Centre Party to condemn that new constitution. Most, if not all of those right-wingers would, however, have voted for a republic. This would help explain the discrepancy between the two 'yes' votes. On the following Sunday, 22 June, the Governor called another 'Advisory Council' at Government House. Present were Malvern, Fynn, Dugmore, McDowell, Caldicott, Barrow and Pestell who had attended the previous meeting; they were joined by Sir Robert Tredgold, Evan Campbell, Sir Edmund Bacon, Mike Currie and Sidney Sawyer, with sons Jeremy and Nigel in attendance. Tributes were paid to the Governor, and all were agreed that as no useful purpose could now be served by staying on, it was hoped that the Queen would soon release him from his post, and it was hoped that he would be able to travel to London to take personal leave of Her Majesty. All that remained now was to await formal notification from

London, which came two days later with a statement in the House by Michael
Stewart, the Foreign Secretary. He confirmed that he had been in touch with
the Governor, and that 'it would not be justifiable to ask [him] to remain
any longer at his post'. He added the Governor and Lady Gibbs would fly
to Britain in the near future to take leave of the Queen personally. He
announced also that the time had come to close the residual mission in
Salisbury.[764] On the same day the Governor delivered his own statement to
the press and television. 'With his voice cracking with emotion and at times
appearing to be on the verge of breaking down', Sir Humphrey confirmed
that he would be stepping down, as 'it is apparent that the majority of the
electorate has demonstrated that it wants Rhodesia to break all ties, not only
with Her Majesty the Queen, but also with Britain and the Commonwealth'.
His final words, after his thanks to the staff of Government House and to
'loyal, kind and generous Rhodesians from all walks of life', not only
expressed noble sentiments, but also pointed to an optimism which he could
scarcely have felt at the time, yet which was to inform his activities for the
rest of his life:[765]

> I lay down my office with sadness, but without bitterness or rancour, and
> I look forward to the day when the deep divisions of this country are
> replaced by feelings of goodwill and friendship – when a united people,
> without fear and prejudice, will lead this young country forward to peace
> and prosperity for all.

The *Rhodesia Herald* carried a leader praising his tenure of office and
headed 'Tenacious of Purpose' (*tenax propositi*, the Gibbs family motto).
On the day the newspapers carried the Governor's statement, Lady Gibbs
was taken to hospital; 'she has had a near nervous breakdown – poor thing',
John Pestell recorded in his diary.

There was still work to be done. The British Mission in Salisbury was soon
to close, so there were documents to transfer for onward transmission to
London. At Government House, the Governor's Fund had business to attend
to, and Lord Malvern called a meeting on Saturday 26 June, attended by Sir
Malcolm Barrow. Malvern and Barrow were founding trustees of the fund
which had been set up in 1966. John Pestell and Mindy Bacon attended as
well, and generous grants were made to the various members of the Governor's
staff. On the next day – Sunday – Humphrey attended the cathedral as usual,
though Molly could not be with him. Something else was different: '- no
front pew – sat some way back – [Sir Humphrey] quite resigned to new
position'. With those words John Pestell ended his diary, and handed it over
for safe keeping to Peter Carter at the residual British Mission. One further
ceremony took place within Government House. On 4 July there was a

drinks party before lunch. Sir Humphrey called for a toast to the Queen. Lord Malvern, on the eve of his eighty-sixth birthday, presented an illuminated scroll to Sir Humphrey and Lady Gibbs. It was from the Trustees of the Governor's Fund – and signed by Lord Malvern, Dr Robert Fynn and Sidney Sawyer on behalf of Sir Malcolm Barrow. Lord Malvern's eyesight was so poor that he called upon Robert Fynn to read out the inscription, which praised both Humphrey and Molly for their 'courage, steadfastness and Christian devotion to duty throughout [their] most difficult period of office'.[766] The next day, Saturday, saw a smaller but equally moving ceremony: Sir Humphrey watched as the Union Jack was lowered for the last time in his presence in the late afternoon sunshine. On Sunday morning he and Molly attended the cathedral for 8.00 a.m. service. At 9.30 a.m. they drove out of Government House. Well-wishers crowded the pavement. Before them lay a journey of 380 miles to their home, Bonisa, which they had not seen for four years, and had not lived in for ten. Back at Government House, John Pestell set about packing up and settling accounts.

AFTERMATH

'I feel better already, just because I am home', Molly announced when they arrived at Bonisa, though she soon had to take to her bed again. It was, as Roy Welensky wrote, just a part of 'the price you had to pay for carrying on'.[767] With Molly ill, and Tim effectively running the farm as he had been doing, there was little for Humphrey to do in the immediate future. There must have been, also, the inevitable let-down after years of being at least in some senses 'centre-stage'. Good news arrived with the announcement from 10 Downing Street on 9 July that Humphrey was to be awarded the GCVO (Knight Grand Cross of the Royal Victorian Order) and was to become a member of the Privy Council. He would in future be 'the Right Honourable'. There had been talk of a peerage, and there were reports that he had no wish to accept one.[768] However, the Royal Victorian Order was in Her Majesty's personal gift, and he was to become a member of her Privy Council – perhaps those were enough, underlining as they did Humphrey's insistence that he was a servant of the Queen, and not of the British government. He and Molly had only a short time at Bonisa before they flew to England for an extended holiday and a round of official engagements. They were meanwhile able to watch on television what seemed, at the time, to be a potent symbol of a new era – an era far removed from colonialism and honours and the pageantry of empire and Commonwealth. On 21 July Neil Armstrong, the American astronaut, became the first man to set foot on the moon.

Back on earth it was while en route for England that Molly had her unexpected bit of good news. During a stopover at Blantyre, they were met by the British High Commissioner to Malawi, who gave her a message from Downing Street informing her of the Queen's intention to appoint her a Dame Commander of the Order of the British Empire – an honour, and title, for her in her own right. The news was to be released after they had arrived in London.[769] They landed at Heathrow on 20 August and were met by a Commonwealth Office minister, Lord Shepherd. Humphrey lost no time in making an official call at the Foreign and Commonwealth Office, and there were then a few days for seeing family and friends before they flew north to Deeside, for a weekend at Balmoral, where Humphrey was to take leave of the Queen officially. There they were duly invested with their respective honours, and joined in the sort of country house weekend that Humphrey must have remembered from his youth. Alec Douglas-Home was there, as was Lord Plunket, who 'had a passion for royal entertaining' and 'made everyone feel comfortable'.[770] Humphrey and Molly knew his brother well: Robin Plunket lived at Melsetter and had predicted before they left that his brother, who had been Deputy Master of the Queen's Household since 1954, would 'do his best to be on duty when you see the Queen'.[771] They met the heir to the throne for the first time. Prince Charles had just been through the ordeal of his Investiture as Prince of Wales, and was about to return for his final year at Trinity College, Cambridge, which Humphrey had left forty-seven years before. The Prince drove them ('too fast' said Molly) for tea with the Queen Mother whom they had last seen in happier times before UDI. It was a wonderful weekend for the Gibbses, only slightly spoiled by the fact that Molly arrived at her bedroom to find her case unpacked and the bath not only prepared for her, but overflowing, with water running down the corridor.

Other engagements were fitted in around visits to family and friends. In late September there was a visit to Birmingham University where Humphrey received the degree of Doctor of Laws. There was a particularly happy link with this university, since it had validated medical degrees for the University College of Rhodesia since its inception. And the Vice-Chancellor of Birmingham was a distinguished medical man. There was a shadow over the proceedings, however, as students protested about giving a degree to 'a man who is a white settler'.[772] A similar event took place a month later when the University of East Anglia also awarded Humphrey an LL.D. Mindy Bacon, who was its Pro-Chancellor, was similarly honoured, though he denied that he had had any hand in the proposal to honour Humphrey.[773] Again there were scuffles. While Humphrey had suffered what might be called formal humiliations in Salisbury, he had not been subjected to this sort of personal attack before – except possibly from the students at University College just before UDI. On that occasion, and on these, it is ironical that he should have become the butt of student protesters who were demonstrating against a UDI which he had personally stood against. But he was a symbol to be attacked; just as Brian Jones, the former Rolling Stone who died in 1969, was a symbol to be worshipped by a quarter of a million young people who turned up in Hyde Park in July. Instead of being welcomed in his homeland as an upholder of British values, Humphrey became – albeit briefly – a symbol of all that was stuffy and reactionary in the older generation. These incidents at Birmingham and East Anglia pale into insignificance, however, when set against the widespread and often violent student protests of the late 1960s.[774]

One other formal event awaited the Gibbses before their return home. They were invited to a dinner in their honour at 10 Downing Street. They had dined with Harold Wilson before, or rather he had dined with them, during his rather stormy visit to Salisbury just before UDI. Downing Street provided a cooler and even more splendid setting for a black tie dinner. Humphrey sat on Harold Wilson's right, opposite Alec Douglas-Home, and next to the Foreign Secretary's wife, Mrs Stewart. George Thomson was there, as were the Thorpes. It was a generous tribute. A week later they were seen off at Waterloo by Maurice Foley, Parliamentary Under-Secretary at the Foreign and Commonwealth Office (FCO). Neither Humphrey not Molly was feeling particularly well, the train journey was 'slightly depressing', and they arrived in Southampton to find it was snowing.[775] However, their spirits lifted since Simon was there to see them off, they were given VIP status and were able to 'dodge customs and immigration' before boarding the *Pendennis Castle*. The gift of a crate of champagne awaiting them in their cabin further lifted their spirits. But as they were enjoying their journey to warmer climes, an embarrassing row blew up in England.

Mindy Bacon had been working quietly behind the scenes to ensure that there was some suitable financial settlement for the ex-Governor, who had received no income during the UDI years. He had therefore felt obliged to pay for the entire establishment at Government House from his own resources and those supplied by the Governor's Fund. Mindy had discussed the matter of funding when he was in Rhodesia, but had found during his 1966 and 1967 visits that Humphrey had been reluctant to talk about it, and unwilling to think about what might happen when he retired. But in 1969, after the referendum, Mindy had been able to take the subject further. Although Humphrey would be due a Governor's pension (of some £1800 per annum) Mindy felt that in addition he was due 'a sum of money equal to that of which he was out of pocket'.[776] The matter had already been raised in the House of Commons by Michael Hamilton who had asked, following the announcement that the Governor would retire, if 'the personal financial sacrifice of the Governor [would] be remedied'. Michael Stewart had replied, 'that is perhaps not a matter for discussion here, but I have it in mind'.[777] So events were already in train when Bacon visited the Foreign and Commonwealth Office early in July, immediately after returning from Salisbury, and had discussions with James Bottomley, who had of course seen for himself the situation at Government House during the Thomson visit of November 1968.[778] Mindy was able to tell Humphrey in August that a financial settlement would indeed be forthcoming, and advised him to place his financial affairs in the hands of experts in London. Having consulted Deloittes, Humphrey was directed to a legal firm, Linklaters, who were commissioned to make whatever arrangements were needed, especially in view of the fact that Humphrey did not want the money for himself, but was determined that it should go into a trust for the benefit of his wife and children. This point he made forcibly when he visited the FCO to talk with Bottomley the day before his departure from England.[779] Bottomley also told Humphrey that the announcement of the award would be made 'by means of an arranged Parliamentary Question and written answer before the Christmas recess', without waiting for details of the proposed trust to be worked out.

The announcement was duly made on Friday 19 December.[780] By means of a written answer, Mr Foley stated that 'a suitable grant should be made as an expression of gratitude to Sir Humphrey for his outstanding record of service to the Crown in Southern Rhodesia'. The press headlines that followed put an unfortunate gloss on the award: 'Golden handout for "our man in Rhodesia"';[781] 'Sir Humphrey gets £66,000 for loyalty';[782] '£66,000 gift to Gibbs puzzles MPs'.[783] The *Daily Mirror* was nearer the mark with 'Gibbs "wasn't paid for 4 years"'.[784] But, as Eric Faulkner of Lloyds Bank noted, the problem arose from the impression that the award to Sir Humphrey, and those to his staff which were included in the total, were seen as 'grants in appreciation'.[785] This was not entirely Mr Foley's fault; in fact the fault lay with Sir Alec Douglas-Home who had tabled the question, which had asked what financial arrangements were being made 'to mark appreciation of the loyal services to the Crown of Sir Humphrey Gibbs and the former members of his household'. The impression given was that the money was a reward for loyalty. Different wording would have made clear that it was to make up for lost earnings and expenses incurred. Given the wording used, however, the reaction to the announcement was predictable. It was denounced by Canon Collins and the Anti-Apartheid Movement, and by the Labour former Cabinet Minister, Richard Marsh – perhaps still smarting from his demotion from the Cabinet. A different sort of reaction came from Mr and Mrs Barbanell, who in a letter to *The Times* praised Sir Humphrey's stand during UDI, but asked plaintively whether since 'exchange controls can be circumvented in this case', they could also be relaxed in favour of people like themselves, who had left Rhodesia with no more than the permitted £100 of their assets.[786] The Tory back-bencher, John Biggs-Davidson, always a scourge of the government in matters relating to Rhodesia, said that he would be raising the matter of the award to Sir Humphrey in the House of Commons after the Christmas recess. Perhaps someone had a word with him, because when parliament reassembled his question to the Foreign Secretary was merely, 'may we be told when the sanctions will begin to bite?'[787] The timing of the announcement had been clever, even if the wording had not been, because no more was heard of the matter in public after the Christmas break.

However, although there was no further public debate about the award, the complexities of sorting it out ran on for years. There was the question of how much should be paid, and with what justification. This meant furnishing details of the payments made from the Governor's own bank account. But it also meant calculating how much of – for instance – the £6500 spend during the UDI years on liquor and tobacco was expense incurred as a result of UDI. The calculation was not that the strain of UDI had necessitated heavier smoking and drinking, but rather that the Governor had had to pay tax on these articles, which before UDI he had been entitled to purchase tax-free. The sum owing to him, therefore, would be the tax element, which in this case was calculated at some £3000. It then emerged that the total settlement would incur tax in Rhodesia, and since a Governor's income was untaxed, there was a need to adjust the settlement to cover the tax which the Rhodesian authorities were unwilling to waive. The decision had been taken early on by the Governor that he would receive nothing, and that the whole sum would be for the benefit of Lady Gibbs and their children. It was not until March 1973 that the final payments into the trust, as well as the tax liability in Rhodesia, were finally settled, and Mindy Bacon was able to report to Sir Alec Douglas-Home (now once again Foreign Secretary) that the matter was closed.[788] In fact it was not closed as far as the Government House staff were concerned, since they belatedly found themselves liable to tax in Rhodesia for payments made to them under the parliamentary grant. Like Sir Humphrey, they found that the legal and tax experts in Salisbury were unable to shift the regime in this matter, and they appealed to the British government. Finally, in November 1974, the issue was resolved for John Pestell, Belle Baxter the secretary, and Christopher Owen the ADC, when the British government agreed to make up the difference.[789] Over five years after the closure of Government House in Salisbury, the Government House staff could finally regard their service there as having been fully recognised and compensated.

14   Retirement at Bonisa

Humphrey was sixty-seven when he and Molly returned from England at the end of their long visit in late 1969. It was a matter now of adjusting to the normal features of retirement. There were the financial problems, still unresolved as far as the British government's grant was concerned, and exacerbated by a run of poor seasons on the farm. Humphrey managed to pick up a few directorships – notably the Chairmanship of Barclays Bank in Rhodesia – but at his age could not contemplate amassing the sort of portfolio he had enjoyed in the 1950s. There were the deaths of his contemporaries. Archbishop Paget died in April 1971 at the age of eighty-five, and there were memorial services for him in the cathedrals at Bulawayo and Salisbury. A month later, Lord Malvern, 'Huggie', died, just two months short of his eighty-eighth birthday. Humphrey had attended his last birthday celebration the year before, in company with a fine selection of the old guard who had survived from happier days: Sir Roy Welensky, Sir Robert Tredgold, Sir Ernest Guest and Sir Malcolm Barrow. At the funeral service for Huggie in Salisbury Cathedral, Father Holderness linked those two giants of Federation days together in Paradise – 'Think of that vigorous comradeship going on.'[790] Edgar Whitehead, a few years younger than Humphrey, also died in 1971, having left the country to settle with his sister in England, increasingly cut off from his friends and the world by his continuing deafness and worsening blindness. Humphrey unveiled a plaque to him in the Cathedral Cloisters in Salisbury in 1972. There were other more personal losses. In July 1975, his brother Geoffrey died, as did his sister-in-law Helen four years later. They had been close to Humphrey and Molly, and had brought good cheer and comfort to Government House during the UDI period. Another close friend and relative died in 1976 – Charles Ponsonby, his brother-in-law, whom Humphrey could remember in that cricket match at Hunsdon as the First World War broke out. Then in 1978 Beatrix, his eldest brother's widow, died. But old age brings not only the passing of contemporaries, but the birth of a new generation. Two grandchildren were born in 1970 – a son to Nigel and a daughter to Kenneth. Nigel's second son was born in 1972, and Kenneth's first a year later. Further grandchildren were to be expected, when Simon married in 1974 and Tim in 1978.

Humphrey was himself fitter now than he had been. As life slipped back into a more even and quiet rhythm at Bonisa, he began to put on some weight, perhaps aided by the fact that early in 1971 he gave up smoking.[791] He had been a sixty-a-day man, in a country where smoking was, by English standards, incredibly inexpensive. Perhaps the stress of the UDI years had sent his consumption up. Now there were fewer worries. As the 1970s wore on, one small worry arose. Humphrey and Molly decided that they had no longer any need for their collection of silver, much of which had come out from England after their marriage. They now sent it back to England for distribution among the three children who were there. But the consignment, worth, it was estimated, some £4000, was impounded by Customs, on the grounds that imports from Rhodesia were prohibited, even though all the proper paperwork had been completed. Dame Molly decided that this was an issue which she herself would take up.[792] She had shared Humphrey's burdens at Government House, but had always steered clear of involvement in the political and constitutional discussions which went on there. Sometimes she was unaware of the meetings Humphrey was having with Ian Smith or others. Humphrey had always tried to be non-political; she was even more so. Now however she was stirred into action, no longer constrained by her role as Governor's wife. She wrote to *The Times*, and in a reference to recent revelations about the British government turning a blind eye to oil companies circumventing sanctions, she commented: 'It appears sadly ironical to me that the Bingham Report seems to show that Her Majesty's Government knowingly took a course of action that perpetuated a regime in this country that this family has, through two generations and at considerable personal cost, opposed.'[793] Patrick Wall MP took up the issue and put down a question in the House of Commons,[794] but even before it was answered, the Prime Minister himself had become involved. Just after Christmas 1978 he was able to assure Michael Hamilton that in view of 'Sir Humphrey Gibbs's unique position and the exceptional services he has rendered to the Crown', the normal rules were to be waived and the silver released.[795] One of the reasons Molly gave for their wish to send the silver to England was the 'real possibility of our home being destroyed by terrorist action'. This was, as it happens, a very prophetic remark, rather than a realistic assessment of the current situation in Matabeleland. While Humphrey no longer had any official responsibilities within the country, the fact was that the quality of his life in retirement was bound up with the rapidly changing situation in Rhodesia.

Rhodesia had become a Republic on 2 March 1970, 'an event which passed almost without notice inside the country'.[796] Effectively it had been a republic since Humphrey vacated Government House eight months earlier. Soon afterwards, and confounding the pollsters, the Conservatives had come to power in Britain. Alec Douglas-Home, now Foreign and Commonwealth Secretary, again found himself facing up to the challenge of Rhodesia, which he had last had governmental dealings with in 1964 as Prime Minister. Since then, he had visited the country, and despite the odd lapse (such as when he made what Humphrey thought was political capital out of the impounding of Sir Frederick Crawford's passport in 1968) he had supported the Labour governments' handling of the Rhodesia problem. And indeed he made use of the same emissaries Wilson had used before *Fearless*. Sir Max Aitken and Lord Goodman were again dispatched to Salisbury in April 1971. Further visits led to full-scale talks between Ian Smith and a British team headed by Sir Alec, who arrived in November. He signed an agreement with Ian Smith. 'The final product is as good as I think we had any right to expect and a good deal better than often seemed possible', he wrote to Goodman at the conclusion of the talks.[797] There was to be no 'interim government' and no appeal to the Privy Council, but the 'provisional settlement was within the Five Principles – if only just within'.[798] In the long run, the Africans would have a majority, and not merely parity, in the Assembly. The 'long run' was however likely to be a lot longer than had been envisaged at *Tiger* or *Fearless*. A critical aspect was that there was to be a test of acceptability of the proposals, and in early 1972 a team headed by Lord Pearce arrived to implement that test. They travelled the country. They took soundings. They received submissions. One was from Sir Humphrey Gibbs. He had had no involvement with politics since his departure from Government House, but here at last there seemed to be the possibility of a settlement. It would be particularly pleasing if it were to be one that had been crafted by his old friend, Alec. In a letter to the Commission on 16 February Humphrey wrote:

> While I was Governor and since leaving Government House I have been careful to avoid giving anyone an opportunity to accuse me of taking any part in politics. It would have been wrong for Her Majesty's representative to do so while in office and I think for several years afterwards as well.
>
> However, having been asked by the Press and many others for my views on the settlement proposals, which I regard as a National rather than a political matter, I have decided that it is my duty to make this short statement.
>
> Ever since the day of UDI I have been hoping for a settlement of our dispute with the United Kingdom and we now have a very good chance to break the deadlock in which we find ourselves. There is no point in discussing the merits or otherwise of UDI. The past is past and it is the future of Rhodesia which is our concern.
>
> The choice before us appears to me to be a very simple one – we can only do one of two things: firstly, we can say 'No' to the proposals and continue as we are under the 1969 Constitution; secondly, we can accept the proposals as they are but without any amendment.

I think some of us have got a bit confused and think that by saying 'No' we may be able to improve on the settlement terms.

It is quite clear to me that the choice is between 'Yes' or 'No' only and Lord Pearce and his Commission have stressed this on many occasions.

What is possible, however is that if we say 'Yes', the settlement proposals can be improved on by common consent as found desirable, at any time in the future. Amendments have to be agreed by both the Africans and Europeans voting separately.

A 'Yes' vote, therefore, as opposed to a 'No' vote does mean that the door is open.

Normal trading relations with other countries can be renewed, our exports will no longer be restricted by sanctions. We will regain recognition by other countries. Our economy must advance more quickly with the boost it will have, not only from the United Kingdom's £50,000,000 grant over ten years for education and TTL development, but also from increased investment from the private sector.

I therefore recommend the proposals most earnestly to my fellow Rhodesians I would stress again that in my view this matter is a national one of great concern to us all.[799]

The new proposals were welcomed widely within the white community; Humphrey was voicing the concerns and hopes that were felt not only by 'liberals', but by a widening constituency of whites, particularly in the business and farming communities. Overwhelmingly the new proposals were accepted by the whites, though the Centre Party did register its qualified 'Yes' on the basis of 'our acceptance of Hobson's choice'.[800] But the Pearce Report concluded that 'we have no doubt from all the facts and circumstances and our own observation that ... the Africans' rejection by a substantial majority was a genuine expression of opinion'.[801] It marked the end of a road travelled by the British and Rhodesian governments ever since the first contact between the two had been established, via the Governor, in the months after UDI. Joshua Nkomo, while saying 'No', declared that the Africans were 'prepared to work resolutely for a constitutional settlement that will give peace and security to all citizens of our country irrespective of colour'.[802] But for the next seven years in Rhodesia, the motor of change would not be discussion and debate – though there would be much of that – but rather military and external factors.

The guerrilla war intensified. In mid-1975 the call-up was extended to all white eighteen-year-old school leavers. The newspapers were full of stories of death and destruction, affecting both the whites, particularly farmers and soldiers, and blacks, especially the rural population. The death toll mounted.

And the balance of power shifted dramatically within white Southern Africa. A month before the Pearce Report was published, the authoritarian regime in Portugal was overthrown, and the new left wing government pledged itself to abandoning its African empire. As a result, by the end of 1975 Mozambique was in the hands of a revolutionary left-wing government under Samora Machel, thus exposing the whole of Rhodesia's eastern border to terrorist (or freedom fighter) incursions. Humphrey Gibbs was merely an anxious onlooker as these events unfolded, though there was a family involvement in the affairs of state, as Tim had become a leading light in the Rhodesia Party. This emerged in 1973, replacing the virtually defunct Centre Party as the main vehicle for 'liberal' opinion. It polled 22.4 per cent of the vote in the 1974 general election and although 'we were disappointed', Tim Gibbs wrote that nevertheless 'we have come out of this as a Party like there has not been since UDI'.[803] As with so many 'liberal' hopes in Rhodesia in the thirty years since the world war it proved to be a chimera. Yet there were evident grounds for such hope. There was discontent within the white community, especially among the farmers who bore the brunt of the bush war on the white side. They had been a powerful influence in shifting the balance politically towards the Rhodesian Front. They had a stake in the country which was more permanent than, say, that of the business community. If they were discontented, if they thought that an alternative government would serve their, and their country's, interests better than the Smith regime, then there was hope that change might be possible. They were not – in most cases – liberals, but they might add weight to that cause. But liberal white opinion, which had always tended to express itself with a 20–25 per cent vote at the polls, was as divided as it had been in the mid-1960s. A classic example of this was the debacle in the Highlands North constituency – possibly a winnable seat for a 'liberal'. At the general election in 1974 the now tiny Centre Party put up a candidate, as did Tim Gibbs' Rhodesia Party. But Allan Savory, former RP leader and now further to the left, also stood. The three way split ensured the election of the Rhodesian Front candidate.[804] Humphrey must have felt a certain *déjà vu* as he watched that, thinking of all the 'lost chances' in Rhodesia over the previous twenty years. No longer the intermediary, he was an observer of the shuttle diplomacy of the mid-1970s. Tim himself got involved in that when he flew to Gaborone in 1975 to meet James Callaghan, the British Foreign Secretary, who just over a year later was to succeed Harold Wilson as Prime Minister. For Tim it was a visit 'aimed at achieving greater understanding on all sides', and at 'putting across the varied points of view of Rhodesian Europeans'.[805] The Callaghan mission achieved little or nothing to further negotiations, and indeed the British were somewhat peripheral to the subsequent talks which took place. Smith's negotiations in these years involved meetings with the various leaders of African opinion, Nkomo in 1975 and Abel Muzorewa in 1978. David Owen, the young British Foreign Secretary, made Britain's voice heard, but he was outclassed by two Americans, Andrew Young and Henry Kissinger who had become involved in the negotiations. The huge difference now with these talks and visits was that, unlike those of the 1960s in which Humphrey had been involved, they took place against a background of mounting violence as the bush war intensified. Even in the midst of Tim's involvement as President of the Rhodesia Party, however, Humphrey felt little confidence in the outcome. Despite his experiences in the 1960s, then and later he had tended to be upbeat. But that was no longer the case. The bush war, and particularly the massacres of missionaries, school children, and farmers, must have been painful to read about. 'At last', John Pestell reported in August 1975, 'Humphrey's unbounded optimism about Rhodesia's future has come to an end', for 'Smith was saying the same old things and getting nowhere'.[806] Perhaps Humphrey's outlook was affected by personal problems. There was the 'very bad spell on the farm' which he was experiencing that year. It was all 'pretty disastrous', he wrote, after an 'unusual heavy rainy season which weakened the cattle'.[807]

1977 was the year of Queen's Silver Jubilee. Rhodesia was now a republic but for Humphrey and his like, that was a technicality. They still felt loyalty to the British monarch. Robin Plunket conceived the idea of sending a presentation to the Queen to mark the occasion, though he was aware that there were difficulties and it would have to be clear that not all Rhodesians were or would want to be involved.[808] Humphrey, who had spoken recently on television about the forthcoming jubilee, was even more apprehensive, and suggested instead that there should be a message of loyalty from himself, Tredgold and Welensky – her three Privy Councillors in Rhodesia. 'I omit Hugh Beadle', he wrote, 'as I expect none of us would sign if his signature was included.' As there were no official channels of communication between Britain and Rhodesia, Humphrey felt that such a message would be more appropriate, and that Robin Plunket would be sure to know how to have it delivered personally to the Queen's Private Secretary.[809] Roy Welensky had gone ahead, however, and purchased a silver salver which would be inscribed 'a gift to Her Majesty Queen Elizabeth the Second to mark her Silver Jubilee and is presented by a number of her Rhodesian subjects'. Welensky invited a small contribution, but he made the point that there should be no publicity.[810] Humphrey and Robbie Tredgold were still dubious about the wisdom of such a presentation, but Welensky had worked quickly and in the event his letters to potential subscribers had been so successful that neither of them was required to contribute.[811] The loyal address was however also dispatched, and Martin Charteris, the Queen's Private Secretary, wrote – tongue in cheek – to thank them for the address from 'the "great majority" of Rhodesia's Privy Counsellors!'[812]

Shuttle diplomacy on the national scene, as well as guerrilla warfare, continued unabated throughout 1977 and 1978. But 1979 saw the period of most dramatic changes. The year opened with a referendum. A decade before, it had been a referendum which gave a resounding 'yes' to a republic and brought Humphrey's governorship to a close. This time there was an equally firm 'yes' to majority rule.[813] Soon there followed a government decision to end all forms of racial discrimination.[814] On 1 June 1979 Zimbabwe-Rhodesia was born, and a black president took office. By the end of the year, a new Conservative government was in office in Britain, but this time there would be no negotiations with the Rhodesian government. After the Commonwealth Heads of Government summit at Lusaka in August 1979, the new Foreign Secretary Lord Carrington issued invitations to all parties to constitutional talks at Lancaster House in London. The aim was to establish a form of government which would be acceptable to the world community as well as to all the peoples of what was now again regarded as a colony. A British Governor was to be dispatched to Salisbury. It was as if the clock had been turned back to June 1969. Or, more dramatically it could be said that 'it was the first time in the history of decolonization that a black President had been displaced by a white Governor'.[815] It was an astonishing year, not least in terms of heads of state. In January the President was Jack Pithey, who as President of the Senate had taken over from Lieutenant-Colonel Henry Everard, who resigned in November 1978 at the age of eighty-one, and in failing health. He had been acting President since the death (or as many believed, the suicide) of John Wrathall the previous August. In May the first black head of state, Josiah Gumede, was sworn in. So in the space of seventeen months the country had four heads of state, when in December, Queen Elizabeth again exercised that role, with as her representative in the colony Lord Soames, son-in-law of Winston Churchill.[816] And on 12 December, Humphrey Gibbs was again at Government House. A decade before, a crowd had gathered there to see him off. Now he was a part of the crowd that assembled to welcome his successor as Governor of the colony. As Christopher Soames arrived to take up residence in Government House, Humphrey waved along with the rest. Beside him, a woman was waving a large and faded Union Jack. In its corner was the signature, 'Humphrey Gibbs'. It was the flag that had been lowered on Humphrey's last day as Governor. Ian Smith's attitude to Soames' arrival was rather different. 'When he drove to Government House', Smith later wrote, 'there was a handful of people with a Union Jack to welcome him – the same old bunch of starry-eyed liberals who had always been petrified at the thought of standing alone in this world. They now heaved a sigh of relief at once more being able to cling on to the mother country's apron strings.'[817]

A whole decade had passed and Humphrey had been on the sidelines, watching and hoping as talks were followed by talks, and as yet more awful massacres took place, even in this last year before the restoration of British rule. There were some resonances from the past. Harold Wilson had been accused of dragging the Queen into politics, and certainly he had tried playing the royal card in a bid to trump Ian Smith. It had not worked. Now in 1979, and with only the lukewarm support of her Prime Minister, the Queen had attended the Lusaka summit of the Commonwealth Heads of Government, which resulted in the convening of the Lancaster House talks. 'The fact that she was there made it happen', the Commonwealth Secretary General asserted.[818] But some things did not change. As Humphrey stood outside Government House to welcome his successor, Ian Smith had 'decided to boycott' Soames' arrival, despite having been invited to be present on the tarmac. He had, however, been present in parliament the previous day to observe the passing of the bill which finally terminated his fourteen years of UDI.[819]

Later on the day of Soames' arrival, Humphrey and Molly entered Government House again for the first time in a decade. They were present at the Governor's drinks party. Christopher Soames, who had not met Humphrey before, commented of his predecessor afterwards, 'What a magnificent man.'[820] There was further contact between the two. The next day, Humphrey wrote to Soames to suggest the names of people the new Governor might find helpful to meet: people like Bishop Burrough, Ken Mew, Sir Henry McDowell, and C. G. Tracey.[821] Humphrey did not have an opportunity to follow this up as well as he might. When Lord and Lady Soames attended a lunch in their honour at the Bulawayo Club on 4 January 1980, their intention had been to go on to spend a night at Bonisa with Humphrey and Molly. However the security situation was such that the Governor felt he ought to cut short his stay and get back to Salisbury as soon as possible. Humphrey nevertheless gave some assistance in suggesting names for possible honours. It was a roll-call of what might be called the last remains of the liberal establishment: Evan Campbell, Sir Henry McDowell, Bob Newson, Bob Williams, the RC Archbishop and the Anglican Bishop, General Sam Putterill, Brian O'Connell, Muriel Rosin, and Ken Mew.[822] He warmed to his subject in further letters both to Sir Antony Duff at Government House, and to others from whom he took soundings. But in the end he accepted that, as Sir Antony wrote, 'it would be very difficult and probably unacceptably invidious to attempt to pick out now those people who, over the years, have deserved well of HMG'. The Governor had decided therefore that the matter should be left for the moment, but that the incoming British High Commissioner should be apprised of the situation, so that he could furnish some of the names as part of his half-yearly lists of recommendations.[823]

Humphrey and Molly attended the great reception at Government House just prior to independence, and took the opportunity to meet some of their black staff who were still employed there. It was probably the last great colonial occasion in the country, as the Gibbses and Todds and Putterills mingled with the new black ministers designate. A week later, the Union Jack came down finally at Rufaro Stadium on 18 April, and Prince Charles represented his mother at this the last such ceremony on the continent of Africa. Eleven years earlier, Humphrey had watched what he must have thought was the last lowering of the Union flag, on the evening before his departure from Government House. Then, he had been depressed and saddened by the events which had driven him into retirement; it had been as if he was being exiled to his farm in the new Republic of Rhodesia. Now Molly and Humphrey returned to Bonisa as citizens of the new Republic of Zimbabwe.

Now, perhaps, a proper and peaceful retirement could begin. Humphrey was seventy-eight when the new country was born. Tim could run the farm, and Humphrey and Molly could enjoy their ever increasing number of grandchildren, one of whom – Tim's son – was with them at Bonisa. Humphrey and Molly both had plenty of interests to keep them occupied, and their range of charitable activities was impressive. The Red Cross, St John Ambulance, the Bulawayo Orchestra, the Matabeleland Sea Cadet Corps, the Leprosy Mission, the Gun Dog Club, the Tree Society, the St Joseph's House for Boys, the Wildlife Protection Society, Jairos Jiri (an organisation for helping the handicapped) – these were a few of the good causes which they continued to support. Humphrey had been Patron or President of some seventy organisations while Governor,[824] and he and Molly were still called upon to help, patronise and support many of these. Humphrey in addition kept up his membership of the Bulawayo Club (and reciprocal membership of the Salisbury Club), and was still active in the affairs of Peterhouse and of the Ruzawi Group of Schools. And of course, despite their advancing years and the length of the drive, Humphrey and Molly were still to be found in their pew at Sunday worship each week in Bulawayo Cathedral.

Their new country enjoyed an auspicious start. Mugabe and Nkomo agreed to form a coalition government. Even before his victory at the polls, Robert Mugabe was calling upon the whites to stay in the country.[825] When he formed his government, white ministers were appointed. Two of them, David Smith and Chris Andersen, had served in Ian Smith's administration. Denis Norman, a former President of the Rhodesia National Farmers Union, became Minister of Agriculture, much to the relief of the powerful white farming community. There were still twenty seats reserved for whites in the assembly. *The Times* noted approvingly the 'middle way' which the new Prime Minister seemed to be adopting between communism and capitalism.[826] The new republic joined the Commonwealth. and was declared to be 'non-aligned'. And it was given a propitious start by the weather: good rains ensured a bumper harvest during the first two years of the new regime.

For some, though not for Humphrey and Molly, the transition was too much to take. It was a time 'when old value systems had been up-ended and old devils had suddenly become gods; when witch doctors became traditional healers and formed their own trade union; when servants insisted on being called domestic workers, joined the Party, acquired a surname and demanded the minimum wage. When you could be prosecuted for calling a black adult "boy" and thrown into jail if you breathed the word "kaffir".'[827] Many whites could not stomach the changes, and left. Many, however, stayed, and some returned from abroad to take part in the new multiracial experiment. Sadly however, there was trouble on the horizon, and tragically for the Gibbs family – as for many others – it centred on Matabeleland. That south-western part of the country had seen only a little of the guerrilla war: the north and east of the country had suffered most during the 1970s. Now however a different problem arose. Less than two years after independence, the 'thin membrane of the tribal alliance' between the followers of Mugabe and the followers of Nkomo was 'ripped apart'.[828] Joshua Nkomo, Minister of Home Affairs and effectively deputy Prime Minister, was accused by Mugabe of plotting a *coup d'état*. Arms caches, ostensibly belonging to Nkomo's followers, were found in Matabeleland.[829] The North Korean trained 'Fifth Brigade' was soon to move through the province hunting out people who had come to be called 'dissidents'.

The tribal vendetta which by early 1983 seemed to be under way in Matabeleland, was overshadowed for whites by other events. In March 1982 the government had 'disclosed' that former Army commander Peter Walls was in South Africa 'organising a gang plotting to carry out acts of sabotage in Zimbabwe'.[830] In June there was a mortar attack on the official residence of the Prime Minister. In July the Zimbabwe Air Force lost a quarter of its aircraft, blown up on the ground at Thornhill airbase near Gweru. Seven white Air Force officers were arrested, and though they did not come to trial for almost a year, there were disturbing reports soon after their arrest that they had been tortured.[831] Whites came under attack. A farmer was shot dead at

Headlands (in the eastern part of the country) in June, and in early August two British tourists were murdered a half-hour drive further east near the tourist area of Inyanga. Towards the end of the year, there was a gun battle near Nyamandhlovu when seven 'dissidents' were killed in a skirmish with paratroopers. The year ended with two chilling events, all too reminiscent of the incidents which had marked the guerrilla war in the 1970s. There was the murder of a white Lonhro farm manager, his two young sons, and three Africans, on the main Bulawayo–Victoria Falls road. And there was the abduction of two farmers near Turk Mine, about forty miles east of Bonisa, one of whom was later found beheaded. Christmas on the farm for the Gibbses was overshadowed by this mounting local violence. In the New Year things did not improve. In March 1983 a white farmer and his wife, along with their grand-daughters aged ten and eleven, were murdered not far from Bonisa. There was growing fear among the four hundred or so white farmers in Matabeleland that they were 'being targeted for revenge killings following the recent ruthless campaign by government troops which left many Ndebele civilians dead'.[832] They decided to form their own militia to protect themselves, moderated later to reliance upon Fawcett's Security, a private firm, employing guards under government licence. Humphrey and Molly had to carry guns as they went about the farm – no life for a retired couple. It was one of these guards who 'went berserk while drunk' and took pot-shots at Molly's car.[833] He was disarmed before any more damage was done, but it was a disturbing incident. In their locality, the number of white farmers declined: some were killed, and others left and put their farms up for sale. At independence there were sixty white farmers in the Nyamandhlovu area; by mid-1983 the number had dropped to about twenty-five.[834]

Among those who decided to leave were the Gibbses. For Tim and his family, the obvious answer was to join his other brothers in England, and see what employment he could find there. For Humphrey and Molly, the matter was not so simple. When the newspapers first got hold of the story, they reported that they were to 'leave Zimbabwe ... because they no longer feel safe here'.[835] However within a few days it was reported that Humphrey had 'changed his mind about leaving Zimbabwe ... [and] intended to buy a house in Harare'.[836] It was obvious that they should leave Matabeleland, but to leave the country which had been Humphrey's home for over half a century was not so attractive a prospect. It soon became clear that they would be able to stay in the country with a decent standard of living, and with the means to fly to see their family on an annual basis should they wish to, if Bonisa were sold and the funds invested. It was a long and complicated business. The farm had been in quarantine since June because of foot and mouth, which hampered selling the herd off as a separate entity, at least for the present. There were not all that many people around with some $500,000 available to purchase the property, and of course the dissident threat was the chief disincentive to purchasers.[837] By October they had decided that they would move to a comfortable house in the Salisbury suburb of Borrowdale, and live off the invested income when the farm was sold.

In early 1984, they settled into their new house in Dornie Road, Borrowdale. It was a modest property by northern suburbs standards – in effect a large bungalow such as might be found in the south-east of England, though with a larger garden than its British equivalent. In other roads nearby, great Cape Dutch villas and residences of ambassadorial proportions gave the suburb an air of millionaires' row in the tropics, a sort of Beverly Hills crossed with Hampstead. Good local shops and plentiful servants ensured a pleasant lifestyle for the inhabitants of Borrowdale. Although Molly still had her painting, Humphrey no longer had a farm to look after, or even to prowl around. It is not surprising therefore that he found a new interest in life – fund-raising for the school of which he had been a governor since its inception. He had been on the initial planning committee for Peterhouse in 1953.

15 Epilogue

It was said in the early 1980s that all too many white Rhodesians who still lived in the country had not yet emigrated to Zimbabwe: that is, they remained at heart – and sometimes vocally too – committed to a way of life and a country that no longer existed. That was not true of Humphrey and Molly Gibbs. They moved from Matabeleland to Harare. They had already emigrated, mentally and spiritually, from a Rhodesia which for fifteen years had not been the sort of country they wanted to live in, to the new Zimbabwe, which was the country to which they were now committed.

Just as the Gibbses were moving to Harare, I emigrated to Zimbabwe. I was moving, with my wife and two children, from a housemastership in a Surrey public school to the headship of a school in a country which I did not know. I had been appointed Rector of Peterhouse, the school of which Sir Humphrey had been a governor since its inception. We moved into the Rector's Lodge at Peterhouse late in 1983. As we were settling in, some fifty miles away Humphrey and Molly were moving into their new house in Dornie Road, Borrowdale, in the northern suburbs of Harare. Humphrey had been on the initial planning committee for Peterhouse in 1953, even before it had a name, or a site. He had attended its Speech Days regularly, and even during the UDI years when he could not attend, his regret at being unable to do so was always put on record. He became fired by the idea of aiding the further development of the school.

Just as he was deciding to move from Matabeleland, and as I was preparing to move from England, the independent schools in Zimbabwe were in a state of crisis. It was a crisis caused by the Prime Minister. When he had taken office in 1980, Robert Mugabe had declared publicly that 'fee-paying non-racial church schools like Peterhouse would not be touched'.[838] It came as a shock, therefore, when he was reported to have attacked independent schools at various political rallies in the 'communal areas'.[839] His concern, subsequently spelt out by the Minister of Education in November 1983, focused on the 'racist' nature of these schools. There were only some thirty of them in the country, and like their counterparts in Britain, they charged high fees, had small classes, mostly had Christian foundations, and catered mainly for the economic and social elite. The Minister recognised that during the UDI years 'the independent schools saw themselves not only as fighting for the underdog, but also as pioneering attempts at creating a just and equitable society in which harmony and co-operation between the races would ensure a prosperous and peaceful future for the country as a whole'.[840]

That was a fair, even generous summary. All the independent schools in theory, and most in practice, had followed the lead set by Peterhouse and St George's (the Roman Catholic school in Harare) in admitting black pupils after 1964. Despite obstacles placed in their way by the government, most had taken in the maximum they could within the law – a mere 6 per cent. The Minister was concerned that after independence these schools 'froze in their tracks and, in many cases, back-pedalled'. This was not entirely true, though it may have looked that way. The year 1979 saw the opening up of the former white 'government' (that is, state) schools to all races. These were schools with excellent facilities and staff. Many black parents lost any desire they might have had to send their children to independent schools (either as full fee-paying or on bursaries) when for minimal cost they could use these former preserves of the whites. Black pupils at Peterhouse, for instance, accounted for 13 per cent of the school in 1980. This had fallen to 12 per cent in 1983, not because Peterhouse discouraged them, but because they did not want to come. After much negotiation the crisis passed. My first few months as a headmaster in Zimbabwe were taken up with meetings with Ministry of Education officials, and occasionally with the Minister himself. Subsequently independent schools made more overt and energetic attempts to recruit more non-European pupils. Nevertheless the 'scare' of 1983/84 had made independent schools, and their governing bodies, more aware of their responsibilities to Zimbabwe, and more conscious of the high profile they would necessarily have in a new nation which took education very seriously and on which it spent more in its budget than on any other single item.

In the light of all this, Peterhouse expanded. Not only was there a continuing demand from whites, but there was an increasing demand from blacks, as the government schools became overcrowded. They also suffered an ongoing haemorrhage of good and experienced teachers, mainly white ones who emigrated, but also black ones who found more lucrative employment in other areas. In 1984 Peterhouse acquired a redundant school and its campus. Springvale Preparatory School, just across the main road from Peterhouse, had closed during the bush war, and now its 1000 acres and its buildings were available for our use. In 1985 a preparatory school opened there. In 1986 the beginnings of a girls' school started on the same site. By the beginning of the academic year in 1987, there were 515 boys at Peterhouse (as opposed to the 383 there had been in 1983); in addition the prep school had 170 pupils, and the newly started girls' school had 34. It was becoming obvious that an enormous injection of funds was required if the schools were to thrive and develop. Funding was required in two significant areas: one was to provide the new buildings needed by all three sections of the growing Peterhouse enterprise; the other was to provide sufficient bursarial help for those – especially blacks – who desired and would benefit from a Peterhouse education, but whose parents could not afford the fees.

A campaign was devised under the patronage of three of the school's governors: Didymus Mutasa, the first black Speaker of the House of Assembly, Peter Hatendi, the first black Bishop of Mashonaland (soon to be renamed Harare), and Sir Humphrey Gibbs. It was Humphrey who, as well as patronising the appeal, threw himself into supporting and encouraging it most actively. His range of contacts in the United Kingdom and in Zimbabwe was extensive. While plans were devised for a major fund-raising appeal, largely using those contacts, Robert Mugabe agreed to attend the school's Speech Day in 1987. There were those, particularly among the farming community who formed a significant sector of the parents, who were dubious about the invitation. But the Board of Governors was enthusiastic. His visit – despite the mammoth security precautions which disrupted school life before and during the day – was a huge success. Mr Mugabe spoke enthusiastically of the school as a 'trail-blazer' in Zimbabwe, which, he continued, 'still needs your contribution: your pupils must continue to achieve high standards in the classroom, on the games field, and in terms of racial harmony'. And in an uncharacteristically jocular way he praised the school for expanding, especially into girls' education, and said that 'It is to be hoped, nay urged, that other schools which may still be wedded to the old pro-male approach will see the light and go the Peterhouse way.'[841] At the end of the ceremony, as Bob Williams prepared to lead the Prime Minister down the aisle of the large school chapel where the proceedings had taken place, I was concerned to see the founding Rector, Fred Snell, dart from his place in the front pews and dash down the aisle. Fred Snell had retired as Rector in 1968 and although he was a year younger than Humphrey, he now seemed older and more frail. When the platform party reached the great west door of the chapel, Fred Snell embraced the Prime Minister and said, with tears streaming down his face, 'This is a moment I have lived for.' Humphrey and I looked on, and one was reminded of the prophetic words that Fred Snell had himself spoken, which had been sent to the Prime Minister and had been quoted by him just half an hour before, of 'the hope of the emergence in the next twenty years of a state which is based not on domination but on co-operation. To build any bridges between the races is to increase that hope.' Those words had been spoken in August 1964, in the context of an announcement that Peterhouse was to admit black pupils, and in the presence of Sir Humphrey Gibbs, Chairman of the Board of Governors. Now, just a few years late, those words had come true, and the Prime Minister responded with some emotion to the embrace of the man who had first spoken them. There was a light-hearted sequel to that moment. The platform party made its way to the Rector's Lodge for lunch. To the consternation of the Rector's wife, at least twice the number expected now turned up – including police chiefs and members of the Cabinet. There was enough food – the school's caterer always notoriously over-catered. But we ran out of crockery and cutlery. The abiding image of the lunch is the sight of the ex-Governor of Rhodesia, sitting a few feet away from the Prime Minister of Zimbabwe, and unselfconsciously tackling his main course from a pudding bowl, wielding a spoon as the only utensil to hand. The discomfiture, as Humphrey would have been the first to admit, had been worth it. The *Herald* only four years before had been deriding the independent schools for 'their objective [which] is all too transparent: keep classrooms predominantly white by keeping fees high'.[842] Now it changed its tune, and declared that 'any schools still operating along unacceptable lines, and there are many, should take a leaf out of Peterhouse's book and start "building bridges" for the sake of our future generations ... Peterhouse, although not perfect, cannot be accused of not playing a positive role.'[843]

Sir Humphrey's enthusiasm for the Appeal had been mentioned at Speech Day. His eagerness for the school's expansion had received prime ministerial support. In the letter he wrote to possible donors – and it was entirely his own composition – Humphrey said that 'after sixty years in this country, I remain an enthusiastic Zimbabwean and have great faith in its future'. Then, to allay any fears which the recipients might have, he wrote that the 'Government is, of course, wedded to socialism but it is a mild form which encourages co-operatives and individual enterprise'. 'Our Prime Minister's appeal for reconciliation', he continued, 'is being successful, and he is continually expressing support for important matters such as family planning and the conservation of our natural resources – two areas that appear to be neglected in many other African countries.'[844] So Humphrey managed, in appealing for funds for the school, to mention the concern which had been one of the main themes in his life. While now he might be concentrating on an educational initiative, he could not forget that the land, the soil and the country's natural resources had meant much to him for half a century, and had been the focus of much of his personal and political activity.

It was at a Peterhouse Board of Governors meeting in July 1989 that the question first arose of my writing this biography. After the meeting, over drinks, I was chatting to Humphrey's old friend, Dr Robert Fynn. He had been a Trustee of the Governor's Fund, and a great support to Humphrey during the UDI years. His own father, Sir Percy Fynn, had been Minister of Finance in the 1920s and a founder-member of the United Party. Pointing to Humphrey across the room, Dr Fynn said to me that a biography ought to be written. I agreed, and volunteered to do the job myself. Robert Fynn promised to approach Humphrey. This he did, and I followed up that approach with a letter explaining what I might hope to do. The result was the following letter:[845]

Dear Alan,

Many thanks for your letter of the 22nd September. I can, of course, appreciate your desire to write the history of the UDI period and the end of the federal one and there is no doubt you would do it extremely well. I have often been asked to record the part I played in this but as it was only a very minor one, I have not thought it worthwhile to do so. In any case, my memory is quite appalling. However, as you have been kind enough to approach me about this I would like to give you the background and my reasons for refusing.

In the first place I was astonished at being asked to be Governor by Edgar Whitehead, but after discussing this with Molly we decided that it was our duty to accept in spite of the fact that I felt completely unfitted to the task. I had been in Rhodesia for 30 odd years farming (rather badly), but had been active in the Farmers Union helping to bring the two ends of the country together in one Union and eventually becoming its President. I had also been a silent member of Parliament for the Wankie Constituency for six years and Chairman of the Natural Resources Board. I had also been active in Church affairs under Bishop Paget on his Diocesan Board. I was also a Director of lot of companies. However, I had not the slightest idea of the duties of a Governor.

Before taking the post we went over to the UK to get some idea of my responsibilities as far as the UK were concerned and I have called on the Permanent Head of the Colonial Office to have them explained to me. He asked me how long I had been in Rhodesia and when I told him he said 'You must know much more about Rhodesia then I do, so I can't help you'.

When we got back I went to try to get some advice from Lord Malvern. He was a bit vague, but said the Governors liked to be kept informed about what is going on: so keep in touch with your Prime Minister.

I took his advice and had a weekly session with Edgar Whitehead and I rubber stamped all the papers I had to sign. But I tried to educate myself more about the country and spent time visiting all the main centres and the communal areas to see their farming and to visit the Missions and Schools. I also visited the various mining ventures: gold, asbestos, etc. and as many factories as possible to see what we were producing. It was a very interesting period and I did the usual laying of foundation stones and opening buildings. I resigned all my directorships and Chairmanship of Peterhouse Executive, but remained a Governor of Peterhouse and Ruzawi School.

In May 1963 Dalhousie left and I acted as Governor-General of the federation for its final seven months. That, however, was all winding-up formalities. During the run up to UDI we had a last minute visit from Harold Wilson who brought a letter from the Queen for Ian Smith which I handed to him before the large dinner party we had arranged for the first evening of the visit. He did not open it straight away, so I took him aside after dinner and asked him to do so and show it to me. It was a short letter expressing the hope for success of the negotiations between our two countries.

After this visit, Hughie Beadle went to the UK with Smith's blessing to try and further the negotiations, but just before Beadle landed back with new proposals, Smith had declared his UDI.

I had my proclamation ready in the event of the UDI, and we rushed it down to the Herald for publication, only to find that censorship was already in action. The proclamation, of course, apart from sacking Smith and his cabinet, appealed to the Armed Forces, Judges and Police and Civil Service to continue their duties, but not to assist the rebellion in any way.

My duty then, as I saw it, was to remain at Government House as a rallying point for loyalists and to assist in any way I could to get Smith and the UK Government to negotiate a return to legality and the end of the rebellion.

So that is all I did for the next three and a half years. We had many visits from the UK Ministers and officials and arranged for the Tiger and Fearless talks at Gibraltar.

My own view was that Smith would have accepted the Fearless terms if it had not been for some of his more extreme colleagues and Dupont. However, all the negotiations failed and Smith organised a referendum on whether or not to become a republic. A majority wanted a Republic and there was no point in my remaining any longer at Government House.

I had therefore failed to prevent UDI and also failed to get a negotiated settlement, whereas if a stronger and more persuasive person had been in my place he might well have been successful.

I hope, if you have waded through this letter, you will now agree that I am right in not wanting my part recorded as it was both a very minor part and unsuccessful as well!

Any memoranda I had or other papers were lodged in the UK archive, together with letters from the Queen which I greatly valued.

Sir John Pestell remained with us at Government House after UDI and was my main support: he kept a diary of events and he may be publishing a book on this period of UDI. You might like to meet him when you are in the UK some time.

All good wishes to you both,
Yours ever,

Humphrey

That, however, was not the end of the matter. Fortunately, Dame Molly was convinced that her husband's life and contribution to the country ought to be put on record. So while she encouraged me, and despite Humphrey's unwillingness, I began to collect material. That letter was a starting point. It underlines the essential honesty and modesty of the man, and it also represents something of a *cri de coeur* – 'I failed ... I failed ... .' It did not seem to me then, nor does it seem to me now, that such a verdict should be recorded. Nor does it seem to me that even the 'what if' school of history could come up with a convincing alternative scenario of what might have happened if that one aspect of the jigsaw puzzle – the character of the Governor at the time of UDI – had been different. Indeed there is an alternative view: that any man with less of a sense of integrity, loyalty and transparent decency would have failed to achieve what Humphrey did. What did he achieve? His achievements before UDI were in themselves significant. But during the UDI years – the period to which his 'I failed ... I failed ... ' applies – his achievement was to represent the Crown in an unprecedented situation, to maintain a focus of loyalty which was beyond politics, and to act as a trusted conduit between Salisbury and London in a series of negotiations which might just have succeeded. That they did not was not the fault of the Governor.

Sir Humphrey did not live to see the final success of his appeal on behalf of Peterhouse. Just over a year after he had written to me, after a short illness, he died in Harare in November 1990, and his funeral took place in Harare Cathedral. Six years later, as a result of a further appeal, a great new range of buildings was added to the school which he had served for so long. It was called the 'Humphrey Gibbs Centre', and was opened on 1 November 1996 – All Saints Day.

Humphrey Gibbs may not have been a saint, but he was a good man in Africa. He was the last colonial governor there, the last to wear the uniform of cocked hat and sword. His trilby-hatted, blue-suited successor, Lord Soames, did a magnificent job in very different circumstances, and with a very specific role. But he was hardly a colonial governor in a tradition which had started with Sir Bartle Frere in South Africa in 1877. Since then there had been some 140 British governors or governors-general in the African continent, not counting Commissioners, Residents and Resident Commissioners. In Southern Rhodesia itself there had been seven before Humphrey, the first being Sir John Chancellor who took up office in 1923, and who resigned in the year that Humphrey arrived in the country.[846] The startling shortness of the British Empire in Africa – or parts of it – is underlined by the fact that Southern Rhodesia was only colonised twelve years before Humphrey's birth, and had become an independent state a decade before his death. The achievements of Humphrey – and people like him – in the country which is now Zimbabwe are even more remarkable when judged in this light. All they had achieved – in education, in farming, in finance and construction – had taken place virtually within a single lifetime. Their achievements were skewed by an increasingly racist political system within a world where such racism was increasingly disreputable. And where once, even as late as when Humphrey became Governor, there was a hope that at least a part of Africa would thrive both economically and politically, there was, by the time of his death, a deep pessimism about the continent. Martin Meredith sums up a general feeling:

> The rewards of independence all too evidently were reaped for the most part by small, privileged groups at the pinnacle of power ... Huge sums were squandered for reasons of pomp and prestige. Meanwhile the gap between the rich and poor grew conspicuously wider. Peasant farmers and urban poor alike suffered from neglect. More than two thirds of the people of Africa were estimated to live in conditions of extreme poverty; and their ranks increased all the time. Added to such misery was the toll taken by natural disasters like drought and famine and by the spasms of violence which persistently wracked Africa. Indeed, by the late 1970s, a mood of despair about the fate of Africa had begun to take hold.[847]

Such was the mood and the analysis as Humphrey entered the last decade of his life, and Zimbabwe its first. As a young man, he had contributed to the development of the new colony of Southern Rhodesia. As an MP he had thought it legitimate to hope that British Central Africa could show the world how a peaceful, just and non-racial society might emerge within the 'Dark Continent'. As acting Governor-General of the Federation he had seen those dreams fade away, and as Governor of his country had seen them replaced by a drive towards a more unjust and divided society. But in his last years, he found reason to hope once more, that new generations of young people would indeed create a land of co-operative effort and prosperity, where the natural resources were conserved and utilised for the good of all.

Like his earlier aspirations, that is a good and laudable hope. It is a hope that could not possibly have been framed in the world into which Humphrey was born in 1902. It was not a hope that he could have carried out with him to Africa in 1928. Nevertheless a tenacity of purpose is evident throughout his career. For while in many ways he lived a privileged and comfortable life, his purposes in Africa were altruistic and, according to their lights, progressive. That he made a huge contribution to organisations which sought to help and develop both the land and its people is not in doubt. There is of course the shadow cast over his life, and that of his adopted country, by the UDI years. But that Humphrey tried, in his own rather undramatic and cautious way, to temper political myopia with kindness, honesty, decency and integrity is a significant reason for calling him a good man in Africa. It is also the reason why his life and contribution should not be forgotten.

Notes

CHAPTER 1

1. See, for example, Read, *Edwardian England*, esp. chapter 2.
2. BonhamCarter, *Winston Churchill as I Knew Him*, p. 134.
3. *Ibid*, p. 133.
4. Stone and Stone, *An Open Elite? England 1540–1880*, p. 115; see also pp. 204 and 268 for the significance of Hertfordshire to the banking elite.
5. See Kynaston, *The City of London Volume 1: A World of its Own*, p. 297 and passim.
6. See for example: H. H. Gibbs (first Baron Aldenham) 'The Gold Standard and the Fall of Prices', *National Review*, vol. I, no. 5 (July 1883) pp. 658–76; 'The Bi-metallic Standard of Value' in *Fortnightly Review*, no. ccxxxviii, new series (Oct 1886) pp. 481–97; H. C. Gibbs, 'Bimetallism', *Blackwood's Magazine*, no. DCCXCVIII (Aug 1890) pp. 268–84; see also Kynaston, *The City of London Volume II*, especially chapter 6.
7. Zebel, *Balfour*, p. 92; the debate has recently been reopened by historians; see A. C. Howe, 'Bimetallism, c1880–1898: a controversy re-opened?', *English Historical Review*, vol. CV, no. 415 (April 1990) pp. 377–91.
8. 'Golden Years' is the title of Kynaston's *The City of London Volume II*.
9. See his obituary in *The Times*, 13 January 1932.
10. *Ibid*, Vicary's 'standard was so high that weeds were scarce'.
11. Stone, *op.cit.*, p. 115.
12. *Ibid*, p. 116.
13. Unlike the continental landed classes, 'the British peerage was a very small and very exclusive caste indeed, and even if the baronetage and the landed gentry were included, it remained an astonishingly tight and tiny status elite'. Cannadine, *The Decline and Fall of the British Aristocracy*, p. 20.
14. *Ibid*, pp. 255–64 and 487–98.
15. St Albans Abbey became a cathedral when the new diocese was created in 1877.
16. *Journal of the General Synod of the Church of Ireland*, 1917, p. 28.
17. HVG MSS, Address by the Bishop of St Albans in Hunsdon Church, 28 May 1935; see also HVG MSS, Address by Canon Wilson in St Michael's, Cornmarket.
18. Ironically, Humphrey was Chairman for many years of Barclays Bank in Rhodesia.
19. Keppel, *Edwardian Daughter*, p. 6.
20. Magnus, *King Edward the Seventh*, p. 456.
21. See *Ponsonby Remembers*; the book contains a picture of the author's wife which bears a stunning resemblance to Humphrey.
22. Ollard, *An English Education*, p. 99.
23. See Card, *Eton Renewed;* also Ollard, *An English Education*.
24. These are the comments of Lord Home in his *The Way the Wind Blows*, p. 27 – though, curiously, Home misspells Broke's name!

25. Thorpe, *Alec Douglas-Home*, p. 23; Whitworth died in 1976.
26. Fergusson, *Eton Portrait*, p. 91.
27. HVG MSS, Sir John Maud to HVG, 31 July 1959.
28. *Eton College Chronicle*, 2 June 1921, p. 34.
29. Howarth, *Cambridge Between two Wars*, p. 28.
30. While Humphrey was incarcerated in Government House, Salisbury, in the mid to late 1960s, F. A. Simpson could still be spotted in Trinity Great Court, going round dead-heading the roses, and often mistaken for a gardener.
31. Trevelyan (quoting Professor Bragg) in *Trinity College: An Historical Sketch*, p. 115.
32. Lindsay, *Sir Edmund Bacon; A Norfolk Life*, p. 30.
33. HVG MSS, Butler to HVG, 7 October 1979; they hoped he would attend a Feast in his honour, but he was unable to make it.
34. Governor of Sierra Leone, 1904–10; of Barbados, 1910–18; of Jamaica, 1918–24.
35. Churchill, *The World Crisis*, p. 1242.
36. See, for instance, S. W. Roskill in Taylor, *History of World War 1*, p. 227.
37. Coupland, *The Empire in These Days*, p. 9.
38. Robert Boutflour was Principal of the Royal Agricultural College, Cirencester, from 1931–9, and 1945–58.
39. Roberts, *'The Holy Fox': A Biography of Lord Halifax*. p. 17; Wood himself seems to agree. In his autobiography he comments, 'Luckily I did not have to contend with Agriculture very long', The Earl of Halifax, *Fullness of Days*, p. 101.
40. See McIntosh, *Echoes of Enterprise: A History of the Enterprise District*, p. 120.

CHAPTER 2

41. Kitson Clark, *An Expanding Society: Britain 1830–1900*.
42. See Faber, *The Vision and the Need: Late Victorian Imperialist Aims*, pp. 15–16; also 'Commerce and Christianity: the rise and fall of a nineteenth century missionary slogan', *Historical Journal*, 28, 3 (1985) pp. 597–621.
43. Princess Elizabeth used the phrase during her twenty-first birthday radio broadcast to the Empire and Commonwealth, transmitted from South Africa in 1947; Bradford, *Elizabeth*, p. 120.
44. James, *The Rise and Fall of the British Empire*, p. 318.
45. Kennedy, *The Rise and Fall of the Great Powers*, p. 277.
46. *Royal Commission on the Dominions* (Chairman, Edgar Vincent, first Lord D'Abernon); see especially the First *Interim Report* (28 December 1912) 1912/3 Cd.6515; *Minutes of Evidence, part 1: migration*, 1912/3 Cd.6516; *Final Report* (21 February 1917) 1917/8 Cd.8462.
47. Quoted in Plant, *Oversea Settlement: Migration from the United Kingdom to the Dominions* (London 1951) which is useful on this whole subject; Martin Gilbert's magisterial volume on Churchill during this period, *Winston S Churchill Volume IV 1916–1922* (London 1975) has nothing to say about this

aspect of Churchill as Colonial Secretary; it concentrates instead on Ireland and the Middle East.

48. See *United Empire* (Journal of the Royal Empire Society) vol. xxi (September 1930) no. 9, p. xii.
49. Constantine, *Emigrants and Empire*, p. 186.
50. Bean and Melville, *Lost Children of the Empire*, p. 80; also Humphreys, *Empty Cradles*, pp. 145–53.
51. *Handbook of Commonwealth Organisations*, published by the Federation of Commonwealth Chambers of Commerce (1965) pp. 183–6.
52. See Morris, *Pax Britannica: The Climax of an Empire* (London 1968) – the second of three marvellous volumes dealing with the history of the empire.
53. Meredith, 'Imperial Images: The Empire Marketing Board 1926–32', *History Today*, vol. 37 (Jan 1987) pp. 30–6.
54. Christopher, *Colonial Africa*, p. 122.
55. *United Empire*, vol. xix, no. 1 (January 1928) p. 55.
56. *Ibid*, vol. xxi, no. 1 (January 1930) p. 15.
57. See for example the lecture by Robert Coupland, Oxford's Beit Professor of Colonial History, delivered in 1924; Coupland, *The Empire in these Days*, pp. 44–8.
58. See Cartwright, *Valley of Gold*, pp. 13–14 and passim.
59. This is convincingly argued by Hyam, 'The Geopolitical Origins of the Central African Federation: Britain, Rhodesia and South Africa 1948–1953', *Historical Journal*, 30, 1 (1987) pp. 145–72; see also Chanock, *Unconsummated Union*.
60. Lessing, *African Laughter*, p. 253; the word 'chef' was coined in the mid-1980s to describe the new variety of 'chiefs' or blacks who were on the make, or rather had made it; perhaps there is a connotation of 'cooking the books' as well.
61. Cloete, *The African Giant*, p. 42.
62. This is the title of an enthusiastic article by E. J. Hutton Brown in *United Empire*, vol. xxi, no. 1, January 1930.
63. Gann and Duignan (eds) *Colonialism in Africa 1870–1960 Volume 2*, p. 58.
64. Baldock, 'Sir John Chancellor and the Moffat Succession', *Rhodesian History*, vol. 3 (1972) pp. 41–52.
65. Knight, *Rhodesia of Today*, p. 21; the idea of 'health-giving' breezes was a key Victorian belief. Public schools sometimes boasted of their exposed geographical situation because it counteracted the smells from sewers and drains which were thought to cause diphtheria and scarlet fever. See Megahey, *A History of Cranleigh School*, chapter 6: 'Health and Hygiene'.
66. Anonymous writer in *Blackwood's Magazine*, no. MXXXVII , vol. CLXXI (March 1902) p. 427.
67. Macdonald, *Martie and Others in Rhodesia*, p. 158; so impressed was she by the sentiments expressed in this letter that she reprinted them in her other book published in the same year, *Sally in Rhodesia*, p. 145.
68. *Ibid*, p. 161.
69. Churton Inge, 'Recapturing Rhodesia', *United Empire*, vol. xxvi, no. 9 (September 1935) p. 559.
70. Lord, *Ghosts of King Solomon's Mines*, p. xiii.
71. de la Harpe, *Msasa Morning*, p. 250.

72. Dibb, *Ivory, Apes and Peacocks*, p. 2.
73. Parker, *Rhodesia: Little White Island*, p. 25.
74. Brettell, *Side-gate and Style*, p. 75.
75. *Empire Review*, vol. lxii, no. 414 (July 1935) p. 74.
76. Gunther, *Inside Africa*, p. 611.
77. Lucas, *England and Englishness*, pp. 203–4.
78. *Empire Review*, vol. 52, no. 358 (Nov 1930) p. 361.
79. Salmon, editor of *United Empire*, so described it at length in 'My Rhodesian Tour', vol. xxx, no. 12 (December 1939) pp. cxix–cxxiii.
80. *Official Year Book of Southern Rhodesia 1952*, ch. V; the 'native' population in 1931 was reckoned to be 1,081,000, though Mosley (*Agricultural Development and Government Policy in Settler Economies*, p. 408) claims that this official estimate falls short of the true picture by some 353,000.
81. Gann, *A History of Southern Rhodesia*, p. 315.
82. Hastings, 'Southern Rhodesia Today', *Empire Review*, vol. 52, no. 358 (November 1930) p. 362.
83. Gann and Gelfand, *Huggins of Rhodesia*, p. 70.

CHAPTER 3

84. Whitehead Papers, MSS Afr s 1482/1 – Original Typescript of Autobiography, p. 14.
85. HVG MSS, D. E. McLoughlin, Assistant Agriculturist, Salisbury to HVG, 12 December 1932.
86. HVG MSS, D. E. McLoughlin, Agriculturist, Salisbury to HVG, 20 January 1933.
87. HVG (UK) MSS, Lady Hunsdon to HVG, nd (probably autumn 1933).
88. Hutton Brown in *United Empire*, vol. xxi, no. 1 (January 1930) p. 22.
89. Quoted in Victor, *The Salient of South Africa*, p. 177.
90. See Phimister, 'The Political Economy of Tribal Animosity', *Journal of Southern African Studies*, vol. 6, no. 1 (October 1979) pp. 1–43.
91. See Christopher, *Colonial Africa*, p. 57.
92. Palmer, *Land and Racial Discrimination in Rhodesia*, p. 210.
93. See Phimister, *An Economic and Social History of Zimbabwe*, pp. 184–93, and Murray, *The Governmental System in Southern Rhodesia*, pp. 76–83.
94. Murray, *op. cit.*, p. 72.
95. *Rhodesian Woman's Journal*, 15 February 1934.
96. HVG (UK) MSS, Lady Hunsdon to HVG, (October) 1934.
97. 'Rhodesian boilers' are still used on many farms to this day, and older whites still call them by their original name.
98. HVG MSS, HVG to Molly Gibbs, 1 June 1946.
99. Mr S M Lanigan O'Keeffe, at a luncheon in November 1940; quoted in *United Empire*, vol. xxxii, no. 1 (January 1941) p. 6.
100. Anderson, *The Toe Rags*, p. 340.
101. Meredith, 'The Rhodesian Air Training Group 1940–1945', *Rhodesiana*, no. 28 (July 1973) pp. 16–29. This is a semi-official memorandum written at the behest of Lord Malvern.

102. See *African Affairs*, vol. 48, no. 193 (October 1949) p. 321.
103. HVG MSS, [Eric] to HVG, 19 June 1940.
104. *Ibid*; Douglas-Home claims that Huggins was not best pleased at this.
105. Quoted in Douglas-Home, *Evelyn Baring*, p. 136.
106. *Ibid*, p. 119.
107. W. D. Gale, *The Rhodesian Press*, p. 166.
108. *President's Monthly Newsletter*, 7 June 1940.
109. *Vuka*, October 1941.
110. *Ibid*, February 1942.
111. *Ibid*, July 1942.
112. RNFU Minute Book, Report of the proceedings of the Second Annual Congress (18–19 September 1945).
113. See for example HVG's presidential address in 1946, RNFU Minute Book (9–10 Sept 1946).
114. Phimister, *An Economic and Social History of Zimbabwe*, p. 234.
115. Quoted in *ibid*, p. 229.
116. Christopher, *Colonial Africa*, p. 90.
117. See Davidson, *Wankie: The Story of a Great Game Reserve*.
118. See Beinart, 'Empire, Hunting and Ecological Change in Southern and Central Africa', *Past and Present*, no. 128 (August 1990) pp. 162–86.
119. Heseltine, *Remaking Africa*, p. 69.
120. *Report of the Secretary, Department of Agriculture and Lands, for the years 1941, 1942, 1943, 1944, 1945* (CSR 15-1947) p. 2. To save paper, the reports for 1941 to 1945 were all printed together after the end of the war.
121. See, for instance, Smyth, 'Britain's African Colonies and British Propaganda during the Second World War', *Journal of Imperial and Commonwealth History*, vol. xiv, no. 1 (October 1985) pp. 65–82.
122. *Annual Report of the Natural Resources Board for the year ended 31 December 1946*, (CSR 36–1947) p. 2.
123. *Ibid*, p. 3.
124. *Ibid*, p. 4.
125. This comment is quoted by, among others, Flower, *Serving Secretly*, p. 280.
126. Tanser, *A Sequence of Time*, p. 130.
127. See Paget and Crum, *Francis Paget*.
128. Chadwick, *The Victorian Church Part II*, p. 146.
129. See Gibbon, *Paget of Rhodesia*.
130. In his autobiography, Driberg claims that 'had I not had this rebuff, [I] would have controlled my private conduct so that it would be more acceptable to the school authorities'. As it was, he was caught indulging in activities for which he later became notorious. He was demoted. Driberg, *Ruling Passions*, pp. 50–1.
131. Harare Diocesan Archives, *Finance: Memorandum from the Committee appointed by the Diocesan Standing Committee*, 1931.
132. Quoted in Gibbon, *Paget of Rhodesia*, p. 47.
133. Harare Diocesan Archives, *Progress of the Anglican Community in Southern Rhodesia 1921–36* (1936).
134. Bishop's Letter in *Southern Rhodesia Church Magazine*, 28 December 1938.
135. The Revd G. E. P. Broderick was appointed; Arnold, *Here to Stay*, p. 81.
136. *Southern Rhodesia Church Magazine*, 22 May 1940.

137. Harare Diocesan Archives, HVG (on behalf of the Diocesan Finance Board) to all Priests in Charge and Parish and Mission Councils, 27 February 1942.
138. Harare Diocesan Archives, Broderick to HVG, 21 December 1942.
139. *The Link*, February 1943.
140. Harare Diocesan Archives, *Report of the Division of the Diocese Committee set up by the Authority of the Lord Bishop with the Archdeacon of Matabeleland as Chairman in the year 1943*, 6 June 1946.
141. Harare Diocesan Archives, *Report of the Committee set up by the Standing Committee to Consider and Report on the proposed Division of the Diocese of Southern Rhodesia*, 5 April 1947; see also Arnold, *Here to Stay*, p. 84.
142. Roberts, *The Colonial Moment in Africa*, p. 187.
143. *Ibid*, p. 60.
144. *The Link*, June 1947; article entitled 'Her Majesty at Cyrene!'
145. *The Link*, August 1947.

CHAPTER 4

146. Phimister, *Economic and Social History of Zimbabwe*, p. 173.
147. *Ibid*, p. 230.
148. Immigrants could not vote until they had three years' residence, so they could not have affected the results in 1946, and it is unlikely that they did in 1948 either.
149. G. W. Rudland's phrase, NAZ ORAL RU/3, p. 37; see also Wetherell, 'NH Wilson: Populism in Rhodesian Politics', *Rhodesian History*, vol. 6 (1975) pp. 65–6.
150. Stumbles, *Some Recollections of a Rhodesian Speaker*, p. 49; Stumbles was not very forthcoming about the incident when interviewed for the National Archives (NAZ, ORAL/ST 6) in 1973; he died in 1978 by which time he had written of the 'Bulawayo Plot' in his memoirs published posthumously in 1980.
151. HVG gives a brief account of the whole episode in his Autobiography.
152. It was over an issue 'of no great importance'; see Blake, *A History of Rhodesia*, p. 241.
153. Rudland was in fact the Cabinet member in 1964 who 'leaked' the news that Field's downfall was imminent: see Blake, *op. cit.*, pp. 359–60.
154. NAZ, Rudland Memoirs, ORAL RU/3, p. 17.
155. See Pasmore and Mitchell, *Source Book of Parliamentary Elections*, 160ff.
156. Gann and Gelfand, *Huggins of Rhodesia*, p. 207.
157. A. R. W. Stumbles recollected, 'as far as I know the only speech he made was to say "Hear, hear!" He said it himself'; NAZ, Stumbles Memoirs, ORAL/ST 6, p. 47.
158. NAZ, Todd memoirs, ORAL/TO 1, p. 27.
159. *Southern Rhodesia Legislative Assembly Debates*, vol. 29, col. 437 (30 November 1948).
160. *Ibid*, cols 673–701 (7 December 1948).
161. *Southern Rhodesia Legislative Assembly Debates*, vol. 30, col. 2882 (21 October 1949); full details of the legislation are given in the *Official Year Book of Southern Rhodesia 1952*, pp. 483–5.

162. *Southern Rhodesia Legislative Assembly Debates*, vol. 29, cols 557–8.
163. *Ibid*, vol. 31, col. 1865.
164. *Ibid*, vol. 32, col. 828 (2 May 1951) when he said that 'the Government have done a great deal for the farming industry over the past ten years or so'.
165. See Joyce, *Anatomy of a Rebel*, pp. 66–7, on this, and on Ian Smith's attitude – he was of course a member of the opposition, having entered parliament in the 1948 election.
166. The word used by Leys, *European Politics in Southern Rhodesia*, p. 68.
167. This seventh Assembly lasted from 16 November 1948 until 13 October 1953.
168. *Report of the Commission on closer union of the dependencies in eastern and central Africa* (Hilton Young Report) (17 October 1928) Cmd.3234.
169. Quoted in Hanna, *The Story of the Rhodesias and Nyasaland*, p. 246; see also *Empire Review*, vol. lxiv, no. 426 (July 1936).
170. *Report of the Royal Commission on Rhodesia and Nyasaland* (Bledisloe Report) (1 March 1939) Cmd.5949.
171. 'It brought Nyasaland, from the point of view of future planning, away from the East African and into the Central African orbit', Wills, *The History of Central Africa*, p. 312.
172. Blake, *A History of Rhodesia,* p. 226.
173. HVG (UK) MSS, Lady Hunsdon to HVG, nd (1938).
174. Silk, 'The Bledisloe Medal', *Heritage*, no. 8 (1989) pp. 94–6.
175. Welensky, *Welensky's Four Thousand Days*, p. 23.
176. 'I wanted us to go in with South Africa', Guest recalled later; 'that is what I stood for – for amalgamation. I was very keen on that'; NAZ, ORAL/GU 1.
177. Cmd. 8573 (18 June 1952).
178. Judd, *Empire*, p. 356.
179. Chandos, *The Memoirs of Lord Chandos*, p. 388.
180. *Southern Rhodesia Legislative Assembly Debates*, vol. 33, col. 2579 (26 June 1952).
181. Gann and Gelfand, *Huggins of Rhodesia*, p. 234.
182. Hyam, 'The Geopolitical Origins of the Central African Federation', *Historical Journal*, 30, 1 (1987) pp. 145–72.
183. Butler, *The Art of the Possible*, p. 209.
184. *Rhodesia Herald*, 15 August 1953.
185. Greenfield, *Testimony of a Federal*, pp. 134–6.
186. NAZ, Todd Memoirs, ORAL/TO 1, p. 27.
187. See *United Empire*, vol. xli, no. 3 (May–June 1950) p. 173.
188. *African Affairs*, vol. 51, no. 205 (October 1952) p. 289.
189. *Ibid*, vol. 51, no. 203 (April 1952) p. 112.
190. Creighton, *The Anatomy of Partnership*, p. 127.
191. Holderness, *Lost Chance*, p. 119.
192. *Ibid*, p. 124.
193. NAZ, Lloyd Memoirs, ORAL/LL 2, p. 18.
194. Creighton, *The Anatomy of Partnership*, p. 97.
195. Capricorn Africa Society, *Contract*, p. 1.
196. *Sunday Mail*, 17 June 1956.
197. Herbert was murdered in mysterious circumstances in 1975; his wife became a minister in Robert Mugabe's government.

198. Or perhaps 'Prince Charles' guru'; Dimbleby, *The Prince of Wales*, pp. 249–53 and passim.
199. Paget writing in 1953, quoted in Gibbon, *Paget of Rhodesia*, p. 112.
200. *The Link*, March 1946, quoting his Bishop's Letter of 12 February 1946.

CHAPTER 5

201. Brettell, *Side-gate and Style*, p. 75.
202. The history of the 'English Private Schools' in South Africa is recorded by Randall, *Little England on the Veld,* published in 1982 – its cover decorated with the Union Jack.
203. McIntyre, *The Diocesan College*, p. 94.
204. HVG MSS, Circular letter dated 14 July 1954.
205. Hodder-Williams, *White Farmers in Rhodesia*, p. 171.
206. The RAU was the forerunner of the RNFU; the writer is specifically speaking of the 1930s and 1940s, but his remarks apply equally to the 1950s.
207. Hodder-Williams, 'White attitudes and the Unilateral Declaration of Independence', *Journal of Commonwealth Political Studies*, 8 (1970) p. 243.
208. See Atkinson, *Teaching Rhodesians*.
209. Brown, *Bye bye Shangri-la*, p. 123.
210. Caute, *Under the Skin*, pp. 402–3; this was Umtali Boys' High School in 1980.
211. Waugh, *A Tourist in Africa*, p. 144.
212. Lessing, *African Laughter*, p. 25; as was Ruzawi for her brother.
213. *Peterhouse Magazine*, 1955, p. 8.
214. Bothashof was, tactfully, renamed Eaglesvale after independence in 1980.
215. Author's possession: Paget to Snell, 26 November and 1 December 1951; 28 November 1951; Snell to Paget, 28 November 1951.
216. Welensky MSS, Letter from HVG (13 May 1953) MS 49,5,70; Minutes of the Executive Council of NR (9 June 1953) MS 49,5,92.
217. Hunt, *Oxford to Zimbabwe*, p. 177.
218. K. M. Goodenough in a talk given on 27 July 1949; printed in *African Affairs*, vol. 48, no. 193 (October 1949) pp. 318–23.
219. Tredgold, *The Rhodesia that was my Life*, p. 224.
220. Colville, *The Fringes of Power*, p. 488.
221. *The Times*, 9 May 1955.
222. See Hastings, *A History of English Christianity*, p. 434. Fisher had been headmaster of Repton 1914–32; one of his pupils there was Michael Ramsey, who as Archbishop of Canterbury had very different views on Africa from those of his old headmaster.
223. He had been Bishop of Lebombo 1921–8 and Bishop of Natal 1928–51.
224. Headmistress of St Winifred's Diocesan School in the Cape, from 1944–6; Limuru Girls' School in Kenya from 1949–57; Arundel School in Salisbury from 1958–62; thereafter she was Headmistress of Wycombe Abbey School in England.
225. Charles Fisher was soon to move to Australia to become Headmaster of Geelong Grammar School, where Prince Charles was to be one of his pupils.

226. Paget House later acquired the Archbishop's military and civil medals, which are still on show there.

227. Symonds, *Oxford and Empire*, p. xi.

228. Gelfand, *A Non-racial island of Learning*, p. 70.

229. Dunn, *Central African Witness*, p. 151.

230. The franchise story is an extremely complicated one, impossible to summarise briefly. Details are given in Leys, *European Politics in Southern Rhodesia*, pp. 212–40; Blake, *History of Rhodesia*, pp. 302–4; Holderness, *Lost Chance*, chapters 14 and 15.

231. He was willing to allow an amendment on the basis of a motion which had passed in the house, and which he personally had opposed, 'that the Immorality and Indecency Suppression Act be amended to prohibit illegal sexual intercourse between a European male and an African female': see Holderness, *op. cit.*, pp. 184–7.

232. Holderness, *op. cit.*, p. 207.

233. *Spectator*, 6 December 1957.

234. Whitehead Papers, Butler to Whitehead, 19 June 1953.

235. Home, *The Way the Wind Blows*, p. 130; Dorneywood was the official country residence of the Foreign Secretary.

236. Brown, *Bye bye Shangri-la*, p. 167.

237. Lord, *Ghosts of King Solomon's Mines*, pp. 53–4.

238. Clements, *Rhodesia: The Course to Collision*, p. 138.

239. Lord, *The Ghosts of King Solomon's Mines*, p. 113.

240. Creighton, *The Anatomy of Partnership*, p. 193.

241. Home, *The Way the Wind Blows*, p. 125.

242. *Spectator*, 17 January 1958.

243. *Southern Rhodesia Legislative Debates*, vol. 41, cols 1209–1212 (3 February 1959).

244. *Ibid*, cols 1212–1214.

245. *Ibid*, vol. 43, col. 566 (23 July 1959); Minister of Labour, A. E. Abrahamson, speaking.

246. Leys and Pratt, *A New Deal in Central Africa*, p. 101.

247. Blake, *History of Rhodesia*, p. 325.

248. Darwin, 'The Central African Emergency 1959', *Journal of Imperial and Commonwealth History*, vol. xxi, no. 3 (September 1993) p. 218.

249. Quoted in Horne, *Macmillan 1957–1986*, p. 181.

250. *Central African Examiner*, 28 March 1959.

251. Home, *The Way the Wind Blows*, p. 131.

252. Horne, *Macmillan 1957–1986*, p. 179.

253. Letter quoted in Douglas-Home, *Evelyn Baring*, p. 285.

254. Welensky, *Welensky's 4000 Days*, p. 144.

255. Quoted in Italiaander, *The New Leaders of Africa*, p. 90.

CHAPTER 6

256. DO 35/7450; 'Brief for the Secretary of State', Central Africa Department, 30 August 1960.

257. DO 35/7471; Lennox-Boyd to Home, 4 July 1956.
258. DO 35/7471; Internal memo dated 5 June 1958.
259. DO 35/7471; British High Commissioner in Salisbury to the Permanent Secretary, CRO, 23 December 1958.
260. DO 35/7471; Dalhousie to Home, 20 February 1959.
261. DO 35/7471; Home to Whitehead, 29 May 1959.
262. *Rhodesia Herald*, 13 July 1959; leading article.
263. *Sunday News*, 12 July 1959.
264. HVG MSS, Baring to HVG, 22 July 1959.
265. HVG MSS, Maud to HVG, 31 July 1959.
266. HVG MSS, Home to HVG, 20 August 1959.
267. HVG MSS, J. E. S. Green (Natal, South Africa) to HVG, 16 August 1959.
268. Of the 138 British colonial governors who served in Africa, only five apart from Gibbs served for a decade or longer, and all were pre-First World War appointments; see Kirk-Greene, *A Biographical Dictionary of the British Colonial Governor Volume 1: Africa*.
269. *Rhodesia Herald*, 14 January 1960.
270. Storry, *Jubilee Scrapbook*, gives details of the work of the Order in Rhodesia. The link between Sir Humphrey and the Order was evident in 1990, when several members, clad in their robes, attended his funeral in Harare Cathedral.
271. See Jackson, *Historic Buildings of Harare*, p. 118; the building later became a government training centre.
272. *Ibid*, pp. 100–1.
273. Morris, *Farewell the Trumpets*, p. 530.
274. *Ibid*, p. 537.
275. *Rhodesia Herald*, 13 January 1960.
276. *Ibid,* 27 and 30 January 1960.
277. *Ibid,* 4, 12, 18 February 1960.
278. The Governor's Programme for March was published in *Rhodesia Herald*, 2 March 1960.
279. *Ibid,* 5 April 1960.
280. *Ibid,* 9 April 1960.
281. *Ibid,* 9, 12 April 1960.
282. Ziegler, *King Edward VIII*, p. 160.
283. Frew, *Prince George's African Tour*, p. 182 and passim.
284. Lionel was brother of Sir Stafford, who was to become Chancellor of the Exchequer in 1945.
285. *Bulawayo Chronicle*, 15 April 1947.
286. Pimlott, *The Queen*, p. 119.
287. Lacey, *Majesty*, chapter 17.
288. Stewart, 'The Last Royal Train', in *Heritage of Zimbabwe*, no. 14 (1995) p. 17.
289. See Bean and Melville, *Lost Children of the Empire* and Humphreys, *Empty Cradles*; in the course of her research in the 1980s trying to trace child migrants, Margaret Humphreys visited the Gibbses who – as she puts it – told her 'This could all become very embarrassing ... you won't be doing these people any favours' (p. 148).
290. DO 35/7718, Sir Michael Adeane to the Commonwealth Office, 11 September 1955.

291. DO 35/7718, Welensky to Home, 4 October 1958; Adeane to Home, 4 March 1959.
292. Bradford, *Elizabeth*, p. 283.
293. And he adds, 'even after UDI'; Lacey, *Majesty*, p. 364.
294. In the 1980s Salisbury – now Harare – was accused of the same thing by Bulawayo.
295. Leys and Pratt, *A New Deal in Central Africa*, p. 78.
296. *Rhodesia Herald*, 12 May 1960; NAZ, Barrow papers, MS 841/28; Sir Malcolm Barrow was the federal minister in charge of the tour.
297. *Rhodesia Herald*, 25 May 1960; since the beginning of the year, the Scout movement had been formally non-racial, *Ibid*, 21 December 1959.
298. *Rhodesia Herald*, 25 May 1960.
299. Macmillan, *Riding the Storm*, p. 736.
300. *Ibid*, p. 735.
301. Diary entry for 28 July 1959 quoted in *Ibid*, p. 738.
302. Callaghan, *Time and Chance*, p. 143.
303. *Central African Examiner*, 10 October 1959; Editorial entitled 'That "Let's have a party" feeling'.
304. Low (Smuts Professor of the History of the British Commonwealth at Cambridge), *Eclipse of Empire*, p. 214.
305. Horne, *Macmillan 1957–1986*, p. 391.
306. Welensky, *Welensky's 4000 Days*, p. 171.
307. His article in the *Daily Mail* was reported, not disapprovingly, in *Rhodesia Herald*, 13 January 1960.
308. Horne, *Macmillan 1957–1986*, p. 191.
309. Macmillan, *Pointing the Way*, p. 130.
310. Speech by Harold Macmillan to the Joint Commonwealth Associations on 13 April 1960; reported in *African Affairs*, vol. 59, no. 236 (July 1960) p. 196.
311. *Ibid*, p. 147.
312. *Rhodesia Herald*, 4 February 1960; the long report on the speech contains no mention of 'the wind of change' phrase.
313. Horne, *Macmillan 1957–1986*, p. 194.
314. *Ibid*, p. 195.
315. Lessing, *African Laughter*, p. 31.
316. Welensky, *Welensky's 4000 Days*, pp. 179–82.
317. *Rhodesia Herald*, 17 February 1960.
318. *Ibid*, 24 February 1960.
319. Home, *The Way the Wind Blows*, p. 77.
320. Quoted in Welensky, *Welensky's 4000 Days*, pp. 185–6.

CHAPTER 7

321. *Evening Standard*, 28 April 1960; the first black Anglican priest, Samuel Muhlanga, was ordained in 1919, and the next two were Sagonda and S. Hatendi in 1923. Father Muhlanga had become a Canon, retired in 1950, and was the first African in S. Rhodesia to be awarded the MBE: see Weller, *Mainstream Christianity*, p. 74. (The first black RC priest was not ordained until 1939.)

322. *Rhodesia Herald*, 28 June 1960; strictly accurately, the newspaper headline referred to the opening of the 'Territorial House', though with less accuracy proclaimed its being opened by the 'Colony's First Rhodesian Governor'.
323. *Guardian*, 6 July 1960.
324. *Central African Examiner*, Editorial, 30 July 1960.
325. *Ibid*, article entitled 'The Case of African X'.
326. The British High Commissioner in Salisbury reporting on a dinner party conversation; he had dined with the Welenskys the night the trouble broke out; DO 35/7600, 22 July 1960.
327. HVG MSS; typescript of radio broadcast speech.
328. *Southern Rhodesia Legislative Assembly Debates*, vol. 46 (2 November 1960) cols 2731–2.
329. *Guardian*, 27 July 1960.
330. DO 35/7600; 28 July 1960.
331. *Keesing's Contemporary Archives*, 1959/1960, p. 17624.
332. *Southern Rhodesia Legislative Assembly Debates,* vol. 46 (20 October 1960, col. 2303.
333. *Ibid*, (15 November 1960) col. 3183.
334. Bowman, *Politics in Rhodesia*, p. 58.
335. Tredgold, *The Rhodesia that was my Life*, pp. 229–30.
336. Tredgold MSS, Welensky to Tredgold, 26 October 1960.
337. DO 35/7660, Welensky to Sandys, 7 November 1960.
338. Tredgold MSS, Clutton-Brock to Tredgold, 2 November 1960; see also Welensky to Tredgold, 16 November 1960.
339. Three regimes later, 'these notorious provisions are still on our statute books'; article entitled 'Scrap this Act' in *Horizon*, January 1992.
340. Welensky, *Welensky's 4000 Days*, p. 272.
341. *Rhodesia Herald*, 8 October 1960.
342. Welensky, *Welensky's 4000 Days*, p. 275.
343. The details were subsequently spelled out in *Southern Rhodesia Constitution,* [Cmnd 1399,1400], June 1961.
344. Macmillan, *At the End of the Day*, p. 307.
345. Butler Papers, RAB G 40, Bernard to Butler, 12 January 1963. Bernard, a Southern Rhodesian relative of Butler (through the Courtauld connection) sent Rab this long confidential assessment of the situation in SR.
346. Welensky, *Welensky's 4000 Days*, p. 309.
347. Brown, *Bye Bye Shangri-la*, p. 184.
348. Quoted in Barber, *Rhodesia: The Road to Rebellion*, p. 95.
349. Young, *Rhodesia and Independence*, p. 55.
350. Blake, *A History of Rhodesia*, p. 334.
351. Thyne Papers, Welensky to Thyne, 21 August 1961.
352. *The Memoirs of Lord Chandos*, p. 393 (the book was published in 1962).
353. *Rhodesia Herald*, 13 January 1962.
354. *Report of the S. Rhodesia Education Commission* (Judges Report) CSR 37–1963.
355. Peterhouse Archives, *Confidential Memorandum*, October 1962.
356. *Rhodesia Herald*, 7 February 1962.
357. *Rhodesia Herald*, 31 October 1961.

358. Macmillan to Home, 24 February 1962; quoted in Macmillan, *At the End of the Day*, p. 320.
359. *Rhodesia Herald*, 14 August 1962.
360. Tredgold, *The Rhodesia that was my Life*, p. 232.
361. Hanna, *The Story of the Rhodesias and Nyasaland*, p. 310.
362. Macmillan's diary entry for 24 March quoted in his *At the End of the Day*, p. 322.
363. Butler Papers, RAB G 41/26: Welensky to Butler, 3 January 1963.
364. Bowman, *Politics in Rhodesia*, p. 42.
365. Flower, *Serving Secretly*, p. 12.
366. NAZ, ORAL/LI 2 pp. 18–19; interview with Mrs Barbara Ann Field.
367. Holderness, *Lost Chance*, p. 167.
368. Alport, *Sudden Assignment*, p. 222.
369. Butler, *The Art of the Possible*, p. 220.
370. Wells, *History of Central Africa*, p. 357.
371. Flower, *Serving Secretly*, p. 12.
372. *Rhodesia Herald*, 6 December 1962; despite this, Chinamano's sons were soon to attend Peterhouse on scholarships, and were thus among the first black boys at any white school in Rhodesia.
373. *Daily News*, 18 December 1962.
374. *Ibid*;. small wonder that this newspaper was banned by Ian Smith's government in 1964.
375. Alport, *Sudden Assignment*, p. 230.
376. *Central African Examiner*, 10 October 1959.
377. 26 December 1962; in Macmillan, *At the End of the Day*, p. 324.
378. Butler, *The Art of the Possible*, p. 225.
379. Welensky, *Welensky's 4000 Days*, p. 359.
380. Greenfield, *Testimony of a Rhodesian Federal*, p. 211.
381. Field to Butler, 29 March 1963, quoted in Young, *Rhodesia and Independence*, p. 75.
382. Butler Papers, RAB F100/8, Dalhousie to Butler, 12 April 1963.
383. CAB 129/113, Field to Butler, 20 April 1963.
384. Federal Press Statement, 11 May 1963, quoted in Bowman, *Politics in Rhodesia*, p. 63.
385. Wood, *The Welensky Papers*, p. 1232.
386. Ian Smith; interview with the author, November 1993.
387. Lord, *Ghosts of King Solomon's Mines*, p. 103.
388. Wilson Papers, Wilson to Boyd, 15 November 1963.
389. Wilson Papers, Wilson to Douglas-Home, 30 December 1963.
390. Quoted in Springhall, *Youth, Empire and Society*, p. 58.
391. See, for example, 'Southern Rhodesia – Unilateral Independence', a paper discussed by officials of the Foreign and Central Africa Offices, December 1963 – FO 371/167126.
392. Alderson Papers, NAZ AL/7/6/20: entry for Thursday 10 December 1963.
393. Anglo-American Archives, HVG to Sir Albert Robinson, 21 December 1963.

CHAPTER 8

394. Creighton, *The Anatomy of Partnership*, p. 29 and footnote 2.
395. Alport, *Sudden Assignment*, pp. 150–1; Alport's book was published in 1965 – that is, before UDI.
396. Peterhouse Archives, HVG to Snell, 6 December 1962.
397. Peterhouse Archives, Minutes of the Executive Committee, November 1962; and 'Memorandum recording the Executive Committee's Discussion on March 21, 1963, on the Admission of Africans', 1 April 1963.
398. *Peterhouse Magazine*, 1962, p. 14.
399. Peterhouse Archives: Letter from the Rector 'To all members of the Board and Executive', 30 July 1963.
400. *Peterhouse Magazine*, 1963, pp. 6–14.
401. See Atkinson, *Teaching Rhodesians*, pp. 191–4.
402. Fothergill, *Laboratory for Peace*, p. 46.
403. *Ibid*, p. 107.
404. *Bulawayo Chronicle*, 3 May 1960.
405. Butler Papers, RAB G 40, Bernard to Butler, 12 January 1963.
406. The Diary and Notes of the Chief Justice, quoted in Goldin, *The Judge, the Prince and the Usurper*, pp. 26–8.
407. *Rhodesia Herald*, 1 February 1964 (editorial).
408. Butler, *The Art of the Possible*, p. 226: 'I know perfectly well that I did not give the Southern Rhodesians an assurance of independence ... .'
409. Ian Smith claimed that there was no possibility that he had misunderstood Butler; interview with the author, November 1993.
410. Quoted in Goldin, *The Judge, the Prince and the Usurper*, p. 26.
411. Young, *Rhodesia and Independence*, p. 101; Nevile Henderson, it will be remembered, stands accused of having sent back from Berlin in the late 1930s reports which encouraged Chamberlain to believe that he could achieve his aim of peace by negotiating with Hitler.
412. Campbell to Field, 11 February 1964; quoted in Blake, *Rhodesia*, p. 357; this and other exchanges between the British and Rhodesian governments are recorded in Cmnd 2807 (November 1965).
413. Quoted in Young, *Rhodesia and Independence*, p. 104.
414. Bishop Alderson's Notebook, entry for 13 March 1964; NAZ 7/6/20.
415. Memorandum dated 14 February 1964 and tabled for discussion at Cabinet on 18 February; CAB 129/116.
416. Goldin, *op.cit.*, p. 27.
417. Flower, *Serving Secretly*, p. 23.
418. Young, *Rhodesia and Independence*, p. 106.
419. HVG MSS, Field to Gibbs, 16 April 1964.
420. DO 183/306; British High Commissioner, Salisbury, to Secretary of State for Commonwealth Relations, 12 June 1964: 'Southern Rhodesia: Situation Report'.
421. Douglas-Home to HVG, 8 June 1964; quoted in Thorpe, *Alec Douglas-Home*, p. 351.
422. *Rhodesia Herald*, 13 April 1964.
423. Blake, *Rhodesia*, p. 366.

424. PREM 13/085, British High Commissioner, Salisbury to CRO, 16 October 1964.
425. *Ibid.*
426. *Ibid.*
427. PREM 13/085, Commonwealth Relations Office to High Commissioner, Salisbury, 23 October 1964.
428. PREM 13/086, Wilson to HVG, 4 November 1964.
429. *Rhodesia Herald*, 28 October 1964.
430. CAB 130/209, 'Possible Appointment of a New Governor in the event of the Arrest of the Present Governor'.
431. CAB 130/208.
432. *Rhodesia Herald*, 30 October 1964.
433. Caute, *Under the Skin*, p. 90.
434. Morris, *Pax Britannica*, p. 284.
435. Bishop Alderson's Notebook, entry for 30 January 1965; NAZ AL 7/6/21.
436. Wilson, *The Labour Government 1964–1970*, p. 73.
437. *Ibid.*
438. Berlyn, *The Quiet Man*, p. 148.
439. Joyce, *Anatomy of a Rebel*, p. 185.
440. Wilson, *The Labour Government 1964–1970,* p. 143; a sixth principle, NIBMAR or 'No independence before majority rule', was added, initially on a provisional basis, in December 1966; see *ibid*, p. 286.
441. Headline in *Sunday Mail*, 1 August 1965, quoting extensively from the British press.
442. *African Affairs*, vol. 64, no. 256 (July 1965).
443. PREM 13/555: a note prepared for Harold Wilson before Campbell's leave-taking.
444. PREM 13/555: Note to CRO from the PM's Office, 15 June 1965.
445. Beadle's diary notes covering these events is printed in Golden, *The Judge, The Prince and the Usurper*, p. 29.
446. Hall, *The High Price of Principles*, p. 102.
447. See *Illustrated London News*, 24 April 1965.
448. Windrich, *Britain and the Politics of Rhodesian Independence*, p. 37.
449. Henderson, 'White Populism in Southern Rhodesia', *Comparative Studies in History and Society*, vol. 14, no. 4 (September 1972) p. 399.
450. Quoted in Godwin and Hancock, *Rhodesians Never Die*, o 73.
451. *Bulawayo Chronicle*, 29 April 1965.
452. Hintz, 'The Political Transformation of Rhodesia 1858-1965', *African Studies Review*, vol. 15, no. 2 (1972) p. 182.
453. DO 183/306, High Commissioner, Salisbury to CRO, 12 June 1964.
454. The author, doing a locum, found himself as Robert Birley's parish priest in Somerton, Somerset in 1972. The post-prandial entertainment was watching and commenting upon these films.
455. Hearnden, *Red Robert: A Life of Robert Birley*, p. 50.
456. Holderness, *Lost Chance*, p. 40.
457. Bobbie Pritchett to Whitehead, Whitehead papers, Rhodes House MSS Afr s 1482/2c.

CHAPTER 9

458. Gelfand, *A Non-Racial Island of Learning*, p. 251; what follows relies on Gelfand's narrative.
459. Goldin, *The Prince, The Judge and The Usurper*, p. 32.
460. *Ibid*, p. 33; the irony is that Judge MacDonald later emerged as an RF supporter.
461. Flower, *Serving Secretly*, p. 283.
462. Castle, *Diaries*, p. 61.
463. Wilson, *The Labour Government 1964–1970*, p. 151.
464. See below, p. 112; the documents in the Public Record Office suggest that the Mountbatten Plan was both conceived of, and then dropped, in November.
465. *Rhodesia Herald*, 20 October 1965.
466. HVG MSS, Welensky to Lady Gibbs, 22 October 1965.
467. HVG MSS, *Report on CBI Mission to Rhodesia October 1965*.
468. Wilson, *op. cit.*, p. 155.
469. PREM 13/556: preliminary annotated drafts, and final message from the Queen to Smith, 24 October 1965.
470. *Daily Mirror*, 29 October 1965.
471. *Rhodesia Herald*, 26 June 1971.
472. Birkenhead, *Monckton*, p. 345.
473. Wilson, *The Labour Government*, p. 155; 'I had not at that time learned to discount his optimism', Wilson records, 'nor ... how supple, indeed devious, he was prepared to be to get us to concede a settlement'.
474. *Op. cit.*, p. 156.
475. PREM 13/556, Ian Smith to the Queen, 27 October 1965.
476. Wilson, *op. cit.*, p. 159.
477. Wilson, *op. cit.*, p. 162.
478. Wilson understandably forbears to recount that the dance involved the noble Duke clutching a coin between his cheeks – that is, in the lower part of his anatomy: private information to the author, from one of the British Prime Minister's party.
479. Skeen, *Prelude to Independence*, p. 115.
480. *Hansard*, vol. 720 (11 November 1965) col. 360.
481. Pimlott, *Harold Wilson*, p. 375.
482. Donnelly is scathing about 'Wilson's vainglory', and Smith's 'understandable' stance, in *Gadarene '68*, chapter VI, 'Weeks rather than months' .
483. Article in *News of the World* (17 October 1965) quoted by Nabarro in his *NAB 1: Portrait of a Politician*, p. 243.
484. For a moving account of Richard Cecil's gun-carrying reporting from Rhodesia, and his death, see Caute, *Under the Skin*, pp. 49–52.
485. Quoted in Pimlott, *Harold Wilson*, p. 371.
486. Flower, *Serving Secretly*, p. 51.
487. Chadwick, *Michael Ramsey*, p. 245.
488. Young, *The Road to Rebellion*, p. 259.
489. HVG MSS, William-Powlett to HVG, 27 October 1965.
490. Callaghan, *Time and Chance*, p. 145.
491. Wyllie, *The Influence of British Arms*, pp. 80–81.
492. Castle, *Diaries*, p. 61.

493. Minutes of the Rhodesian Cabinet (1 November 1965); printed in Flower, *Serving Secretly*, pp. 286–91.

494. The Governor wrote a minute giving the details of his exchange with Mr Smith, and subsequent events in November (cited hereafter as *Governor's Note*): HVG Archives, SB/3.

495. Ian Smith in conversation with the author, 12 November 1993.

496. Young claimed (*Rhodesia and Independence*, p. 277) that 'Gibbs himself never made such allegations' – that is, that he had been misled by his Prime Minister, as Harold Wilson later claimed (10 December) in the House of Commons. It is clear from Sir Humphrey's account that he did in fact believe himself to have been misled but certainly in 1967 (when Young's book was published) he had never said so publicly.

497. *Southern Rhodesia: Documents relating to the negotiations* ... [Cmnd. 2807] p. 141; message from Wilson to Smith dated Monday 7 December 1965.

498. *Ibid*, p. 142; message from Smith to Wilson, dated 8 November 1965.

499. PREM 13/556, Rhodesian Cabinet to the Queen, 8 November 1965.

500. Skeen, *Prelude to Independence*, p. 144.

501. PREM 13/556, CRO to Governor, 10 November 1965.

502. Skeen, *op. cit.*, p. 147.

503. Ian Smith claimed (interview with the author) that he remembered these as the exact words. They ring true. Other aspects of Smith's recollection of the interview seem to me to be less reliable; see Smith, *The Great Betrayal*, p. 104.

504. NAZ: Record of interview with Clifford Dupont, ORAL/DU.

505. NAZ: Record of interview with G. W. Rudland, ORAL/RU2.

506. Wilson, *The Labour Government 1964–1970*, p. 157.

507. Fothergill, *Mirror over Rhodesia*, p. 400.

508. *Hansard*, vol. 720 (11 November 1965) col. 360.

509. *Guardian Weekly*, 18 November 1990.

510. Flower, *Serving Secretly*, p. 59.

511. DO 13/085, High Commissioner, Salisbury to CRO, 23 October 1964.

512. PREM 13/085, MoD Memorandum, [23?] October 1964.

513. NAZ: Record of interview with Sir Hugh Beadle, ORAL BE/2.

514. See *Governor's Note*; Smith's own subsequent rather disingenuous comment on the Governor's determination to stay at his post is ' ... because of the new constitution which we had brought in, his authority no longer existed, and the maintenance of his presence was of little concern to us'. Smith, *The Great Betrayal*, p. 109.

515. Author's interview with Ian Smith, 12 November 1993.

516. Flower, *Serving Secretly*, p. 79.

517. PREM 13/556, Ian Smith to the Queen, 3 December 1965.

518. *Ibid*, CRO to Governor, for transmission to the illegal regime, 3 December 1965.

519. PREM 13/553, 'Secret – Note for the Record', Derek Mitchell, 18 November 1965.

520. *Ibid*, 'Proposed Special Visit to Rhodesia', 21 November 1965.

521. *Ibid*, 'Secret – For the Record', 24 November 1965.

522. *Governor's Note*.

523. Crossman, *Diaries vol. 1*, p. 393 (28 November 1965).

524. Flower, *Serving Secretly*, p. 59.
525. Castle, *The Castle Diaries*, p. 76 (7 December 1965).
526. Crossman, *Diaries vol. 1*, p. 403 (7 December 1965).
527. Flower, *Serving Secretly*, p. 62.
528. PREM 13/621, Wilson to HVG, 24 December 1965.

CHAPTER 10

529. *Cape Times*, 14 January 1966 The claim had been made by the left-of-centre Conservative MP Humphrey Berkeley, who had spent a week in Rhodesia in early to mid January.
530. Skeen, *Prelude to Independence*, p. 172.
531. *Rhodesia Herald*, 4 January 1966.
532. *Daily Telegraph*, 7 January 1966 (reporting a statement by the Governor's ADC, Captain Owen); and *Rhodesia Herald*, 22 January 1966 (reporting a statement by Lady Ponsonby, Humphrey's sister).
533. *Rhodesia Herald*, 3 February 1966.
534. *Bulawayo Chronicle*, 2 March 1966.
535. *Citizen*, 4 March 1966. This article was illustrated with the picture of Harold Wilson shaking hands with Ian Smith, with Sir Humphrey looking on. However Ian Smith was cut out of the picture, which was then captioned 'Wilson and Humphrey', and was used on a number of occasions thereafter.
536. Goldin, *The Judge, the Prince and the Usurper*, p. 28.
537. PREM 13/085, A note by the Attorney General, 21 October 1964.
538. DO 183/334, Arthur Bottomley (Commonwealth Secretary) to Wilson, 20 November 1964.
539. *Ibid*, and DO 183/334, Oliver Wright to P. Moon (CRO) 24 November 1964.
540. DO 183/336, CRO to High Commissions, 19 November 1964.
541. See above, p. 95.
542. HVG MSS, F W Fynn to HVG, 19 November 1965.
543. Castle, *Diaries*, p. 72 (29 November 1965).
544. Wilson, *The Labour Government,* p. 196.
545. And it achieved much wider circulation by being repeated in *Argus*, 20 January 1966.
546. *Daily Telegraph*, 21 January 1966.
547. *Sunday Express*, 30 January 1966.
548. *Daily Mail*, 1 February 1966.
549. *Sunday Telegraph*, 6 February 1966.
550. *Cape Times*, 3 February 1966.
551. *Observer*, 23 May 1993.
552. Tredgold MSS, Rhodes House, I, 253.
553. This would appear to be a misspelt reference to Professor G. Kay, head of the Geography Department at the University College of Rhodesia.
554. *Cape Times*, 5 February 1966.
555. 5 February 1966.
556. *Daily Mail*, 9 February 1966; *Rhodesia Herald*, 9 February 1966.
557. *Sunday Mail*, 6 February 1966; *Cape Times*, 22 February 1966.

558. Report in the local Marandellas newspaper, *The Country Times*, 27 May 1966.
559. In HVG MSS, PC6, January 1966.
560. HVG MSS, Anonymous telegram from Rondebosch (Cape Town) dated 9 March 1966.
561. See reports of the incident in *Cape Times*, *Bulawayo Chronicle* and *Daily Mail*, 11 March 1966; John Pestell makes no mention of the incident in his diary.
562. *Bulawayo Chronicle*, 1 April 1966.
563. Wilson, *The Labour Government*, p. 218.
564. *Ibid*, p. 222.
565. HVG quoted in Black, *Sable: The Story of the Salisbury Club*, p. 222.
566. Quotations from the article by Paget, *Daily Mail*, 25 January 1966.
567. See David Steel's account in *Against Goliath*, pp. 56–7 and chapter 5.
568. King, *Closest Correspondence*, p. 147.
569. *Bulawayo Chronicle*, 13 January 1966.
570. *Cape Times*, 13 January 1966.
571. Thorpe, *Selwyn Lloyd*, p. 402.
572. Communiqué issued on 12 January 1966 at the Commonwealth Prime Ministers' Conference in Lagos; quoted in Young, *Rhodesia and Independence*, p. 370.
573. Skeen, *Prelude to Independence*, p. 172.
574. Berlyn, *The Quiet Man*, p. 155.
575. *Rhodesia: Documents relating to Proposals for a Settlement 1966* [Cmnd. 3171] p. 4.
576. PREM 13/621, Wilson to HVG, 24 December 1965.
577. *Bulawayo Chronicle*, 14 January 1966.
578. Wilson, *The Labour Government*, p. 200.
579. Pestell Diary, 7 April 1966.
580. *Rhodesia Herald*, 16 April 1966.
581. *Daily Telegraph*, 28 April 1966.
582. *Hansard*, vol. 727 (27 April 1966) col. 708.
583. Castle, *Diaries*, p. 120 (28 April 1966).
584. See Flower, *Serving Secretly*, p. 40.
585. *The Times*, 9 May 1966.
586. Pestell Diary, 7 May 1966.
587. *Daily Telegraph*, 4 June 1966.
588. *Daily Dispatch*, 4 June 1966.
589. *The Times*, 25 June 1966.
590. *Daily Mail*, 25 June 1966.
591. HVG MSS, Oliver Wright to HVG, 31 August 1966.
592. Editorial in *The Times*, 16 September 1966; the editorial concluded however that 'a new and realistic chapter of Commonwealth relations has opened'.
593. Wilson, *The Labour Government*, p. 287.
594. *Rhodesia: Documents relating to Proposals for a Settlement 1966* [Cmnd. 3171] p. 14.
595. *The Times*, 15 September 1966.
596. *Cape Times*, 19 September 1966.
597. *Bulawayo Chronicle*, 29 September 1966.
598. O'Neill, *The Autobiography of Terence O'Neill*, p. 86.

599. *Ibid*, p. 83.
600. Donal Lowry, 'Ulster resistance and loyalist rebellion in the Empire', in *'An Irish Empire'? Aspects of Ireland and the British Empire*, p. 206 and passim.
601. O'Neill, *The Autobiography of Terence O'Neill*, pp. 86–7; O'Neill mistakenly suggests that his dinner party with Molly happened before UDI – leading to his first approach to Harold Wilson, and that UDI then led to his 'recuperation' suggestion. He misplaces Molly's visit to October 1965 instead of October 1966.
602. TV broadcast, 9 December 1968; quoted in O'Neill, *op. cit.*, p. 147.
603. Castle, *Diaries*, p. 189 (24 November 1966).
604. Crossman, *Diaries of a Cabinet Minister Vol 2*, p. 139 (27 November 1966).
605. *Rhodesia: Documents relating to proposals for a Settlement 1966* [Cmnd. 3171] p. 28.
606. *Bulawayo Chronicle*, 26 November 1966.
607. Wilson, *The Labour Government*, p. 315.
608. *Rhodesia: Documents Relating to Proposals for a Settlement 1966* [Cmnd. 3171] p. 103.
609. *Sunday Times*, 11 December 1966 ('Insight' report).
610. Blake, *A History of Rhodesia*, pp. 398–9; Janet Smith, however, always claimed that her husband 'was infuriating, as he never gave a glimmer that he accepted or rejected what I was saying', *Daily Telegraph* obituary of Janet Smith, 3 December 1994.
611. Quoted in Ziegler, *Wilson*, p. 239.
612. The Sunday Times 'Insight' team in *Sunday Times*, 13 February 1977.

CHAPTER 11

613. CIO Note on the Position of Sir Humphrey Gibbs (23 November 1966), quoted in Flower, *Serving Secretly*, pp. 83–4.
614. Hancock, *White Liberals, Moderates and Radicals in Rhodesia*, p. 2.
615. HVG MSS, Barbara Tredgold to 'Ros and Kitty', 7 April 1980.
616. de la Harpe, *Msasa Morning*, p. 175.
617. Godwin and Hancock, *Rhodesians Never Die*, p. 26.
618. Hodder-Williams, 'White Attitudes and the Unilateral Declaration of Independence', *Journal of Commonwealth Political Studies*, no. 8 (1970) p. 258.
619. de la Harpe, *op. cit.*
620. *Rhodesia Herald*, 9 December 1966; a prominent article alongside the leader, entitled 'Cabinet would accept the Working Document if its meaning were clarified'.
621. Berlyn, *Rhodesia: Beleaguered Country*, p. 107.
622. Fothergill, *Mirror over Rhodesia*, p. 417.
623. *Scope*, 26 August 1966.
624. Pestell Diary, 10 June 1967.
625. *The Times*, 10 June 1968.
626. *Sunday Mail*, 9 June 1968.
627. Reed, *Battle for Rhodesia*, p. 75.

628. Quoted in Lapsley, *Neutrality or Co-option*, p. 25.
629. Quoted in Hancock, *White Liberals, Moderates and Radicals in Rhodesia*, p. 114.
630. Hancock, *op. cit.*, p. 107.
631. 'A New Year's message to my fellow-Africans', *Rhodesia Herald*, 20 January 1967.
632. Joyce, *Anatomy of a Rebel*, p. 382.
633. Pestell Diary, 5 January 1967.
634. Quoted in Flower, *Serving Secretly*, p. 94.
635. *Ibid*, p. 85.
636. *Rhodesia Herald*, 14 January 1967.
637. *Sunday Mail*, 15 January 1965.
638. *Bulawayo Chronicle*, 28 January 1967.
639. *The Times*, 7 February 1967.
640. *Ibid*, 6 February 1967.
641. HVG MSS, Antony Gibbs & Sons Ltd to HVG, 24 February 1967.
642. HVG MSS, Rhodesia Economic Department of the CRO to British High Commission, Salisbury, 6 April 1967.
643. *Sunday Mail*, 23 April 1967.
644. *Rhodesian Herald*, 29 June 1967.
645. Pestell Diary, 13 February 1967.
646. *Ibid*, 14 February 1967.
647. *Ibid*, 20 February 1967.
648. *The Times*, 11 May 1967.
649. Quoted in Goldin, *The Prince, The Judge and the Usurper*, p. 88.
650. *Hansard*, vol. 748 (13 June 1967) col. 305.
651. *Ibid*, col. 306.
652. *Rhodesia Herald*, 14 June 1967.
653. So described by Roy Jenkins, who as Home Secretary called him in as a special adviser in connection with the Prevention of Terrorism Act (after the Guildford bombings) in 1974: *A Life at the Centre*, p. 394.
654. *Ibid*, 19 June 1967.
655. Leading article, 25 June 1967.
656. Castle, *Diaries*, pp. 281-2.
657. *Hansard*, vol. 751 (25 July 1967) col. 327.
658. See especially the editorials in *Rhodesia Herald* and *Bulawayo Chronicle*, 27 July 1967.
659. The Governor's letter to Thomson (21 September 1967), and the conciliatory reply (13 October 1967) are quoted in Goldin, *The Prince, The Judge and the Usurper*, p. 92.
660. *Rhodesia Herald*, 30 September 1967.
661. *Ibid*, 2 October 1967.
662. *Bulawayo Chronicle*, 7 October 1967.
663. Private Information; Everard acted as 'President' briefly from August until November 1978.
664. Cosgrave, *The Strange Death of Socialist Britain*, p. 118.
665. Joyce, *Anatomy of a Rebel*, p. 386.

CHAPTER 12

666. Pestell Diary, 20 January 1968.
667. Cross, *The Fall of the British Empire*, p. 365.
668. Peter Godwin, in his *Mukiwa*, describes the murder in chapter 1; Oberhalzer was his next-door neighbour, and his father was the MO who attended the scene of the crime.
669. Goldin, *The Prince, The Judge and the Usurper*, p. 102.
670. *Ibid*, p. 63.
671. *Ibid*, p. 69.
672. Fieldsend MS, p. 66; grateful thanks to Mr Justice Fieldsend who allowed me to see his unpublished memoir of the case, which I refer to as Fieldsend MS.
673. Allister Sparks, who in an article entitled 'Slow Drama of Rhodesia's hangings' gave a succinct account of the cases: *Rand Daily Mail*, 16 March 1968.
674. Fieldsend MS, p. 73.
675. *Ibid*, p. 72.
676. *The Times*, 30 January 1968.
677. Pestell Diary, 5 January 1968.
678. Ibid, 10 January 1968.
679. Ibid, 29 January 1968.
680. Ibid, 31 January 1968.
681. *The Times*, 16 July 1994, reporting that 'Trinidad defies London judges and hangs murderer' and declaring this as 'unprecedented' – forgetting the Rhodesian precedent. It also noted that the Privy Council 'still serves 16 Commonwealth countries and another 17 territories and dependencies'.
682. Fieldsend MS, p. 82.
683. Pestell Diary, 3 March 1968.
684. From the Epistle for Lent 1, *2 Corinthians* 6, vv 4–5.
685. Quoted in Goldin, *The Prince, The Judge and the Usurper*, p. 122.
686. Thyne Papers, Beadle to Thyne, 13 March 1968.
687. HVG MSS, HVG to Robert Tredgold, 4 February 1977.
688. Macfarlane, 'Justifying Rebellion', *Journal of Commonwealth Political Studies*, vol. 6, no. 1 (March 1968) p. 361.
689. *Rhodesia Herald*, 6 February 1968.
690. *Ibid*, 26 February 1968.
691. Thorpe, *Alec Douglas-Home*, p. 397.
692. Pestell Diary, 25 February 1968.
693. *The Times*, 28 February 1968.
694. Douglas-Home, *Old Men Remember*, p. 90.
695. *Sunday Mail*, 10 March 1968.
696. *Daily Mirror*, 22 March 1968.
697. *Sunday News*, 24 March 1968; it was just over a week after this that President Johnson announced he would not run in the forthcoming US presidential election.
698. HVG MSS, Douglas-Home to HVG, nd (received, 8 April 1968).
699. *Sunday Mail*, 14 April 1968.
700. *Report of the Constitutional Commission 1968* (the Whaley Report) 3 April 1968.
701. *Financial Times*, 4 July 1968.

702. *Hansard*, vol. 764 (14 May 1968) cols 1059–60.
703. Pestell Diary, 24 May 1968.
704. *The Times*, 4 June 1968.
705. *Rhodesia Herald*, 5 June 1968.
706. *Sunday Mail*, 9 June 1968.
707. *Daily Mail*, 12 August 1968.
708. *Rand Daily Mail*, 16 August 1968.
709. Pestell Diary, 24 April 1968.
710. Wilson to HVG, 29 March 1968; quoted in Zeigler, *Wilson*, p. 320.
711. Wilson, *The Labour Government*, p. 565; see also Goodman, *Tell Them I'm On My Way*, pp. 219–20.
712. Pestell Diary, 16 August 1968.
713. *Ibid*, 20 August 1968; detailed account marked 'Top Secret'.
714. *Ibid*, 20 September 1968.
715. *Ibid*, 23 September 1968.
716. Bower, *Tiny Rowland*, p. 108, and generally chapter 3 ('A Decade of Dreams') for Rowland's activities during UDI.
717. Crossman, *Diaries Volume 3*, p. 216 (8 October 1968).
718. Wilson, *The Labour Government*, p. 568.
719. William Hickey in *Daily Express*, 16 October 1968.
720. Windrich, *Britain and the Politics of Rhodesian Independence*, p. 146 and *passim*.
721. *Rand Daily Mail*, 12 October 1968.
722. *The Economist*, 19 October 1968.
723. Wilson, *The Labour Government*, pp. 576–7.
724. HVG MSS, Palliser to Lady Gibbs, 17 November 1968.

CHAPTER 13

725. 'It looks as though it may be that you are near the end of the road as far as your own gallant effort to serve Rhodesia is concerned', HVG MSS, Alport to HVG, 16 June 1968.
726. HVG MSS, Carter to HVG, 22 November 1968.
727. HVG MSS, Lady Rankin to Lady Ponsonby, 17 December 1968.
728. *Citizen*, 13 December 1968; also Pestell Diary, 11 December 1968; in Britain there was far more concern about what road Ulster would take – Terence O'Neill, the Northern Ireland Prime Minister, had just made his 'Ulster at the Cross-roads' speech.
729. Hancock, *White Liberals, Radicals and Moderates in Rhodesia*, p. 122.
730. *Rhodesia Herald*, 14 December 1968.
731. Windrich, *Britain and the Politics of Rhodesian Independence*, p. 150–1.
732. *Daily Mail*, 13 December 1968.
733. Pestell Diary, 3 January 1969; see also Godwin and Hancock, *Rhodesians Never Die*, pp. 74–5.
734. HVG MSS, Owen to HVG, 7 February 1969; the Commonwealth Relations Office had been wound up and merged with the Foreign Office to create the FCO in October 1968.

735. Pestell Diary, 24 January 1969.
736. *Rhodesia Herald*, 25 January 1969.
737. *Ibid*, 23 January 1969.
738. *Hansard*, vol. 776 (21 January 1969) col. 245.
739. Flower, *Serving Secretly*, p. 95.
740. Pestell Diary, 15 February 1969.
741. *Sunday Mail*, 16 February 1969.
742. *Hansard*, vol. 779 (4 March 1969) col. 211.
743. See *Rhodesia: Report on Exchanges with the regime since Talks held in Salisbury* [Cmnd.4065].
744. *Bulawayo Chronicle,* 4 April 1969.
745. Pestell Diary, 10 May 1969.
746. *Proposals for a new Constitution for Rhodesia* (CSR 32-1969).
747. *Rhodesia: Parliamentary Debates*, vol. 75 (8 October 1969) col. 1190.
748. *Rand Daily Mail*, 30 November 1968.
749. Godwin and Hancock, *Rhodesians Never Die*, p. 71.
750. Terence O'Neill resigned on 29 April, and on 31 April was replaced by James Chichester-Clark, who was in turn replaced by the more hard-line Brian Faulkner in March 1971; fancifully one could say it was a sequence not unlike Whitehead, Field and Smith.
751. *Rhodesia Herald*, 13 June 1969.
752. *Sunday Mail*, Supplement, 15 June 1969.
753. Pastoral Letter headlined in *Sunday Mail*, 8 June 1969.
754. Lapsley, *Neutrality or Co-option?*, p. 28.
755. *Rand Daily Mail*, 14 June 1969.
756. *Sunday Mail*, 1 June 1969.
757. *Rhodesia Herald*, 6 June 1969.
758. *Ibid*, 7 June 1969.
759. Godwin and Hancock, *Rhodesians Never Die*, p. 73, quoting his 1967 Annual Report as Chairman of the RCA.
760. Antony Durant Gibbs now became fifth Baron Aldenham and third Baron Hunsdon; he was Walter's second son, the eldest having been killed in action at Nijmegen in 1944.
761. 'Baffy' Dugmore was a Bulawayo businessman and an old friend of Humphrey.
762. His statement was headlined and printed in full in *Rhodesia Herald*, 12 June 1969.
763. HVG MSS, Bishop Burrough to HVG, 16 June 1969.
764. *Hansard*, vol. 785 (24 June 1969) col. 1219; the announcement of the closure of the mission led to protests from Alec Douglas-Home and Edward Heath.
765. *Rhodesia Herald*, 25 June 1969; the original text of his statement is in HVG Archives, SB 3.
766. *Rhodesia Herald*, 5 July 1969.
767. HVG MSS, Welensky to HVG, 21 July 1969.
768. *Daily Telegraph*, 25 June 1965; *Rhodesia Herald*, 7 July 1969.
769. HVG MSS, undated 'Text of Message from the Prime Minister's Private Secretary to Lady Gibbs'.
770. See Pimlott, *The Queen*, pp. 246–7.
771. HVG MSS, Plunket to HVG, 30 June 1969.
772. *The Times*, 27 September 1969.

773. Bacon MSS, Bacon to HVG, 17 January 1969.
774. In the period from March 1967 to December 1968, for instance, there were 'serious incidents of direct student action' at twenty-three campuses in Britain: Crick and Robson (editors), *Protest and Discontent*, p. 82.
775. Bacon MSS, HVG to Bacon, 30 November 1969.
776. Undated Memorandum (probably October 1970) entitled 'ECB's Visits to Rhodesia' in Bacon MSS.
777. *Hansard*, vol. 785 (24 June 1969) col. 1227; Michael Hamilton was the son-in-law of Charles Ponsonby (Humphrey's brother-in-law) who had delivered the 'stick it out' message from Alec Douglas-Home in April 1968: see above p. 152.
778. Bacon MSS, Bottomley to Bacon, 16 July 1969.
779. *Ibid*, 12 December 1969.
780. *Hansard*, vol. 793 (19 December 1969) col. *446*.
781. *Sun*, 20 December 1969.
782. *Daily Telegraph*, 20 December 1969.
783. *Guardian*, 22 December 1969.
784. *Daily Mirror*, 22 December 1969.
785. Bacon MSS, Faulkner to Bacon, 23 December 1969.
786. *The Times*, 31 December 1969.
787. *Hansard*, vol. 794 (20 January 1970) col. 235.
788. Bacon MSS, Bacon to Douglas-Home, 2 April 1973; the Bacon papers have full details of the various calculations forwarded to the government itemising Government House expenditure during UDI.
789. Copy in Bacon MSS of W. J. Rumble (Rhodesia Dept, FCO) to Pestell, 29 November 1974.

CHAPTER 14

790. Gelfand and Ritchken (eds), *Godfrey Martin Huggins*, p. 50.
791. Bacon MSS, Bacon to Sir Denis Greenhill, 7 April 1971.
792. See *Cape Argus*, 23 November 1978, and other relevant (undated) newspaper reports on the issue in HVG Archives, Scrapbook 3.
793. *The Times*, 21 November 1978.
794. *Hansard*, vol. 960 (18 January 1979) col. 827; see also *Sunday Telegraph*, 31 December 1978.
795. HVG MSS, Callaghan to Hamilton, 27 December 1978.
796. Godwin and Hancock, *Rhodesians never Die*, p. 51.
797. Quoted in Thorpe, *Alec Douglas-Home*, p. 425.
798. Blake, *A History of Rhodesia*, p. 404.
799. *Rhodesia: Report of the Commission on Rhodesian Opinion* [Cmnd. 4964] p. 156.
800. *Ibid*, p. 120.
801. *Ibid*, p. 111.
802. *Ibid*, p. 146.
803. Anglo-American Archives, Gibbs to Sir Albert Robinson, 7 August 1974.
804. See Godwin and Hancock, *Rhodesians Never Die*, pp. 111–12.
805. *RePort* (the RP Newsletter), No 16, January 1975.

806. Bacon MSS, Pestell to Bacon, 31 August 1975.
807. Bacon MSS: HVG to Bacon, 23 May 1975.
808. HVG MSS, Plunket to HVG, 30 January 1977.
809. HVG MSS, HVG to Tredgold, 4 February 1977.
810. HVG MSS, Welensky to HVG, 11 February 1977.
811. HVG MSS, Tredgold to HVG, 4 March 1977; HVG to Tredgold, 10 March 1977.
812. Copy in HVG MSS, Charteris to Welensky, 5 April 1977.
813. *Rhodesia Herald*, 31 January 1979.
814. *Ibid*, 2 February 1979.
815. Caute, *Under the Skin*, p. 383.
816. Dupont had been the first President of the Republic in 1970, and in April 1980 The Revd Canaan Banana became the first President of the Republic of Zimbabwe, so in a decade Rhodesia had nine heads of state. Strictly, however, it could be said that the country only had two – Queen Elizabeth and Canaan Banana – the others were titular heads of an illegal and virtually unrecognised regime.
817. Smith, *The Great Betrayal*, p. 326; see also *The Times*, 13 December 1979.
818. Quoted in Pimlott, *The Queen*, p. 468.
819. *The Times*, 12 December 1979.
820. HVG (UK) MSS, Robin Byatt to Dame Molly, 18 November 1990.
821. HVG MSS: HVG to Soames, 13 December 1979.
822. HVG MSS: HVG to Sir Antony Duff, 31 January 1980 .
823. HVG MSS: Sir Antony to HVG, 8 March 1980.
824. See the full list in HVG MSS: 'Patronages, Presidentships, Honorary Memberships etc: His Excellency, the Honourable Sir Humphrey Gibbs', dated July 1963.
825. *The Times* (headline) 28 January 1980.
826. *Ibid*, 5 March 1980.
827. Godwin, *Mukiwa*, p. 326.
828. *Ibid*, p. 329.
829. *The Herald*, 14 February 1982, in a leader which with rather inappropriate humour was entitled 'Cache Crisis'.
830. *The Herald*, 1 March 1982.
831. *Daily Telegraph*, 1 March 1983.
832. *Ibid*, 21 March 1983.
833. *The Times*, 14 July 1983.
834. *The Times*, 13 July 1983.
835. A reporter for *The Times*, 15 September 1983, quoting Tim's wife.
836. *The Times*, 20 September 1983.
837. HVG MSS, letter to all 'the Brothers' from Tim Gibbs, 4 September 1983, spells out the details of the problem, and the various options open to their parents. Half a million dollars at that time was the equivalent of some £250,000.

CHAPTER 15

838. *The Herald*, 23 May 1980.

839. 'Communal areas' was the new name for the 'Tribal Trust Lands' or TTLs, where most of the African rural population lived.
840. 'The Role of Independent Schools in Zimbabwe: Past, Present and Future', a statement by the Minister of Education and Culture, The Hon D. Mutumbuka, 16 November 1983; copy in Peterhouse Archives.
841. Prime Minister's speech at Speech Day, *Peterhouse Magazine 1987*, p. 11.
842. *The Herald*, 18 November 1983, in an editorial under the title 'Heads in the Sand'.
843. *The Herald*, 23 November 1987, in an editorial headed 'Multi-racial education'.
844. Peterhouse Archives, letter of appeal (undated, 1988) from HVG to potential donors.
845. HVG to the author, 2 October 1989, in the author's possession.
846. See Kirk-Greene, *A Biographical Dictionary of the British Colonial Governor, Volume 1: Africa*.
847. Meredith, *The First Dance of Freedom*, p. 377.

Bibliography

Many of the works in this bibliography relate specifically to Rhodesia/Zimbabwe. That is understandable. But I have also included all the books and other sources which I have used. When a book or article is cited in the footnotes, the reference is kept short, and full details may be found by consulting this bibliography, where the material is arranged thus:

> A Manuscript Materials
>   i. In Zimbabwe
>   ii. In the United Kingdom
>
> B Official Publications
>   i. Rhodesia
>   ii. United Kingdom
>
> C Reference Books and Newspapers
>
> D Books
>
> E Articles, Pamphlets and Theses

A MANUSCRIPT SOURCES

i. In Zimbabwe

(a) The Gibbs Archives:
When Sir Humphrey Gibbs died in 1990, his family deposited all the papers and manuscripts then in Zimbabwe at Peterhouse, the school of which he had been a governor since its inception. An archive room has subsequently been built there (as part of a larger development called the Gibbs Building) and it houses the archive which in outline consists of:

(1) 8 Boxes of correspondence, arranged chronologically
(2) 27 Press Cutting books
(3) 4 scrapbooks
(4) 5 photograph albums
(5) Miscellaneous Files (papers relating to the Governor's Fund; correspondence relating to the family silver 1978–9; HVG's autobiographical sketch; obituaries from newspapers; financial and other matters mainly for the post-1980 period
(6) 4 volumes of press cuttings from the Rhodesian Constitutional Association (donated by its sometime Chairman, Dr N. A. F. Williams).

b) The Peterhouse Archives:
The archives of the school for which Sir Humphrey was a governor from its inception in 1953 until his death. They contain a mass of information about independent schools, multiracial education, and Sir Humphrey's role as a founder and governor of the school. These archives are housed alongside the Gibbs Archives.

(c) The Zimbabwe National Archives:
These contain little material specifically about Sir Humphrey, but house other complementary collections. There is a particularly useful set of transcripts of interviews with various personalities (ORAL/). The portrait of Sir Humphrey which used to hang in the House of Assembly is now stored (along with portraits of other ex-governors) in the National Archives, but is not on display (or wasn't when I was taken to see it in 1993).

ORAL/BE 2	Sir Hugh Beadle (interviewed 1972)
ORAL/DU 4	Clifford Dupont (interviewed 1976/7)
ORAL/FI 2	Mrs Barbara Ann Field (interviewed 1971)
ORAL/GU 1	Sir Ernest Guest (interviewed 1971/2)
ORAL/LL 2	A. D. R. Lloyd (interviewed 1972,1973,1975)
ORAL/RO 2	Sir E. P. Robinson (written responses to questions)
ORAL/RU 3	G. W. Rudland (interviewed 1972)
ORAL/ST 6	A. R. W. Stumbles (interviewed 1973)
ORAL/TO 1	R. S. G. Todd (interviewed 1972)

Alderson Papers: Notebooks of Bishop Alderson, NAZ AL 7
Barrow Papers: Papers of Sir John Barrow, NAZ MSS 841
Other individual manuscript items are fully cited in the footnotes, with the preface NAZ.

(d) The Harare Diocesan Archives:
These (relatively unsorted) papers contain a mass of information, especially regarding Sir Humphrey's activities on behalf of the diocese (then of Southern Rhodesia) in the early 1940s.

(e) The Anglo-American Archive:
This collection contains some material relating to Sir Humphrey, and also much material of peripheral interest, especially regarding the founding of Peterhouse, and the political activities of Sir Albert Robinson.

ii. In the United Kingdom

(a) Public Record Office:
Prime Ministerial (PREM), Cabinet Office (CAB), Dominions Office (DO), Commonwealth Office (CRO) and Foreign Office (FO) papers are fully cited in the footnotes. Probably many of the relevant documents are not yet available for public inspection, even those which fall outside the thirty-year rule.

(b) Rhodes House Library, Oxford:
Tredgold Papers: The Papers of Sir Robert Tredgold MSS Afr s 1632
Welensky Papers: The Papers of Sir Roy Welensky (in course of indexing)
Whitehead Papers: The Papers of Sir Edgar Whitehead MSS Afr s 1482

(c) Trinity College Library, Cambridge:
Butler Papers: The Papers of Lord Butler of Saffron Walden

(d) Borthwick Institute, York:
Haddon Papers: The Papers of Mrs Eileen Haddon
Thyne Papers: The Papers of William Thyne OBE
Wilson Papers: The papers of Sir Ian Wilson

(e) In Private Hands:
(1) The (unpublished) Diary of Sir John Pestell: at the suggestion of Sir Charles Ponsonby he kept a very full day by day diary from 4 March 1966 until 28 June 1969
(2) Correspondence: Lady Hunsdon to HVG, mainly from the 1930s (the Gibbs Family)
(3) The (unpublished) legal memoirs of Mr Justice Fieldsend (in his possession)
(4) Sir Edmund Bacon Papers (in the family archives)

B OFFICIAL PUBLICATIONS

i. Rhodesia

Report of the Secretary, Department of Agriculture and Lands, for the years 1941, 1942, 1943, 1944, 1945 (1947) CSR 15-1947

Annual Report of the Natural Resources Board for the year ended 31 December 1946, (1947) CSR 36-1947

Annual Report of the Natural Resources Board for the year ended 31 December 1947, (1948) CSR 8-1948

Annual Report of the Natural Resources Board for the year ended 31 December 1948, (1949) CSR 24-1949

Southern Rhodesia Legislative Assembly, *Second Report of the Select Committee on the Resettlement of Natives,* (16 August 1960) LASC .3-1960

Rhodesia and Nyasaland Federation: The Southern Rhodesia (Constitution) Order in Council, 1961, Statutory Instrument 1961 No. 2314

Report on the Zimbabwe African Peoples Union (September 1962)

Relations between the Rhodesian Government and the United Kingdom Government November 1965–December 1966, CSR 49-1966

Twenty-Five Years of Progress in Conservation in Rhodesia (Natural Resources Board, Salisbury 1967)

Rhodesia Independence Constitution: Proposals for a Settlement contained in the Working Document produced at the Conference aboard HMS Tiger, CSR 6-1967

Report of the Constitutional Commission 1968 (April 1968) (the Whaley Report)
Judgment delivered in the Appellate Division of the High Court of Rhodesia at Salisbury on Friday 13 September 1968 in the matter between: Archion Ndhlovu and Thirty-One Others, and the Queen, (Judgment No. AD 138/68)

Statement on Anglo-Rhodesian Relations December 1966 to May 1969, CSR 36-1969

ii. United Kingdom

Report of the Commission on closer union of the dependencies in eastern and central Africa (Hilton Young Report) (17 October 1928) Cmnd. 3234
Report of the Royal Commission on Rhodesia and Nyasaland (Bledisloe Report) (1 March 1939) Cmnd. 5949
The Federation of Rhodesia and Nyasaland: Report of a Visit by a Parliamentary Delegation, September 1957
Report of the Advisory Committee on the review of the Constitution of Rhodesia and Nyasaland (Monckton Report) (October 1960) Cmnd. 1148
Southern Rhodesia Constitution: Part 1 – Summary of proposed Changes (June 1961), Cmnd 1399; *Part II – Detailed Provisions*, Cmnd. 1400
Southern Rhodesia: Documents relating to the negotiations between the United Kingdom and the Southern Rhodesian Government November 1963–November 1965 (November 1965) Cmnd. 2807
Rhodesia: Proposals for a Settlement (December 1966) Cmnd. 3159
Rhodesia: Documents relating to Proposals for a Settlement 1966 (December 1966) Cmnd. 3171
Rhodesia: Report on Exchanges with the Regime since the Talks held in Salisbury in November, 1968 (June 1969) Cmnd. 4065
Rhodesia: Report of the Commission on Rhodesian Opinion under the Chairmanship of the Right Honourable the Lord Pearce (May 1972) Cmnd. 4964

C REFERENCE BOOKS AND NEWSPAPERS

i. Reference Books

A Register of Rhodes Scholars 1903–1981 (Oxford 1981)
Brelsford, W. V. (ed). *Handbook to the Federation of Rhodesia and Nyasaland* (Salisbury 1960)
Brown, A. S. and Brown, G. G. *The South and East African Year Book & Guide* (London 1936)
Butler, D. and Freeman, J. *British Political Facts 1900–1967* (London 1968)
Burke's Landed Gentry
Dominions Office and Colonial Office List
Foote, G. *A Chronology of Post War British Politics* (Beckenham, Kent 1988)
Gibbs, R. *Pedigree of the Family of Gibbs* (4th edn 1981)
Handbook of Commonwealth Organisations (London 1965)
Keesing's Contemporary Archives
Kelly's Handbook to the Titled, Landed and Official Classes
Kirk-Greene, A. H. M., *A Biographical Dictionary of the british Colonial Governor Volume 1: Africa* (Stanford, California, 1980)
Official Year Book of Southern Rhodesia
Rasmussen, R. K. and Rubert, S. C. *Historical Dictionary of Zimbabwe* (African Historical Dictionaries no. 46, 2nd edn, Metuchen, NJ, 1990)
Whitaker's Almanack
Who's Who

Who's Who in Southern Africa
Wilding, N. W. *Parliamentary Papers of Rhodesia 1954–1970* (Salisbury 1970)

ii. Newspapers

Numerous South African, British and Rhodesian papers are cited in the footnotes, but the following proved to be most useful:

Bulawayo Chronicle (Bulawayo)
Central African Examiner (Salisbury)
Rhodesia Herald (Salisbury)
The Times (London)
Vuka (The Broadsheet of the Farmers' Union) (Bulawayo)

The Gibbs Archive (at Peterhouse) contains many volumes of press cutting books which were kept up at Government House during UDI by a team of volunteers. It also houses the press cutting books of the RCA (Rhodesian Constitutional Association). Photocopies, or originals, of almost all the newspaper items cited are also in a collection in the author's possession.

D BOOKS

Allighan, H. *The Welensky Story* (Cape Town 1962)
Alport, Lord *The Sudden Assignment: Central Africa 1961–3* (London 1965)
Anderson, D. *The Toe-Rags: A Memoir* ((London 1989)
Alston, M. *Via Gibbs: A Memoir* (London 1921)
Arnold, W. E. *Here to Stay: The Story of the Anglican Church in Zimbabwe* (Lewes, Sussex 1985)
Atkinson, N. D. *Teaching Rhodesians: A History of Educational Policy in Rhodesia* (London 1973)
Armstrong, P. *Tobacco Spiced with Ginger: The Life of Ginger Freeman* (Harare 1987)
Banana, C. S. *Turmoil and Tenacity: Zimbabwe 1890–1990* (Harare 1989)
Barber, J. *Rhodesia: The Road to Rebellion* (Oxford 1967)
Barber, W. J. *The Economy of British Central Africa: a case study of economic development in a dualistic society* (London 1961)
Bartlett, V. *Struggle for Africa* (London 1953)
Bean, P. and Melville, J. *Lost Children of the Empire* (London 1989)
Beit, Sir A. and Lockhart, J. G. *The Will and the Way 1906–1956: being an account of Alfred Beit and the Trust which he founded* (London 1957)
Berlyn, P. *Rhodesia: Beleaguered Country* (London 1967)
Birkenhead, Lord *Walter Monckton* (London 1969)
Black, C. *Sable: The Story of the Salisbury Club* (Salisbury 1980)
Blake, R. *A History of Rhodesia* ((London 1977)
Bonham Carter, V. *Winston Churchill as I Knew Him* (London 1965)
Bower, T. *Tiny Rowland: A Rebel Tycoon* (London 1993)

Bowman, L. W. *Politics in Rhodesia: White Power in an African State* (Cambridge, Mass. 1973)

Bradford, S. *Elizabeth: A Biography of Her Majesty the Queen* (London 1996)

Brettell, N. H. *Side-Gate and Style: An Essay in Autobiography* (Bulawayo 1981)

Brettell, N. H. and others *Ruzawi: The Founding of a School* (Salisbury nd [1968?])

Brown, R. *Bye Bye Shangri-la* (London 1989)

Butler, Lord *The Art of the Possible: The Memoirs of Lord Butler* (London 1971)

Callaghan, Lord *Time and Chance* (London 1987)

Campbell, A. *The Heart of Africa* (London 1954)

Cannadine, D. *The Decline and Fall of the British Aristocracy* (London revised edn 1992)

Card, T. *Eton Renewed: A History from 1860 to the Present Day* (London 1994)

Carrington, Lord *Reflect on Things Past: The Memoirs of Lord Carrington* (London 1988)

Cartwright, A. P. *Valley of Gold* (Cape Town 1961)

Castle, B. *The Castle Diaries 1964–70* (London 1984)

Caute, D. *Under the Skin: The Death of White Rhodesia* (London 1983)

Chadwick, O. *Michael Ramsey: A Life* (Oxford 1990)

Chadwick, O. *The Victorian Church Part II* (London 1970)

Chanock, M. *Unconsummated Union: Britain, Rhodesia and South Africa 1900–45* (Manchester 1977)

Christopher, A. J. *Colonial Africa* (London 1984)

Clark, G. Kitson *An Expanding Society: Britain 1832–1900* (Cambridge 1967)

Clegg, E. *Race and Partnership: Partnership in the Federation of Rhodesia and Nyasaland* (London 1960)

Clements, F. *Rhodesia: The Course to Collision* (London 1969)

Cloete, S. *The African Giant: The Story of a Journey* (London 1956)

Clutton-Brock, G. and M. *Cold Comfort Confronted* (Oxford 1972)

Colville, J. *The Fringes of Power: Downing Street Diaries 1939–1955* (London 1985)

Constantine, S. (ed.) *Emigrants and Empire: British Settlement in the Dominions between the Wars* (Manchester 1990)

Cosgrave, P. *The Strange Death of Socialist Britain: Post-War British Politics* (London 1992)

Coupland, R. *The Empire in These Days; An Interpretation* (London 1935)

Creighton, T. R. M. *The Anatomy of Partnership: Southern Rhodesia and the Central African Federation* (London 1960)

Crick, B. and Robson, W. A. (eds) *Protest and Discontent* (Harmondsworth 1970)

Cross, C. *The Fall of the British Empire 1918–1968* (London 1970)

Crossman, R. *The Diaries of a Cabinet Minister Volume One: Minister of Housing and Local Government 1964–66* (London 1975)

Crossman, R. *The Diaries of a Cabinet Minister Volume Three: Secretary of State for Social Services 1968–70* (London 1977)

Culwick, A. T. *Britannia Waives the Rules* ((Cape Town, 1963)

Davidson, T. *Wankie: The Story of a Great Game Reserve* (Cape Town 1967)

Davies, D. K. *Race Relations in Rhodesia: A Survey for 1972–3* (London 1975)

de la Harpe, M. *Msasa Morning* (Harare 1992)

Dibb, C. E. *Ivory, Apes and Peacocks* (Bulawayo 1981)

Dimbleby, J. *The Prince of Wales: A Biography* (London 1994)

Donnelly, D. *Gadarene '68: The Crimes, Follies and Misfortunes of the Wilson Government* (London 1968)

Dorril, S. and Ramsay, R. *Smear! Wilson and the Secret State* (London 1992)

Douglas-Home, C. *Evelyn Baring – The Last Proconsul* (London 1978)

Douglas-Home, W. *Old Men Remember* (London 1991)

Driberg, T. *Ruling Passions* (London 1977)

Dunn, C. *Central African Witness* (London 1959)

Dupont, C. *The Reluctant President: The Memoirs of the Hon Clifford Dupont* (Bulawayo 1978)

Easton, S. C. *The Twilight of European Colonialism* (London 1961)

Evans, H. St J. T. *The Church in Southern Rhodesia* (London 1945)

Faber, R. *The Vision and the Need: Late Victorian Imperialist Aims* (London 1966)

Farrant, J. *Mashonaland Martyr: Bernard Mizeki and the Pioneer Church* (Cape Town 1966)

Fergusson, B. *Eton Portrait* (London 1937)

Fisher, N. *Iain Macleod* (London 1993)

Flower, K. *Serving Secretly* (London 1987)

Fothergill, R. *Laboratory for Peace: The Story of Ken and Lilian Mew and of Ranche House College, Salisbury* (Bulawayo 1984)

Fothergill, R. *Mirror over Rhodesia: The Rhodesian Press 1962–1980* (Privately printed, Johannesburg 1984)

Franklin, H. *Unholy Wedlock: The Failure of the Central African Federation* (London 1963)

Frew, A. A. *Prince George's African Tour* (London 1934)

Frost, R. *Enigmatic Proconsul: Sir Philip Mitchell and the Twilight of Empire* (London 1992)

Gale, W. D. *The Rhodesian Press: The History of the Rhodesian Printing and Publishing Company* (Salisbury 1962)

Gann, L. H. *A History of Southern Rhodesia – Early Days to 1934* (London 1965)

Gann, L. H. and Duignan, P. (eds) *Colonialism in Africa 1870–1960 Volume 2: The History and Politics of Colonialism 1914–1960* (Cambridge 1970)

Gann, L. H. and Gelfand, M. *Huggins of Rhodesia: The Man and His Country* (London 1964)

Garner, J. *The Commonwealth Office 1925–68* (London 1978)

Gelfand, M. *A Non-Racial Island of Learning: A History of the University College of Rhodesia from its Inception to 1966* (Gwelo 1978)

Gelfand, M. and Ritchken, J. *Godfrey Martin Huggins 1883–1971: His Life and Work* (Salisbury nd)

Gibbon, G. *Paget of Rhodesia* (Bulawayo 1973)

Gibbs, P. *Avalanche in Central Africa* (London 1961)

Godwin, P. *Mukiwa: A White Boy in Africa* (London 1996)

Godwin, P. and Hancock, I. *'Rhodesians Never Die' The Impact of War and Political Change in White Rhodesia c1970–1980* (Oxford 1993)

Goldin, B. *The Judge, The Prince and the Usurper – from UDI to Zimbabwe* (New York 1990)

Goodman, A. *Tell Them I'm On My Way* (London 1993)

Gray, R. *The Two Nations: Aspects of the development of Race Relations in the Rhodesias and Nyasaland* (London 1960)

Grain, T. *Mission Unaccomplished: An Account of the Work of Railway Missions in Southern Africa 1890–1980* (Lingfield, Surrey nd)

Greenfield, J. M. *Testimony of a Rhodesian Federal* (Bulawayo 1978)

Gunther, J. *Inside Africa* (London 1957 edn)

Gussman, B. *Out in the Mid-day Sun* (London 1962)

Halifax, Earl of *Fullness of Days* (London 1957)

Hall, R. *The High Price of Principles: Kaunda and the White South* (London 1969)

Hancock, I. *White Liberals, Moderates and Radicals in Rhodesia 1953–1980* (London 1984)

Hanna, A. J. *The Story of the Rhodesias and Nyasaland* (London 1965)

Hastings, A. *A History of English Christianity 1920–1990* (3rd edn, London 1991)

Hatch, J. *Africa Today – And Tomorrow* (2nd revised edn, London 1965)

Hatch, J. *Everyman's Africa* (London 1959)

Heseltine, N. *Remaking Africa* (London 1961)

Hills, D. *Rebel People* (London 1978)

Hoare, R. *Rhodesian Mosaic* (London 1934)

Hodder-Williams, R. *White Farmers in Rhodesia 1890–1965* (London 1983)

Holderness, H. *Lost Chance: Southern Rhodesia 1945–58* (Harare 1985)

Home, Lord *The Way the Wind Blows: An Autobiography* (London 1976)

Horne, A. *Macmillan 1957–1986: Volume II of the Official Biography* (London 1989)

Howarth, T. E. B. *Cambridge Between Two Wars* (London 1978)

Hudson, M. *Triumph or Tragedy? Rhodesia to Zimbabwe* (London 1981)

Humphreys, M. *Empty Cradles* (London 1995)

Hunt, A. *Oxford to Zimbabwe: A Life's Recall* (Oxford 1994)

Italiaander, R. *The New Leaders of Africa* (London 1961)

Jacobson, D. *The Electronic Elephant: A Southern African Journey* (London 1994)

James, L. *The Rise and Fall of the British Empire* (London 1994)

Jeffery, K. (ed.) *'An Irish Empire'? Aspects of Ireland and the British Empire* (Manchester 1996)

Jenkins, R. *A Life at the Centre* (London 1991)

Joyce, P. *Anatomy of a Rebel – Smith of Rhodesia: A Biography* (Salisbury 1974)

Judd, D. *Empire: The British Imperial Experience, from 1765 to the Present* (London 1996)

Kennedy, D. *Islands of White: Settler Society and Culture in Kenya and Southern Rhodesia, 1890–1939* (Durham, 1987)

Kennedy, P. *The Rise and Fall of the Great Powers* (London 1988)

Keppel, S. *Edwardian Daughter* (London 1958)

King, E. *Closest Correspondence* (Lewes, 1989)

Knight, E. F. *Rhodesia of To-day* (London 1895)

Kynaston, D. *The City of London: vol. 1: A World of its own 1815–1890* (London 1994)

Kynaston, D. *The City of London: vol. 2: Golden Years 1890–1914* (London 1995)

Lacey, R. *Majesty: Elizabeth II and the House of Windsor* (London revised edn 1978)

Lapsley, M. *Neutrality or Co-option?* (Gweru 1986)

Lardner-Burke, D. *Rhodesia: The Story of the Crisis* (London 1966)

Lessing, D. *African Laughter: Four Visits to Zimbabwe* (London 1992)

Leys, C. *European Politics in Southern Rhodesia* (Oxford 1959)

Leys, C. and Pratt, C. (eds) *A New Deal in Central Africa* (London 1960)

Lloyd, F. E. *Rhodesian Patrol* (Ilfracombe 1965)
Lord, G. *Ghosts of King Solomon's Mines – Mozambique and Zimbabwe: A Quest* (London 1991)
Low, D. A. *Eclipse of Empire* (Cambridge 1991)
Lucas, J. *England and Englishness* (Iowa 1990)
Macdonald, S. *Martie and Others in Rhodesia* (London 1927)
Macdonald, S. *Sally in Rhodesia* (Bulawayo 1970 – reprint of 1927 edition)
McIntosh, K. *Echoes of Enterprise: A History of the Enterprise District* (Harare 1987?)
McIntyre, D. *The Diocesan College, Rondebosch: A Century of 'Bishops'* (Cape Town 1940)
Macmillan, H. *At the End of the Day 1961–1963* (London 1973)
Macmillan, H. *Pointing the Way 1959–61* (London 1972)
Macmillan, H. *Riding the Storm 1956–1959* (London 1971)
Mason, P. *Year of Decision: Rhodesia and Nyasaland in 1960* (London 1960)
Megahey, A. J. *A History of Cranleigh School* (London 1983)
Meredith, M. *The First Dance of Freedom: Black Africa in the Postwar Era* (London 1984)
Meredith, M. *The Past is Another Country – Rhodesia: UDI to Zimbabwe* (London 1980 edn)
Miracle, M. P. *Maize in Tropical Africa* (Madison 1966)
Moorcraft, P. L. *A Short Thousand Years:The End of Rhodesia's Rebellion* (Salisbury 1979)
Morris, J. *Pax Britannica: The Climax of an Empire* (London 1968)
Mosley, P. *The Settler Economies: Studies in the Economic History of Kenya and Southern Rhodesia* (Cambridge 1983)
Mungazi, D. A. *Colonial Policy and Conflict in Zimbabwe: A Study of Cultures in Collision 1890–1979* (New York 1992)
Mungazi, D. A. *Education and Government Control in Zimbabwe: A Study of the Commissions of Enquiry 1908–1974* (New York 1990)
Murphree, M. W. (ed.) *Education, Race and Employment in Rhodesia* (Salisbury 1965)
Murray, D. J. *The Governmental System in Southern Rhodesia* (Oxford 1970)
Muzorewa, A. T. *Rise up and Walk: An Autobiography* (London 1978)
Nabarro, Sir G. *Nab 1: Portrait of a Politician* (London 1969)
Nkomo, J. *The Story of My Life* (London 1984)
Ollard, R. *An English Education: A Perspective of Eton* (London 1982)
O'Neill, Lord *The Autobiography of Terence O'Neill* (London 1972)
Paget, S. and Crum, J. M. C. *Francis Paget Bishop of Oxford* (London 1912)
Palley, C. *The Constitutional History and Law of Southern Rhodesia 1888–1965 with special reference to imperial control* (Oxford 1966)
Palmer, R. *Land and Racial Discrimination in Rhodesia* (London 1977)
Parker, J. *Rhodesia: Little White Island* (London 1972)
Paver, B. G. *Zimbabwe Cavalcade: Rhodesia's Romance* (London 1957)
Peck, A. J. A. *Rhodesia Accuses* (Salisbury 1966)
Peck, A. J. A. *Rhodesia Condemns* (Salisbury 1967)
Phimister, I. *An Economic and Social History of Zimbabwe 1890–1948: Capital accumulation and class struggle* (London 1988)
Pimlott, B. *The Queen: A Biography of Elizabeth II* (London 1996)
Pimlott, B. *Harold Wilson* (London 1992)

Plant, G. F. *Overseas Settlement: Migration from the United Kingdom to the Dominions* (London 1951)

Ponsonby, Sir C. *Ponsonby Remembers* (Oxford 1965)

Prain, Sir R. *Reflections on an Era: Fifty Years of Mining in Changing Africa* (Metal Bulletin Books 1981)

Randall, P. *Little England on the Veld: The English Private School System in South Africa* (Johannesburg 1982)

Ranger, T. O. (ed.) *Aspects of Central African History* (London 1968)

Rea, F. B. (ed.) *Southern Rhodesia: The Price of Freedom* (Bulawayo 1964)

Reed, D. *The Battle for Rhodesia* (Cape Town 1966)

Richards, J. *My War – And After* (London 1995)

Roberts, A. (ed.) *The Colonial Moment in Africa: Essays on the Movement of Minds and Materials, 1900–1940* (Cambridge 1990)

Roberts, A. *'The Holy Fox': A biography of Lord Halifax* (London 1991)

Robinson, K. *The Dilemmas of Trusteeship: Aspects of British Colonial Policy between the Wars* (London 1965)

Rogers, C. A. and Frantz, C. *Racial Themes in Southern Rhodesia* (New Haven 1962)

Saunders, C. *Murray MacDougall and the Story of Triangle* (Triangle, Rhodesia 1977)

Seymour, J. *One Man's Africa* (London 1955)

Shamuyarira, N. *Crisis in Rhodesia* (London 1965)

Skeen, A. *Prelude to Independence: Skeen's 115 Days* (Cape Town 1966)

Smith, D. and Simpson, C *Mugabe* (London 1981)

Smith, I. *The Great Betrayal: The Memoirs of Ian Douglas Smith* (London 1997)

Smith, R. C. *Avondale to Zimbabwe: A Collection of cameos of Rhodesian Towns and Villages* (Salisbury nd)

Snelson, P. *To Independence and Beyond: Memoirs of a Colonial and Commonwealth Civil Servant* (London 1993)

Springhall, J. *Youth, Empire and Society: British Youth Movements 1883–1960* (London 1977)

Steel, D. *Against Goliath: David Steel's Story* (London, 1991)

Steere, D. V. *God's Irregular: Arthur Shearly Cripps* (London 1973)

Stone, J. and Stone, J. C. Fawtier *An Open Elite? England 1540–1880* (Oxford 1984)

Storry, J. G. *Jubilee Scrapbook 1952–1977: The Commandery in Central Africa of the Grand Priory of the Most Venerable Order of the Hospital of St John of Jerusalem* (Salisbury 1977)

Stumbles, A. R. W. *Some Recollections of a Rhodesian Speaker* ((Bulawayo 1980)

Symonds, R. *Oxford and Empire: The Last Lost Cause?* (Oxford 1991)

Tanser, G. H. *A Sequence of Time: The Story of Salisbury, Rhodesia, 1900–1914* (Salisbury 1974)

Taylor, D. *The Rhodesian: The Life of Sir Roy Welensky* (London 1955)

Thorpe, D. R. *Alec Douglas-Home* (London 1996)

Thorpe, D. R. *Selwyn Lloyd* (London 1989)

Todd, J. *Rhodesia* (London 1966)

Todd, J. *The Right to say No: Rhodesia 1972* (Harare 1987)

Tredgold, Sir R. *The Rhodesia that was my Life* (London 1968)

Tredgold, Sir R. *Xhosa: Tales of Life from the African Veld* (London 1973)

Trevelyan, G. M. *Trinity College: An Historical Sketch* (Cambridge 1946)

Turner, V. (ed.) *Colonialism in Africa 1870–1960 Volume 3: Profiles of Change: African Society and Colonial Rule* (Cambridge 1971)

Victor, O. *The Salient of South Africa* (London 1931)

Waugh, E. *A Tourist in Africa* (London 1960)

Welensky, Sir R. *Welensky's 4000 Days: The Life and Death of the Federation of Rhodesia and Nyasaland* (London 1964)

Weller J. and Linden, J. *Mainstream Christianity to 1980 in Malawi, Zambia and Zimbabwe* (Gweru 1984)

Wells, A. W. *Southern Africa To-day and Yesterday* (London 1956)

Wills, A. J. *The History of Central Africa* (3rd edn, Oxford 1973)

Wilson H. *The Labour Government 1964–1970: A Personal Record* (London 1971)

Windrich, E. *Britain and the Politics of Rhodesian Independence* (London 1978)

Windrich, E. *The Rhodesian Problem: A Documentary Record 1923–1973* (London 1975)

Wood, J. R. T. *The Welensky Papers: A History of the Federation of Rhodesia and Nyasaland* (Durban 1983)

Wyllie, J. H. *The Influence of British Arms: An Analysis of British Military Intervention since 1956* (London 1984)

Young, K. *Rhodesia and Independence: A Study in British Colonial Policy* (London 1967)

Ziegler, P. *King Edward VIII: The Official Biography* (London 1990)

Ziegler, P. *Wilson: The Authorised Life of Lord Wilson of Rievaulx* (London 1993)

E ARTICLES, PAMPHLETS AND THESES

Baldock, R. W. 'Sir John Chancellor and the Moffat Succession', *Rhodesian History,* vol. 3 (1972) pp. 41–52

Beinhart, W. 'Empire, Hunting and Ecological Change in Southern and Central Africa', *Past and Present*, no. 128 (August 1990) , pp. 162–86

Capricorn Africa Society: Contract (Salima, Nyasaland – June 1956)

Carbutt, C. L. 'The Union of the Rhodesias', *The Empire Review*, vol. lxiv, no. 429 (October 1936) pp. 213–17

Curtin, T. R. C. *The Future of Rhodesia* (London 1964)

Darwin, J. 'The Central African Emergency 1959', *Journal of Imperial and Commonwealth History,* vol. xxi (September 1993) no. 3, pp. 217–34

Fedorowich, K. 'Anglicization and the Politicization of British Immigration to South Africa, 1899–1929', *Journal of Imperial and Commonwealth History*, vol. xix, no. 2 (1990) pp. 222–46

Gilchrist, R. D. 'Rhodesia's Place in the Native Problem', *Journal of the African Society,* vol. xxxii, no. cxxvii (April 1933) pp. 135–9

Goodenough, K. M. 'Southern Rhodesia Revisited', *African Affairs*, vol. 48, no. 193 (October 1949) pp. 318–23

Hancock, I. R. 'Sane and Pragmatic Liberalism: The Action Group in Bulawayo, 1955–1965', *Rhodesian History* (1976), 7, pp. 65–83

Harvey, R. K. 'The Conservation Movement in Zimbabwe – A Proud Heritage', *Heritage of Zimbabwe*, no. 11 (1992), pp. 91–4

Hastings, L. M. 'Southern Rhodesia To-day', *Empire Review*, vol. 52, no. 358 (November 1930) pp. 360–6

Haw, R. C. *Golden Age for Rhodesia* (Salisbury 1966)

Henderson, I. 'White Populism in Southern Rhodesia', *Comparative Studies in History and Society*, vol. 14, no. 4 (September 1972) pp. 387–99

Hintz, S. E. C. 'The Political Transformation of Rhodesia 1958–1965', *African Studies Review*, vol. 15, no. 2 (1972), pp. 173–83

Hodder-Williams, R. 'White Attitudes and the Unilateral Declaration of Independence: A Case Study', *Journal of Commonwealth Political Studies*, no. 8 (1970), pp. 241–64

Horowitz, D. 'Attitudes of British Conservatives towards Decolonization in Africa', *African Affairs*, vol. 69, no. 274 (January 1970) pp. 9–26

Howman, R. 'Patriotism and Pioneering Problems', *Heritage*, no. 9 (1990), pp. 75–102

Huggins, Sir G. 'Southern Rhodesia', *African Affairs*, vol. 51, no. 203 (April 1952) pp. 143–8

Hulec, O. 'Some Aspects of the 1930s Depression in Rhodesia', *Journal of Modern African Studies,* 7, 1 (1969) pp. 95–105

Hyam, R. 'The Geopolitical Origins of the Central African Federation: Britain, Rhodesia and South Africa, 1948–1953', *The Historical Journal*, 30, 1 (1987) pp. 145–72

Inge, C. 'Recapturing Rhodesia', *United Empire*, vol. xxvi, no. 9 (September 1935) pp. 555–9

Jennings, A. C. 'Land Apportionment in Southern Rhodesia', *Journal of the Royal African Society*, vol. xxxiv, no. cxxxvi (July 1935) pp. 296–312

Lloyd, B. W. 'Black and White in Rhodesia', *The Empire Review*, vol. lxii, no. 414 (July 1935) pp. 27–30

Macfarlane, L. J. 'Justifying Rebellion: Black and White Nationalism in Rhodesia', *Journal of Commonwealth Political Studies*, vol. 6, no. 1 (March 1968) pp. 54–79

Macfarlane, L. J. 'Pronouncing on Rebellion: The Rhodesian Courts and UDI', *Public Law* (Winter 1968) pp. 325–61

Macmillan, W. M. 'Southern Rhodesia and the Development of Africa', *Journal of the Royal African Society*, vol. xxxii, no. cxxviii (July 1933) pp. 294–8

Meredith, Sir C. 'The Rhodesian Air Training Group 1940–1945', *Rhodesiana*, no. 28 (July 1973) pp. 16–29

Meredith, D. 'The Empire Marketing Board 1926–32', *History Today*, vol. 37 (January 1987) pp. 30–6

Mosley, P. 'Agricultural Development and Government Policy in Settler Economies: The Case of Kenya and Southern Rhodesia, 1900–60', *Economic History Review*, 2nd series, vol. xxxv, no. 3 (August 1982) pp. 390–408

Peace through Justice: Pastoral Instruction of the Catholic Bishops of Southern Rhodesia (Gwelo 1961)

Phillips, G. 'The Great Experiment Begins', *African Affairs*, vol. 56, no. 224 (July 1957) pp. 228–31

Phimister, I. and Van Onselen, C. 'The Political Economy of Tribal Animosity: A Case Study of the 1929 Bulawayo Location "Faction Fight"', *Journal of Southern African Studies*, vol. 6, no. 1 (October 1979), pp. 1–43

Ranger, T. 'Taking hold of the Land: Holy Places and Pilgrimages in Twentieth Century Zimbabwe', *Past and Present*, no. 117 (November 1987) pp. 158–94

Rennie, Sir G. 'The First Year of Federation', *African Affairs*, vol. 54, no. 214 (January 1955) pp. 18–26

Rennie, J. K. 'White Farmers, Black Tenants and Landlord Legislation: Southern Rhodesia 1890–1930', *Journal of Southern African Studies*, vol. 5, no. 1 (October 1978) pp. 86–98

Report of the National Convention of Southern Rhodesia (Salisbury 1960)

Rifkind, M. L. 'Land Apportionment in Perspective', *Rhodesian History*, vol. 3 (1972) pp. 54–62

Rudd, R. 'Royalty in Bulawayo', *Heritage of Zimbabwe*, no. 11 (1992), pp. 41–58

Salmon, E. 'My Rhodesian Tour', *United Empire*, vol. xxx, no. 12 (December 1939) pp. cxix–cxxiii

Schutz, B. 'The Theory of Fragment and the Political Development of White Settler Society in Africa', PhD thesis, UCLA, 1972

Schutz, B. and Scott, D. 'Patterns of Polticial Change in fragment regimes: Northern Ireland and Rhodesia', *British Sociological Yearbook vol. 2: The Politics of Race* (London 1975), pp. 26–54

Shropshire, D. 'Native Development in Rhodesia', *Journal of the African Society*, vol. xxxii, no cxxix (October 1933) pp. 409–23

Silk, P. 'The Bledisloe Medal', *Heritage of Zimbabwe*, no. 8 (1989), pp. 94–6

Smyth, R. 'Britain's African Colonies and British Propaganda during the Second World War', *Journal of Imperial and Commonwealth History*, vol. xiv, no. 1 (1985) pp. 65–82

Soames, Lord 'From Rhodesia to Zimbabwe', *International Affairs*, vol. 56, no. 3 (Summer 1980), pp. 405–19

Stewart, G. 'The Last Royal Train', *Heritage of Zimbabwe*, no. 14 (1995), pp. 17–30

Thomson, J. 'The Developing Federation and Partnership – How is it Progressing?', *African Affairs*, vol. 57, no. 229 (October 1958) pp. 266–78

Wetherell, H. I. 'N.H. Wilson: Populism and Rhodesian Politics', *Rhodesian History*, vol. 6 (1975) pp. 54–76

Wood, R. 'A Recent Visit to Central Africa', *African Affairs*, vol. 57, no. 226 (January 1958) pp. 20–6

Zvobgo, C. J. M. 'Southern Rhodesia under Whitehead: 1958–1962', *Journal of Southern African Affairs*, vol. 2, no. 4 (October 1977) pp. 481–92

Index

Everard, Lieutenant-Colonel Henry, 143, 180
Everard, Tim, 143

Fairbridge, Kingsley, 13
farm labourers' wages (1928), 11, 16
Fearless Talks (1968), 157–63, 191
Federation of Rhodesia and Nyasaland, 40–5
Fergusson, Bernard, 6
Field, Winston, 38, 68, 77, 80, 81, 82–3, 88–90, 99, 151, 153
Fieldsend, Judge John, 146, 147–8, 149, 150
Fingland, S.J.G., 91–2, 95, 96, 98, 111, 123
Fisher, Archbishop Geoffrey, 54
Five Principles, 93–4, 176 (*see also* Six Principles)
Fletcher, Sir Patrick, 55–6
Flower, Ken, 79, 80, 90, 99, 104, 106, 107, 108, 111, 112, 114, 133
Foggin, John, 165
Foley, Maurice, 171–2
Forum, the, 151, 153, 160, 165
Franchise Bill (1957), 55
Frazer, Sir James, 8
Frere, Sir Bartle, 193
Fynn, F.W., 116
Fynn, Sir Percy, 189
Fynn, Dr Robert, 116, 119, 166–7, 169, 189

Gardiner, Gerald, 93, 98, 157
Gascoigne, Sir Julian, 63
Gaul, Bishop William, 32–3
General Elections (Rhodesia), (1946), 37, 46; (1948), 38; (1954), 53; (1962), 79–81; (1965), 96; (1974), 178
George, Duke of Kent, 64
George VI, King, 64–5
Gibbs:
  Alban (2nd Baron Aldenham; uncle of HVG)), 1–3
  Alison (daughter-in-law of HVG), 126
  Anna Maria (Lady Hunsdon; mother of HVG), 4, 24
  Antony (5th Baron Aldenham & 3rd Baron Hunsdon; nephew of HVG), 166
  Arabella (grand-daughter of HVG), 96
  Barbara (sister of HVG), 5, 18, 25
  Beatrix (Lady Aldenham; sister-in-law of HVG), 162, 174
  Elizabeth (grand-daughter of HVG), 5, Geoffrey (brother of HVG), 4, 113–14, 174

Helen (sister-in-law of HVG), 174
Henry, 16
Henry Huck (1st Baron Aldenham; grandfather of HVG), 1, 3
Herbert Cockayne (1st Baron Hunsdon; father of HVG), 3, 4
Jeremy (son of HVG), 26, 47, 48, 57, 126, 167
John Michael, 87
Joseph, 16–17
Revd Joseph, 13
Kenneth (son of HVG), 26, 47, 48, 119, 174
Revd Michael (cousin of HVG), 33, 35, 48
Molly (wife of HVG), xiv, 25, 29, 125, 126–7, 128, 131, 139, 152, 154, 159, 160, 168, 169, 170, 175, 182–6, 190, 192
Nigel (son of HVG), 26, 35, 47, 48, 126, 127, 139, 142, 166, 167, 174
Simon (son of HVG), 26, 48, 53, 171, 174
Thomas, 33
Timothy (son of HVG), 26, 47, 48, 166, 169, 174, 178–9, 182, 184
Vicary (uncle of HVG), 2
Walter, (4th Baron Aldenham & 2nd Baron Hunsdon; brother of HVG), 4, 11, 119, 162, 166
Winfred (Lady Ponsonby; sister-in-law of HVG), 5, 139
Gibraltar, 49, 128–9, 157–8
Goldin, Judge Bernie, 146
Goodman, Lord, 155–6, 176
Goromonzi (school), 64
Government House (Bulawayo), 28, 63
Government House (Salisbury), 63, 66, 97, 101, 112, 114, 115, 119, 120, 124, 136, 154, 160, 166, 168–9, 180, 182
Governor's Fund (1960), 73–4
Governor's Fund (1969), 168, 171, 189
Governor's Lodge (Salisbury), 63, 72, 74, 81, 136
Graham, Billy, 71
Graham, Lord (Duke of Montrose), 81, 103, 107, 130, 133
Grahamstown, 10, 16
Grain Marketing Board, 40
Grainger, Colonel, xiv
Graylin, J.C., 123
Greenfield, Cornelius, 124, 128
Greenfield, Julian, 44, 56, 82, 124